P9-BYB-340

WITHDRAWN

Energy Companies and Market Reform

Energy Companies and Market Reform:
How Deregulation Went Wrong

Jeremiah D. Lambert

The recommendations, advice, descriptions, and the methods in this book are presented solely for educational purposes. The author and publisher assume no liability whatsoever for any loss or damage that results from the use of any of the material in this book. Use of the material in this book is solely at the risk of the user.

Copyright© 2006 by
PennWell Corporation
1421 South Sheridan Road
Tulsa, Oklahoma 74112-6600 USA
800.752.9764
+1.918.831.9421
sales@pennwell.com
www.pennwellbooks.com
www.pennwell.com

Director: Mary McGee
Managing Editor: Steve Hill
Production / Operations Manager: Traci Huntsman
Production Editor: Tony Quinn
Cover Designer: Karla Pfeifer
Book Designer: Sheila Brock

Library of Congress Cataloging-in-Publication Data

Lambert, Jeremiah D., 1934–
  Energy companies and market reform : how deregulation went wrong / by Jeremiah D. Lambert.
      p. cm.
  Includes bibliographical references and indexes.
  ISBN-13: 978-1-59370-060-7 (hardcover)
  ISBN-10: 1-59370-060-1 (hardcover)
  1. Electric utilities--Deregulation--United States. 2. Energy industries--Corrupt practices--California. 3. Enron Corp. 4. United States. Federal Energy Regulatory Commission. I. Title.
  HD9685.U5L25 2006
  333.79--dc22

                                                        2006018092

All rights reserved. No part of this book may be reproduced, stored in a retrieval system, or transcribed in any form or by any means, electronic or mechanical, including photocopying and recording, without the prior written permission of the publisher.

Printed in the United States of America

1 2 3 4 5   10 09 08 07 06

This book is dedicated to my wife, Sanda, and my daughters, Nicole, Alix, Leigh, Clare, and Hilary.

Contents

Preface

This book addresses deregulation of U.S. energy markets. It illustrates the contrast between government policy choices favoring competition and the often problematic results of those choices. A central thesis is that, in network industries such as electricity and natural gas, reliance on markets must be carefully introduced and that real-world economic effects trump *a priori* theory. As the history recounted here shows, removal of price and entry constraints, without a clear understanding of the markets being deregulated, is an invitation to manipulation, rent seeking, and, ultimately, unregulated monopoly.

Energy markets are complex. At the wholesale level, bilateral contracts and auctions serve functions once performed internally by vertically integrated utilities under cost-based regulation. To avoid unintended consequences, as in California, it is essential to get markets right. Doing so requires workable market design, an iterative, bottom-up approach, and adequate underlying capacity. In the framing of policy, regulators should also assume that a variant of Murphy's law holds: If the system can be exploited, it will be exploited.

To put flesh on the bones of policy abstraction, this book includes recent case histories detailing massive failures of regulation and corporate governance. As a guide to the future, it also takes account of post-deregulation markets that work, such as PJMs. The book concludes, as two leading academics foresaw over 20 years ago, that energy industry deregulation "must involve a mixture of regulation and competition" (Joskow and Schmalensee. Markets for Power: An Analysis of Electric Utility Deregulation. MIT Press [1983], p. 212).

1 A Short History of Deregulation

Since Enron's demise and the implosion of California's restructured electricity market in 2001, competitive energy markets have exposed huge risks, with consequences far different from those predicted. Many energy companies, investors, and consumers in the post-Enron era have suffered losses, measured in the billions, from market rigging, price spikes, rolling blackouts, massive corporate fraud, and utility bankruptcies. The stubborn persistence of market power in energy industries and widespread abuses flowing from its exercise have called forth broad remedial measures, whose efficacy nonetheless remains open to question. Citing case histories, this book shows how flawed market design, derelict corporate governance, aggressive accounting, and multiple regulatory failures have led to this result. It also evaluates the ensuing reactive reforms, identifies countervailing market-based success stories, and assesses the prospects for continued deregulation of the nation's energy markets.

In a free-enterprise economy, received wisdom dictates that competitive markets respond to customer demand by rewarding investment and innovation better than regulation. In recent decades, market-based competition has increasingly displaced command-and-control government direction as the preferred way to promote consumer welfare and reward entrepreneurial risk taking. As markets commoditized energy products, electricity and gas became a platform for commerce. Investor-owned utilities, once sheltered in exclusive service areas, formed independent power affiliates to commence energy trading as a high-profit (and high-risk) alternative to conventional cost-based energy services. Derivative energy markets blossomed. Many regulators, even those with a stake in preservation of the old order, urged competition as a needed corrective to the perverse economics of cost-based, return-on-investment utility rate making. It was assumed as an article of faith that competition could be designed, created, and made to work in diverse industrial settings, including electricity and other network industries that present inherent structural limitations.[1]

That assumption underlies the Energy Policy Act of 2005, sweeping reform legislation that, among other objectives, seeks to promote "competition within the wholesale and retail market for electric energy in the United States."[2] As this book shows, however, electricity and natural gas are industries whose "technology, organization, and regulation . . . all make competition particularly hard to implement, and sometimes even to identify."[3] Ongoing market changes have facilitated new means of foreclosure, such as anticompetitive use of transmission rights. For reasons rooted in industry history and structure, market liberalization has not led reliably to competitive outcomes, resolved systemic limitations, or even reduced overall regulation. Pivotal suppliers still control prices and services; unbundled electricity and gas markets continue to require administrative oversight; and, following more than two decades of institutional change, enhanced consumer welfare in the energy industry remains more a promise than an accomplished fact.[4]

Recent Regulatory History

Electricity is a tripartite industry with generation, transmission, and distribution components. The Federal Power Commission and its successor, the Federal Energy Regulatory Commission (FERC), historically exercised plenary control over interstate electricity transmission and bulk-power transactions, leaving retail electric service as the exclusive regulatory province of state and local authorities. Until the advent of industry restructuring, vertically integrated electric utilities owned or controlled generation, transmission, and distribution facilities and served customers under a cost-of-service regime within exclusive retail franchises that encompassed local supply, transmission, and distribution. Rate making accounted for embedded costs incurred in constructing capital facilities. Prevailing regulation leveled the impact of rate changes on risk-averse retail customers, imposed on incumbent utilities an obligation to serve, and protected capital investment through assured cost recovery.[5] Despite substantial change, many of the foregoing features continue into the present.

The natural gas industry was also vertically integrated. FERC regulated the wellhead price of gas sold by producers into the interstate market[6] and the rates for transporting that gas, which pipelines typically purchased from affiliated producer entities and resold to end users and local distributors on a bundled basis. Interstate pipelines, functioning concurrently as gas merchants and transportation providers, were not obliged to transport third-party gas (just as utilities were not required to open their transmission facilities to independent power supplies).

The Natural Gas Policy Act of 1978 (NGPA) granted FERC authority over intrastate as well as interstate production, imposed a complex system of price ceilings by category for wellhead first sales of gas, and provided a schedule for eventual price decontrol. The NGPA also raised contract prices for all categories of gas. When gas demand and market prices declined in the early 1980s, however, pipeline purchasers under long-term take-or-pay contracts geared to maximum allowable NGPA rates could not sell the gas they were required to buy. By equating statutory price ceilings and contractual price floors, many pipelines undertook to purchase gas at more than twice the prevailing market price. By the late 1980s, as a result, pipeline take-or-pay liabilities approached $12 billion.[7] During the same period, rising electricity prices outstripped the rate of inflation, leading utilities to build capacity, particularly costly baseload nuclear plants, in anticipation of demand that failed to materialize. Retail prices escalated sharply.

The resulting rate shock politicized the regulatory process.[8] Cost-based rate regulation—once unquestioned at both the federal and state levels—soon attracted a small army of critics in academia and at FERC, who viewed utilities as complacent bureaucracies seeking assured cost recovery for improvident capital projects. Critics saw a traditional utility system characterized by waste, dysfunctional economics, distorted incentives, and widespread utility losses—an imperfectly regulated industry insulated from competitive pressures.[9] Captive ratepayers, accustomed to stable prices, rebelled against bearing the consequences of utility mismanagement.

Perceived solutions to energy industry problems were largely market based and prefigured actual changes. Electricity reformers contemplated equal access to high-voltage transmission lines, nondiscriminatory transmission rates and access, market-based bulk power priced at marginal cost, centralized dispatch of power generation plants, and development of spot and futures markets that would set an equilibrium price for electricity determined by supply and demand. Based on similar logic, a reconstitutive strategy for the natural gas industry called for competitive trading of pipeline transportation capacity rights, policing of pipeline-producer affiliate transactions, decontrol of new gas prices, increased reliance on spot markets, and elimination of artificial demand constraints.[10] During the ensuing decade, the touchstone in each industry was the need to "identify new forms of government intervention that are both more effective and less intrusive than command and control regulation."[11] Interest in competitive solutions drove deregulatory initiatives by Congress, FERC, and state governments. (See table 1–1.)

Table 1–1. Major Events and Milestones in Restructuring the Natural Gas and Electricity Industries[12]

Event	Natural gas industry	Electric industry
Early steps toward completion	Some large consumers in the interstate market started purchasing gas and pipeline transportation separately—mid 1970s.	Utilities file FERC rates with "up to" cost-based formulas—early 1980s. Public Utility Regulatory Policies Act mandates purchases from qualifying facilities—1978.
Exceptions to cost-of-services rates	Natural Gas Policy Act gradually removes some natural gas price ceilings—1978.	PURPA exempted qualifying facilities from cost-of-service regulation. FERC recognizes competitive bidding for new capacity—1988.
Transmission access proposed to dampen anticompetitive behavior and encourage competition	FERC encourages pipelines to provide open-access transportation—1985.	FERC initiates transmission access conditions for market-priced power sales—1990. Energy Policy Act authorizes FERC to order transmission access to encourage competition—1992.
Standards to mitigate monopoly control in transmission announced	Order 636 issued in 1992: • Comparable transmission and storage open-access required. • Functional unbundling of product and transportation sales required. • Pipeline companies allowed to make market-priced gas sales through affiliates. • Firm transportation customers get flexible receipt and delivery points.	Orders 888 and 889 issued in 1996: • Nondiscriminatory, comparable open access required. • Functional unbundling generation and transmission businesses. • Investor-owned utilities required to participate in OASIS. Order 2000 issued in 1999: • Transmission owning utilities encouraged to place transmission facilities under the control of RTO.
Access to information to support market functions	Trade press publishes spot gas prices—1989. FERC mandates individual pipeline electronic bulletin boards—1992. FERC mandates standardized internet communication protocol—1997.	Market-based pricing inclues requirements for electronic bulletin boards—1992. Energy Policy Act requires public capacity reporting—1992. FERC orders OASIS—1996.
Market characteristics evolve	Company consolidation starts—mid 1980s. Product markets active; prices transparent—1987. Gas marketing evolves as an unregulated industry—1987. NYMEX futures contract for Henry Hub gas—1990. Robust market centers/hubs for physical trade—1993. Futures markets mature with large consumer access to transportation available in most states—1994. Internet trading of gas and transmission rights—1999.	Company consolidation starts—late 1980s. Spot and forward markets still largely restricted to utilities—1995. Neither transportation nor product prices are transparent yet—1995. Development of a futures market hindered by a lack of a standardized spot market for benchmarking. New entrants are trying to find/produce niches. Innovators hope to combine gas and electric market instruments for added value—1995.

Source: GAO-02-656, June 2002, p. 27

As these events were unfolding, an active physical gas market had begun to develop. Courts interpreted the antitrust laws to proscribe unreasonable denial of access to essential bottleneck facilities, such as gas pipelines or electric transmission lines.[13] In 1985, FERC separated gas sales from transportation by requiring interstate pipelines to provide equal access to anyone requesting transportation of gas[14] but allowed bundled pipeline sales of gas, transportation, and storage services to local distributors for several years thereafter. Ultimately, FERC separated pipeline sales from transportation and required release of capacity on interstate pipelines. Natural gas was then free to trade as a commodity, decoupled from gas transportation. Federal regulation of interstate natural gas prices finally ended in 1989, following shortages, supply distortions, price anomalies, and ever-growing pipeline take-or-pay liabilities.

On the electric side, deregulation initially hinged on the Public Utilities Regulatory Policy Act of 1978 (PURPA), which, among other provisions, required that utilities buy power from nonutility generators (qualified facilities [QFs]) at long-term avoided cost. This encouraged construction of nonutility power plants, principally to provide cogenerated power to utilities under long-term agreements, often price-advantaged standard contracts mandated by state law. By 1985, in California alone, over 15,000 MW of QF capacity was under contract.[15]

Competitive power markets nonetheless remained largely a theoretical construct until the Energy Policy Act of 1992 required that grid-owning utilities, if ordered by FERC, must provide interstate transmission service over their wires to any jurisdictional supplier, thus undermining what had been for many years a transmission monopoly. It also exempted many independent power producers from the reach of the Public Utility Holding Company Act (PUHCA), a Depression-era statute that regulated activities by utility holding companies. Several years later, FERC authorized market-based pricing for new electric power and issued Order 888, a landmark rule that required vertically integrated utilities to give third parties access to their high-voltage transmission lines under nondiscriminatory tariffs.[16] FERC also encouraged formation of independent system operators and regional transmission organizations to manage bid-based wholesale power markets and provide nondiscriminatory transmission of electricity over operating utilities' high-voltage lines.

In a parallel change that reflected the government-wide impulse to liberalize markets, the Securities and Exchange Commission (SEC) allowed multistate utility holding companies to own energy-related companies, including power marketers, so long as investment fell within specified dollar and percentage limits. It also limited PUHCA's practical impact by approving utility mergers with minimal or nonexistent physical connections. With the collapse of the utility empires of the 1920s only a distant memory, SEC liberalization encouraged formation of new holding company subsidiaries and pyramidal corporate structures.[17]

Market-based reform was also on the march at the state level. In 1993, the California Public Utility Commission recommended statewide deregulation of power generation. Shortly thereafter, California pioneered a competitive market in electric power,[18] an initiative that eventually led 24 states to adopt competition in retail electricity markets. The California market required self-scheduling of generation and loads, a separate Power Exchange, zonal pricing of transmission, and standard electricity products traded at market-clearing prices. To facilitate these changes, California deregulated wholesale power prices, required that jurisdictional utilities sell fossil-fired generation capacity to merchant companies, and capped the power costs utilities could recover from ratepayers. After a benign start, the restructured electricity market in California—ill conceived and easily manipulated—proved a disastrous failure. A major cause of that failure was traceable to the unwillingness of FERC and the California Public Utilities Commission to fix market design flaws contemporaneously identified by the Market Surveillance Committee of the California Independent System Operator, notably load-serving entities' overreliance on the spot market for wholesale energy purchases and the unavailability of long-term forward contracts.[19]

In 2000, the Commodity Futures Modernization Act limited jurisdiction of the Commodity Futures Trading Commission (CFTC) over "contracts of sale of a commodity for future delivery" by exempting a broad range of swap agreements and derivatives from regulation, extending in general terms a specific exemption that the CFTC had previously granted Enron with respect to energy trading contracts. This encouraged hugely increased trade in and arbitrage of electricity and natural gas as merchant commodities. The profits from unregulated and less-than-transparent energy markets were not lost on utilities, pipeline companies, and their energy-trading arms, which soon emerged as significant players. To manage the resulting energy price risks, new entrants used internal controls based on those developed by global financial institutions, often without adjustment for the unique requirements of energy markets.

Enron

Among those keenly interested in the evolving energy marketplace was Enron, formed in 1985 by the merger of Houston Natural and Internorth Natural Gas. In devising its business strategy, Enron "synthesized existing ideas from the Texas oil business, Wall Street and Silicon Valley."[20] Enron Gas Services—soon to become Enron Capital and Trade Resources and thereafter Enron Wholesale Services—created a gas bank, matching assured gas supplies with demand, primarily from gas-fired power units. Enron Risk Management Services hedged the resulting risks, first through swaps and options and later by means of sophisticated financial derivatives. Enron also placed large unhedged bets on gas and electricity prices. In 1997, Enron acquired Portland General Electric, an electric utility, to arbitrage the so-called spark spread, that is, the difference between the price of natural gas as an input to power generation and the price of electricity. In 1999, Enron launched a proprietary Web site, EnronOnline, that captured nearly one-quarter of all electricity and gas trades nationwide and redefined electricity as a tradable commodity, rather than an essential service. To ensure political cooperation, Enron also lobbied effectively in support of the deregulated energy markets it was soon to manipulate and, in many instances, control.

Deregulation

As deregulation of the $220 billion electric industry gathered momentum in the 1990s, it called forth sharply different economic assessments, polarized around markets and central planning. To its advocates, deregulation promised an efficient commoditized market in natural gas and bulk power that would result in lower consumer prices. To its critics, deregulation of natural monopolies was little more than a gateway to market manipulation that only government intervention could control.[21] Critics also doubted that the functions performed by vertically integrated utilities could be replaced by bilateral contracts between generators and large customers or, with retail utilities and other load-serving entities, supported only by multilateral markets for spot trading.[22]

The major industry coalitions—Edison Electric Institute, American Public Power Association, and National Rural Electric Cooperative Association—offered predictably divergent views and lobbied Congress accordingly. Utility interests escalated soft-money political contributions sixfold between 1992 and 1996 and more than doubled such contributions in 2000. In that same year, Enron's political contributions alone exceeded $2 million.[23] Pro-competitive thinking gained traction accordingly, and faith in deregulatory market solutions took hold in legislative corridors, at FERC, and at state commissions.[24]

A perfect storm of interactive causes also propelled deregulation: a decade-long stock market bubble, lax or outdated accounting rules, increased reliance on financial derivatives, emergence of the Internet, indifferent federal oversight, and gross failures of corporate governance. Other causes, paradoxically, were artifacts of the regulatory era that was then drawing to a close: abundant supplies of energy, excess capacity in the pipeline and electric power infrastructure, and stable or modestly falling real prices. Most forecasters saw more of the same for the first decade of the 21st century. Risks were largely obscured by relatively cheap natural gas, excess generating capacity, and low wholesale market prices. In actuality, however, markets failed to perform as predicted—most notably California's, which collapsed in 2001, following unprecedented price spikes, rolling blackouts, and admissions of corporate fraud.[25]

Facts emerging from Enron's bankruptcy in the same year showed how easily energy markets could be manipulated and how unscrupulous corporate managers could assume extraordinary risks at huge cost to markets, companies, consumers, creditors, and share-holders.[26] Enron's spectacular failure revealed a corporate culture that condoned and fostered trading fraud, questionable accounting, abuse of affiliate relationships, and financial misrepresentation. In the words of one commentator, Enron and California together "exposed fundamental problems of mitigating monopoly power, devising restructuring plans that cannot be gamed, and inadequate monitoring by regulatory commissions . . . [leaving] consumers in a far worse position than traditional cost-of-service regulation."[27]

As the nation's primary energy regulator, FERC remained a steadfast proponent of competitive markets but (until the Energy Policy Act) lacked adequate statutory authority to implement a market-based regime. Although it opened the transmission grid to competition and encouraged regional bid-based wholesale power markets, FERC also authorized market-based rates without a pragmatic understanding of market power, market structure, or the interaction between gas and electric markets. In doing so, FERC failed to discharge its core regulatory function of ensuring just and reasonable rates and compounded its errors through a misplaced reliance on standard market design, which discounted or ignored industry-related barriers to electric power competition, including:

> non-storability of electric production, lack of close substitutes, cyclical and seasonal demand, instantaneous clearing of markets, asset specificity, . . . lack of asset mobility, very high inelasticity of short-run consumer demand, and network effects ([under which] increased output at one plant may require a reduction in output at a competitor's plant, either to balance generation and demand or to prevent overload of transmission network facilities).[28]

The Energy Policy Act is in part a response to perceived regulatory shortfalls. It gives FERC new antifraud tools, enforcement power, merger review jurisdiction, and backup transmission-siting authority. It also repeals PUHCA, which for many years served as a constraint on utility mergers and acquisitions, and transfers to FERC the oversight authority formerly exercised by the SEC. In doing so, the Energy Policy Act devolves on FERC critical regulatory functions at a time of increasing industry consolidation. To exercise those functions in aid of competitive markets, FERC must apply enhanced analytical sophistication, based on a grasp of real-world economics, while recognizing that electricity competition depends on improved infrastructure, demand response, and redesign of differentiated services.

Although diminished by sobering experience, energy deregulation is neither dead nor discredited, as the Energy Policy Act reveals. Trade in energy commodities and the use of derivatives continues to grow in parallel with availability of liquid markets and reliable price data. In certain states, power generation and sales are deregulated enterprises, with few price controls. With revisionist hindsight, the California debacle is now attributed to "what happens when politicians believe they can create robust, well-functioning markets out of whole cloth and efficiently manage competition via regulation."[29] The poster child for successful energy markets is PJM Interconnection (PJM), the dominant regional transmission organization in the eastern United States. As the successor to a tight power pool in existence since 1927, PJM runs an efficient bid-based market in bulk power, administers an open-access nondiscriminatory transmission tariff, and monitors anticompetitive behavior in its service area. Wholesale electricity prices in the eastern United States, where an expanded PJM now imports cheaper power from the Midwest, dropped 15% in 2004, confirming to some observers that competitive electricity markets can reduce costs and provide reliable service. Others remain skeptical, linking effective competition in network industries to market power mitigation and other baseline preconditions.[30]

Sorting through the wreckage left in the wake of flawed energy deregulation, therefore, I have been inclined to proceed pragmatically, not ideologically, with a view to what has worked, what has not, and why.

Notes

[1] *Comments of the American Public Power Association,* FERC Docket No. AD05-17-000. Electric Energy Market Competition Task Force (November 18, 2005), mimeo (hereafter *APPA Market Competition Comments*), p. 7.

[2] Public Law No. 119 Stat. 594 (2005), Section 1815(b)(1).

[3] Michaels. "May the Task (Force) Be with You." *New Power Executive Biweekly,* Vol. 9 (October 31, 2005).

[4] *APPA Market Competition Comments,* pp. 5–7, 11.

[5] Chao, Oren, and Wilson. *Restructured Electricity Markets: Reevaluation of Vertical Integration and Unbundling.* White paper (July 1, 2005) (hereafter *Chao et al. Markets*), p. 4.

[6] *Phillips Petroleum Co. v. Wisconsin,* 374 U.S. 672, 677 (1954).

[7] See, e.g., Pierce. "Reconstituting the Natural Gas Industry from Wellhead to Burnertip." *Energy Law Journal,* 9 (1) (1988) (hereafter *Pierce Gas*).

[8] Gray. *The Regulatory Environment and Industrial Restructuring: The Case of U.S. Electric Power* (PhD dissertation, State University of New York, 2004), pp. 33–34. See also Geddes. "A Historical Perspective on Electric Utility Regulation." *The Cato Review of Business and Government,* https://www.cato.org/pubs/regulation/reg15n1-geddes.html (failure of the regulatory system to deal with economic change led to increasing discontent with the natural monopoly theory of market structure).

[9] See, e.g., Pierce. "A Proposal to Deregulate the Market for Bulk Power." *University of Virginia Law Review,* 72: 783, 795 (1986) (hereafter *Pierce Power*), and O'Connor et al. "The Transition to Competition in the Electric Utility Industry." *Journal of Energy Law & Policy,* 223 (8) (1988). Under cost-of-service rate making, a regulated utility has an economic incentive to over-invest in capital assets, the rate base on which its returns are determined. The phenomenon of overinvestment induced by regulation is called the Averch-Johnson effect. Averch and Johnson. "Behavior of the Firm under Regulatory Constraint." *The American Economic Review,* 52: 1053–69 (1962).

[10] See *Pierce Gas.* Spurred by price deregulation, the New York Mercantile Exchange in 1990 launched a gas futures contract that led to development of the over-the-counter financial trading market in natural gas, known as the gas swaps market.

[11] Ibid., p. 52.

[12] *Energy Markets: Concerted Actions Needed by FERC to Confront Challenges That Impede Effective Oversight.* United States General Accounting Office, GAO-02-656 (June 2002), p. 27.

[13] See, e.g., *Otter Tail Power Co. v. United States,* 410 U.S. 366 (1973); *Hecht v. Pro-Football, Inc.,* 570 F.2d 982 (CA DC 1977); *Aspen Highlands Skiing Corp. v. Aspen Skiing Co.,* 738 F.2d 1509 (10th Cir. 1984). For a general perspective, see Lambert and Pedelty. "Mandatory Contract Carriage: The Changing Role of Pipelines in Competitive Natural Gas Markets." *Public Utility Fortnightly* (February 7, 1985).

[14] *Regulation of Natural Gas Pipelines after Partial Wellhead Decontrol,* 50 *Federal Register* 42,408 (1985), *modified,* Order No. 436-A, 50 *Federal Register* 52,217 (1985), *modified,* Order No. 436-B, 51 *Federal Register* 6398 (1986), *vacated Associated Gas Distribs. v. F.E.R.C.,* 824 F.2d 981 (D.C. Cir. 1987) [codified at 18 *Code of Federal Regulations* §§ 284.8(b), 294(b)] (1987).

[15] Blumstein, Friedman, and Green. *The History of Electricity Restructuring in California* (CSEM Working Paper 103) (University of California Energy Institute) (August 2002).

[16] Energy Policy Act of 1992, Public Law No. 102-486, 106 Stat. 2276 (1992); *Kan. City Power & Light Co.,* 67 F.E.R.C. ¶ 61,183, 61,557 (1994); Order 888, *Promoting Wholesale Competition Through Open Access Non-Discriminatory Transmission Services by Public Utilities; Recovery of stranded Costs by Public Utilities and Transmitting Utilities* [Regs. Preambles 1991–1996] F.E.R.C. Stats & Regs. ¶ 31,036 (1996), 61 *Federal Register* 21,541 (May 10, 1996) (to be codified at 18 *Code of Federal Regulations,* pts. 35, 385). The Energy Policy Act authorizes a new category of persons "engaged exclusively in the business of selling energy at wholesale," exempt wholesale generators, to sell power at market-based rates; authorizes FERC to order utilities that own transmission facilities to transmit wholesale power over their systems; but prohibits FERC from ordering access to transmission for unbundled retail power sales. Order 888 requires that interstate utilities file open-access nondiscriminatory transmission tariffs and unbundle

transmission, generation, and power-marketing functions. PUHCA, 15 *U.S. Code* §§ 79 et seq., regulates utility holding companies by localizing ownership and control, simplifying corporate structures, limiting expansion, controlling securities issuances, and policing affiliate transactions. See *The Regulation of Public-Utility Holding Companies.* Division of Investment Management, United States Securities and Exchange Commission (June 1995). The Energy Policy Act partially repealed PUHCA by allowing an electric utility company to own an exempt wholesale generator, by statutory definition a nonutility, if it does not operate in the utility's own service territory. The Energy Policy Act also enabled utility holding companies to own foreign utility companies and to purchase or build generating projects worldwide.

[17] *The Public Utility Holding Company Act.* American Public Power Association (February 2003), pp. 4–5.

[18] Order Instituting Rulemaking, *Re Proposed Policies Governing Restructuring of California's Electric Services Industry and Reforming Regulation,* 1994 Cal. PUC LEXIS 336 (C.P.U.C. Apr. 20, 1994); Cal. Elec. Restructuring Law, Stats 1996, ch. 854 (1996).

[19] Wolak. *Lessons from International Experience with Electricity Market Monitoring.* University of California Energy Institute (June 2004), pp. 6–7.

[20] Fusaro and Miller. *What Went Wrong at Enron.* John Wiley & Sons (2002), p. 75, cited in Weaver. "Can Energy Markets Be Trusted? The Effect of the Rise and Fall of Enron on Energy Markets." *Houston Business and Tax Law Journal,* 1 (4): 17 (2004) (hereafter *Weaver*).

[21] See, e.g., *Policy Debate: Has Deregulation Caused the Energy Shortage in California?* http://business.baylor.edu/Tom_Kelly/California%20Power.htm (citing sources); Krugman. *The Road to Ruin,* http://www.pkarchive. org/column/081903.html; Black and Pierce. "The Choice between Markets and Central Planning in Regulating the U.S. Electricity Industry." *Columbia Law Review,* 93: 1339 (1993). For failure attributed to market design that retains the regulatory inefficiency of average-cost pricing and relies on a large amount of installed capacity, see also *Resource Adequacy and the Cost of Reliability: The Impact of Alternative Policy Approaches on Customers and Electric Market Participants.* Center for the Advancement of Energy Markets and the Distributed Energy Financial Group, LLC) (2005) (hereafter *CAEM Report*), p. ix: "Auction markets and retail competition, imposed on a base of an inefficient capacity market, cannot enhance efficiency in a major way." Joskow. *The Difficult Transition to Competitive Electricity Markets in the U.S.* MIT (May

2003), p. 3: "The California electricity crisis of 2000–2001 . . . , Enron's bankruptcy, the financial collapse of many merchant generating and trading companies, volatile wholesale market prices, rising real retail prices in some states, phantom trading and fraudulent price reporting revelations, accounting abuses, a declining number of competitive retail supply options for residential and small commercial customers in many states, and continuing allegations of market power and market abuses in wholesale markets have all helped to take the glow off... electricity 'deregulation' in many parts of the country."

[22] *Chao et al. Markets,* p. 56.

[23] See *Electricity Deregulation,* http://www.opensecrets.org/news/electricity. htm (January 30, 2001).

[24] Concerted political intervention allowed energy trading companies such as Enron to avoid federal regulation of their dealings in over-the-counter derivative securities. See Bratton. "Enron and the Dark Side of Shareholder Value." *Tulane Law Review* 76 (5) (2002).

[25] Joskow. "U.S. Energy Policy during the 1990's." Paper prepared for the conference American Economic Policy during the 1990's, sponsored by the John F. Kennedy School of Government, Harvard University (June 2001), p. 20. See also Borenstein et al. "Electricity Market Power." *The American Economic Review,* 92: 1398 (2002) (the wholesale market cost of power in California rose from $1.67 billion to $8.98 billion between 1998 and 2000).

[26] See Coffee. "What Caused Enron? A Capsule Social and Economic History of the 1990's." *Columbia Law and Economics Working Paper No. 214* (2003), p. 9: "As of 1990, equity-based compensation for chief executive officers of U.S. public companies appears to have been only around five percent of their total annual compensation, but by 1999, this percentage had risen to an estimated sixty percent."

[27] *Weaver,* p. 25.

[28] *APPA Market Competition Comments,* p. 11.

[29] Taylor. "Lay Off." *The Wall Street Journal,* July 6, 2004.

[30] See, e.g., *CAEM Report,* pp. iii, ix (competitive processes and efficient prices deemed capable of producing a $19 billion annual cost benefit to ultimate U.S. customers); *The Wall Street Journal,* January 26, 2005, p. B2 (price decline from $33.88 to $28.36 per megawatt hour);

Lambert. *Creating Competitive Power Markets: The PJM Model.* PennWell Publishing (2001); Anderson, "The State of Organized Markets." Presentation at CERA Week/Power Day. Houston (February 17, 2005).

2 Corporate Self-Regulation:
Form Versus Substance

Boards of directors are arguably a first line of defense against fraud, misrepresentation, and market manipulation perpetrated or condoned by company managements seeking unjust personal profit and competitive advantage. Company directors assume fiduciary obligations that should, in theory, make them watchdogs in the service of shareholders and the public interest. The era of energy deregulation, which for too long tolerated rigged markets and arcane financial engineering, has sorely tested this theory. Energy company directors have too often proved to be indifferent, co-opted, and passive observers of illegal management schemes. In many instances, although aware of corporate wrongdoing, directors have declined to act. In others, they have been active participants. This chapter cites illustrative case histories. If there is a lesson to be learned, it is that corporate self-regulation cannot be relied on to ensure market integrity.

Governance of publicly held energy companies, like that of other public corporations, requires effective oversight by boards of directors, rendered all the more important because energy is a basic industry that affects the economy at many levels. Boards have ultimate management authority, under law, but delegate business operations to senior management. As fiduciaries, however, boards cannot delegate their duty of care. They must inquire into corporate affairs sufficiently to take necessary action. In determining whether they have done so, courts typically consider such procedural factors as frequency and length of board meetings, board meeting attendance, information provided by management, and follow-on inquiries.[1] However, discharge of fiduciary obligations transcends compliance with procedural norms. Boards must also be proactive and, in the case of public utilities charged with a public interest, protect both shareholders and ratepayers dependent on an essential service.

Adherence to fiduciary standards often places boards squarely in the path of company management. Focused on short-term earnings and price per share (factors that typically determine bonuses and equity compensation), management may, as in Enron's case, misrepresent financial results relied on by investors, regulators, and creditors. Classic techniques involve off-balance-sheet accounting, accelerated revenue recognition, and suppression of financial statement disclosures.[2] Often, but not always, these matters come before boards for review and approval.

The Monitoring Board

Elected by and accountable to shareholders, boards are the focal point of corporate governance, guided by outside accounting firms, law firms, banks, securities analysts, and debt-rating agencies.[3] Boards hire, monitor, compensate, and replace senior management.[4] They also select outside auditors to provide accurate financial reporting. As pillars of shareholder capitalism, boards are expected to remain free of conflicts of interest, exercise due diligence, and ensure the integrity of financial reporting systems.[5] Real-world experience, unfortunately, deviates from this ideal. As the following case histories show, boards have often proved supine, negligent, and unwilling to act in response to obvious danger signs.

Under prevailing legal standards, boards have an affirmative obligation to oversee "the enterprise to assure that [it] functions within the law to achieve its purposes."[6] In so doing, they may approve, modify, or disapprove financial objectives, plans, actions, and applicable accounting principles.[7] Acting through specialized committees, boards also monitor corporate performance.

Board *decisions*—for example, authorization of mergers, changes in capital structure, and compensation of the chief executive officer— are subject to the business judgment rule, which assumes them to be, if not self-interested, the product of a "process that was either deliberately considered in good faith or was otherwise rational."[8] Under this standard, good-faith board decisions are not open to after-the-fact objective review by a court or jury if the formalities of process have been satisfied.

Unconsidered *failure* to act, including failure to elicit information essential for effective monitoring, may also result in losses. Given boards' underlying responsibility to see that companies function within the law, such failure is judged by a more rigorous substantive standard. Boards have an affirmative duty to inquire and must exercise a good-faith judgment that the company's information and reporting system is adequate to ensure "that appropriate information will come to [their] attention in a timely manner."[9] Failure in this respect, whether because of negligence or co-optation by a dominant chief executive, can be more damaging than a board's questionable decisions. Board inaction may also implicitly condone ordinary course but illegal business decisions made by officers and employees "deeper in the interior of the organization."[10]

The monitoring model of corporate governance contemplates an objective, process-based system that, on balance, provides little real assurance of effective oversight. If boards go through the motions of making conscientious informed judgments, neither the degree of attention actually paid nor the quality of decision reached will ordinarily be subject to substantive review. Under the business judgment rule, the primary requirement is evidence that customary procedures were followed. This has been called, at best, a "circumstantial guarantee of good governance."[11] Except for egregious cases, directorial due diligence does not lend itself to *ex post* determination, since business judgment lies beyond the purview of courts and juries. "In the chasm separating the circumstantial guarantee from . . . an actual guarantee," writes one commentator, "[lie] untold billions of lost investment."[12]

The Enron board, a case in point (discussed in a later section of this chapter), contributed to Enron's collapse by tolerating or approving high-risk accounting, conflict-of-interest transactions, extensive off-the-books activities, and inadequate public disclosure.[13] For several years after Enron's demise, notwithstanding multiple lawsuits and government investigations, the Enron board appeared likely to avoid liability. In 2004, however, former Enron directors paid $1.5 million from their own funds as part of a larger settlement of retirement-plan litigation.[14] Similarly, in 2005, 10 of 18 former Enron directors agreed to a $168 million settlement of class-action securities litigation, including $13 million from their own funds.[15] Such settlements, unlike judicial decisions, are not regarded as legal precedents but do reflect concerted efforts by institutional shareholders to hold directors personally responsible for losses. The pendulum may therefore have begun to swing toward greater board accountability.

Considered in the following sections are the governance implications of three energy company case histories, with particular emphasis on the monitoring board of directors, presumed by law to be a primary constraint on illegal or ill-considered corporate conduct. Although their factual circumstances differ, the cases are linked by a common theme: in each case, whether because of negligence, inattention, lack of independence, or structural flaws, the board failed to discharge its fiduciary duty. As a result, self-regulation proved ineffective and failed to avert disastrous consequences for shareholders, creditors, ratepayers, and markets alike.

Northeast Utilities:
A Failed Competitive Strategy[16]

Cost containment

Long before electricity deregulation had become a practical reality in New England, Northeast Utilities (Northeast) foresaw loss of market share to merchant power. In the mid-1980s, Northeast had just under 6,000 MW of generating capacity, largely produced by nuclear plants. As the high-cost supplier in an emerging regional market, Northeast feared that deregulation would allow power sources outside New England to wheel in cheaper conventional power supplies, undercutting local utility prices. Northeast also anticipated competition from large industrial and commercial customers and cogeneration facilities, expecting a 20% load loss within five years.[17] To meet this perceived threat, management adopted—and Northeast's board of trustees endorsed after the fact—an aggressive cost-containment strategy focused on nuclear engineering and operations. Given the central importance of nuclear safety, this response was problematic. It nonetheless became corporate policy without prior board approval.[18] (See table 2–1.)

Table 2–1. Northeast's Competitive Response Strategy[19]

	Northeast's Four-Part Strategy	Corporate Implementation Items
1.	Increase competitiveness of NU's core business	• cut operating and capital costs • improve customer service
2.	Improve financial performance	• establish more competitive rates • increase revenues and earning margins from Part 1 • restructure debt holdings
3.	Expand geographically and focus on electric business	• acquire electric production and distribution outside Southern New England • divest natural gas distribution
4.	Enter new energy-related businesses	• set up new corporate structure for new unregulated service offerings

Source: MacAvoy and Rosenthal, Corporate Profit and Nuclear Safety (Princeton University Press 2005)

Management's cost-containment strategy implicated issues within the purview of the Nuclear Regulatory Commission (NRC), FERC, and the utility commissions of Connecticut and Massachusetts. The NRC monitors nuclear plant operating performance and enforces safety standards. Before the advent of deregulated markets, state commissions determined whether to allow low-cost power to enter franchised monopoly markets, while FERC regulated transmission and proposed compelling incumbent utilities to wheel cheaper third-party power to retail customers. Despite these initiatives, the Connecticut commission did not believe that deregulation was imminent or that Northeast would lose significant load within five years. Nor did other major utilities share Northeast's emphasis on the strategic necessity for cost containment.[20]

For Northeast, however, company-wide cost reduction had two prospective payoffs: preventing load loss to competitive entrants and increasing profits. With fixed regulated prices, each dollar of cost savings would drop to the bottom line. In 1986, such savings increased Northeast's free cash flow by $80 million, added $36 million in after-tax earnings, and increased its net income by more than 21%.

Cost containment versus safety regulation

Nonetheless, Northeast's strategy appeared workable only if high safety ratings could be maintained as costs were contained. Northeast's nuclear plants required multimillion-dollar expenditures annually for engineering, regulatory compliance, and scheduled maintenance unrelated to day-to-day power generation. Cost containment risked degradation of plant safety and raised the prospect of forced outages and shutdowns.[21] Undeterred, management reduced operational support for the company's nuclear plants—a conscious trade-off between cost containment and safety regulation that viewed the risk of nuclear plant shutdowns as a "'hazard' in a duration survival process."[22] Northeast's board of trustees ignored the risk management had explicitly assumed.

In 1990–91, Northeast suffered forced outages, at several Millstone nuclear plants, that were attributable to "management or operational imprudence."[23] The outages reduced Northeast's overall capacity utilization to just over 50% and led the NRC to question its "relative priorities of cost containment and safety."[24] Later, after Northeast had acquired Public Service of New Hampshire (PSNH) out of bankruptcy, the NRC conditioned transfer of the operating license for PSNH's Seabrook nuclear plant by requiring that Northeast first restore its out-of-service Millstone facilities. The NRC also took the unusual step of asking Northeast's board of trustees to intervene, but to no avail: management declined to reverse cost containment at Millstone or modify short-term company-wide profit goals.[25]

Short-term earnings increase

Such disregard was driven by regulatory accounting practice. Production losses attributable to plant shutdowns did not immediately reduce corporate earnings, since costs incurred for repairs and replacement power were allocated to recovery accounts as deferred expenses, recoupable from future revenues. Despite nuclear plant shutdowns, Northeast's earnings increased during the early and mid-1990s. (See table 2–2.)

Short-run gains thus relied on continued budget reductions that deferred loss-producing nuclear renovation costs but posed the risk of an even-more-costly fix in the future.[27] Under the circumstances, it was no coincidence that management compensation depended largely on shareholder returns and cost-of-service containment, rather than avoidance of forced outages. In 1994, Northeast's top two executives realized compensation increases of almost 40%.[28]

Plant safety fell victim, in the words of a study undertaken for the Connecticut commission, "to a preoccupation on the part of executive and senior management with the cost and financial implications of operating its nuclear units, heightened by concerns over the pending deregulation of wholesale and retail electric markets."[29] In 1996, as management projected a further 40% operating-cost reduction over five years, the board remained uninvolved, despite the clear risk of nuclear shutdown. Deeming this a "course of imprudent conduct," the Connecticut commission concluded that, "despite being warned that an excessive focus on budget concerns would ultimately be more costly to the Company than . . . correcting its performance decline, the Company again opted to sacrifice its nuclear program to financial concerns."[30]

Table 2–2. Northeast Utilities Consolidated Financial Performance, 1991–1995 (millions of dollars)[26]

	1991	1992	1993	1994	1995
Operating Revenues	2,754	3,217	3,629	3,643	3,751
Operating Expenses:					
Operation –					
Fuel	674	773	918	832	909
Other	764	828	979	919	967
Maintenance	230	274	266	306	289
Depreciation	239	283	321	335	354
Taxes	377	468	465	541	518
Total Operating Expenses	2,364	2,776	3,158	3,095	3,158
Operating Income	390	442	471	548	592
Interest Charges	191	250	292	281	299
Income (Cont. Operations)	237	256	250	287	282
Long- and Short-Term Debt	2,760	4,942	4,638	4,303	4,022
Preferred and Common Equity	2,441	2,832	2,846	2,923	2,897
Total Capitalization	5,201	7,774	7,483	7,226	6,920
Northeast Utilities' Financial Performance					
Earnings per Common Share ($)	2.12	2.02	1.60	2.30	2.24
Dividends per Share ($)	1.76	1.76	1.76	1.76	1.76
Book Value per Share ($)	15.73	16.24	17.89	18.48	19.08
Market Price per Share ($)	235/8	261/2	233/4	215/8	201/4
Deferred Return on Plants (% of Earnings)	24.7	28.1	37.1	23.8	13.3

Source: Northeast Utilities, annual reports, various years

Shutdown and financial crisis

In 1996, the NRC ordered Northeast to mothball its Millstone nuclear plants until they had been relicensed. As a result, Northeast lost 40% of its generation capacity and had to spend more than $1 billion, almost none of which was recoverable, to qualify the shutdown plants for relicensing. Net income, equal to $39 million in 1996, became negative $130 million the next year, and the price of Northeast's common stock sank to just over half its per-share book value. (See table 2–3.)

Table 2–3. Northeast Utilities Consolidated Financial Performance, (millions of dollars)[31]

	1996	1997
Operating Revenues	$3,792	$3,835
Operating Expenses:		
Operation –		
Fuel	1,140	1,294
Other Operations	1,094	1,104
Maintenance	416	502
Depreciation	360	354
Taxes	352	266
Total Operating Expenses	3,483	3,644
Operating Income	309	191
Interest Charges	278	272
Income (Cont. Operations)	39	(130)
Long- and Short-Term Debt	3,947	4,012
Preferred Stock, Common Equity	2,714	2,622
Total Capitalization	6,661	6,633

Notes: Debt and equity figures for twelve months ended June 3, 1997.

Source: Northeast Utilities, annual reports, various years

The resulting financial crisis compelled Northeast to divest its remaining generating facilities and sell its retail operations. It ceased being the leading producer and distributor of electricity in New England and became a common carrier for other companies.[32]

Although board passivity, indifference, and imprudence had decisively shaped this result, no trustee was forced to resign or incurred financial liability, while Northeast's senior management team, responsible for its disastrous decade-long cost-containment strategy, realized full contract buyouts in the face of regulatory shutdown and corporate collapse. Accordingly, the "company took on the risk of destruction, while the decision-makers were left relatively unscathed."[33] As the ultimate decision-making body, the board remained unaccountable for Northeast's myopic corporate strategy driven by management's focus on short-term compensation. In view of management's concurrent neglect of nuclear maintenance requirements, the board's failure also threatened public safety.

Enron: Abdication of the Board

Background

Until its collapse in 2001, Enron was the seventh-largest U.S. company, with more than $100 billion in gross revenues and 20,000 employees worldwide. From a traditional hard-asset energy base (natural gas pipelines and power plants), Enron had reinvented itself as an energy-based merchant bank.[34] Taking advantage of deregulated energy markets and unregulated energy derivatives, Enron ran an online energy trading business as counterparty rather than broker and traded natural gas and electricity contracts unconstrained by existing controls on investment companies and commodity brokers.

Enron's share price reflected its transformation. Investment in a share of Northern Natural Gas (an Enron predecessor), worth $35 in January 1979, grew to almost $3,700 by late August 2000. Enron's share price peaked at $90, and its market capitalization reached almost $66 billion.[35] Just over a year later, Enron was bankrupt. Several factors sharply accelerated its financial demise. When Enron lost its investment-grade credit rating, counterparties refused to trade, unwound their existing positions, and brought its online business to a halt. Enron's huge off-balance-sheet debt, when finally understood, cut off credit needed to support its trading operations.[36] Its complex business strategies were then revealed to have been critically dependent on an ever-increasing but insupportable valuation for its common stock.

EnronOnline was a principal-based exchange in which all trades involved Enron as counterparty. To settle energy contracts, Enron required significant lines of credit and an investment-grade credit rating, each dependent on its meeting financial statement thresholds.[37] For years, Enron's credit rating remained remarkably stable despite the growing debt burden implicit in its many off-balance-sheet and derivative transactions. Assisted by Arthur Andersen (Andersen), its auditor, Enron used complex financial transactions to enhance reported income and cash flow, inflate asset values, and remove balance sheet liabilities. In final prebankruptcy negotiations with its bankers, Enron revealed debt approaching $40 billion, more than three times the $13 billion previously reported.[38]

The SEC interpreted these financial manipulations as part of an elaborate scheme to defraud, orchestrated by Enron's chief executive and accounting officers, Jeffrey Skilling and Richard Causey, who, it alleged, artificially inflated Enron's stock price by reporting earnings increases of 15–20% per year, facilitated by manufactured earnings, cookie jar reserves, concealed debt, and avoidance of booked losses.[39] A driving motivation was personal gain: between 1998 and 2001, Skilling netted almost $90 million by selling Enron stock.[40] Other officers also made enormous profits.

Financial engineering

Enron's expansion into energy trading and new businesses made it a voracious consumer of cash.[41] To generate cash and satisfy credit-rating criteria, Enron accelerated receivables, translated debt into equity, booked transactions at hypothetical market prices, kept underperforming assets off its books, and—most significantly— used its own stock as collateral.[42] These activities relied on several financial engineering strategies:

- *prepays*, in which third parties paid in advance for natural gas or other energy products to be delivered over a period of years

- hedges to reduce the risk of long-term energy delivery contracts

- pooling and securitizing energy assets through bonds or other financial instruments sold to investors

- selling interests in low-return, capital-intensive assets such as power plants to investors while recording the revenues generated as income

- selling such assets to unconsolidated affiliates not included in Enron's financial statements[43]

Ultimately almost half of Enron's assets, valued at $27 billion, were lodged with such unconsolidated affiliates.[44] As a result, its financial statements bore little resemblance to its actual financial condition or performance.[45]

Ignoring many obvious signals, the Enron board steadfastly supported management:

> All were familiar with the company's "asset light" strategy and actions taken . . . to move billions of dollars in assets off its balance sheet to separate but affiliated companies. All knew that, to accomplish its objectives, Enron had been relying on complicated transactions with convoluted financing and accounting structures, including transactions with multiple special purpose entities, hedges, derivatives, swaps, forward contracts, prepaid contracts, and other forms of structured finance.[46]

The Enron board

In 2001, the Enron board consisted of 15 members, several with 15 or more years of service, described as "experienced, successful businessmen and women" and "experts in areas of finance and accounting."[47] The board functioned through five standing committees, including the Audit and Compliance Committee (which approved its financial statements and was the primary liaison with Andersen), the Finance Committee (responsible for approving transactions of $75 million and above), and the Compensation Committee (which established and monitored Enron's compensation plans and policies for directors, officers, and employees). Enron board members were compensated with cash, restricted stock, phantom stock units, and stock options. In 2000, each director's total cash and equity compensation was valued at $350,000, more than twice the national average for director compensation at U.S. publicly traded companies.[48] Independence was further compromised by financial ties between Enron and certain board members. As of May 2001, such ties meant that 6 of 12 outside directors had potential conflicts of interest and that fewer than half of Enron's board members were independent of management.[49]

Subcommittee findings

A U.S. Senate subcommittee investigating Enron's collapse and bankruptcy identified fundamental failures of its board as a primary cause, including the board's disregard of known red flags.[50] The subcommittee's findings are consistent with those of the Powers Committee, a special investigative body, which determined that the board had "failed ... in its oversight duties" with "serious consequences for Enron, its employees, and its shareholders."[51]

High-risk accounting

Among other failures, the board tolerated high-risk accounting practices that allowed Enron to shift underperforming investments into nonreporting entities to accommodate its need for cash, its reluctance to issue equity, its investment-grade credit rating, and the disparity between reported net income and cash flow from operations.[52] Andersen regularly informed the Audit Committee about the financial reporting risks inherent in Enron's accounting and disclosure judgments. The board knew that Enron's accounting for structured transactions, commodity trading activities, and related-party dealings was problematic.[53] Because aggressive accounting enabled Enron to meet its funds flow and balance sheet ratio targets, however, no board member objected, requested a second opinion, or demanded a more prudent approach.[54] Among Enron's structured transactions, the following contributed significantly to its fraudulent financial reporting.[55]

FAS 140 transactions.[56] Enron viewed such transactions as balance sheet management efforts and as a means of monetizing illiquid assets (e.g., interests in partnerships or limited liability companies) by removing them from its balance sheet while retaining control and beneficial ownership. Typically, an Enron subsidiary sold an asset to an unconsolidated special-purpose entity (SPE) created for the transaction. Under then-applicable accounting rules, Enron did not need to consolidate the SPE on its balance sheet if an independent investor had made a substantive investment (at least equal to 3% of the SPE's equity), was in control of the SPE, and had the risks and rewards of asset ownership. Given these accounting parameters, the SPE could borrow 97% of the ostensible purchase price, issuing equity for the balance. The transferring subsidiary would then receive payment of the amount financed (roughly equal to the purchase price of the transferred asset). Through a total return swap, Enron would agree to pay the SPE amounts equal to scheduled repayments on its borrowing but would remain entitled to all revenues derived from the asset (whether by sale or otherwise). Enron recognized as income on its financial statements all or its share of the difference between the cash proceeds received by its subsidiary and the lower book value of the asset. It also reported subsequent increases or decreases in the value of the asset on its balance sheet and income statement. (See fig. 2–1.)

Enron's bankruptcy examiner concluded that each of its FAS 140 transactions was in fact a loan to Enron, not a sale of assets, and that Enron had incorrectly recognized as income a $350 million gain on the sale of assets transferred, had incorrectly recorded $1.1 billion as cash flow from operating activities, and had failed to disclose in its financial statements $857 million of contingent liabilities under total return swaps and $894 million of debt.[58]

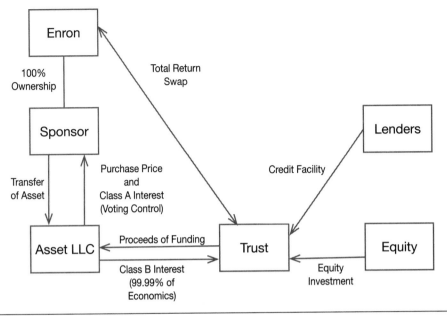

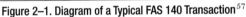

Figure 2–1. Diagram of a Typical FAS 140 Transaction[57]

Source: Second Interim Report of Neal Batson, Court-Appointed Examiner, In re Enron, et. al, U.S. Bankruptcy Court, S.D.N.Y., Case No. 01-16034 (AJG) (January 21, 2003) (Hereafter Batson II), p. 110

Noneconomic hedges. In a series of extremely complex transactions, Enron and related SPEs (the Raptors) entered into equity swaps that hedged Enron's downside risk on publicly traded stocks held in its merchant portfolio.[59] Since the stocks were accounted for as trading securities, any unrealized loss in their value would be deducted from Enron's net earnings. To avoid realizing losses, Enron entered into accounting hedges with the SPEs as counterparties.[60] If the value of Enron's merchant investment declined, the value of the SPE counterparty's hedge would increase by an equal amount, resulting in a wash. Enron funded the SPEs with $1.2 billion of its own stock (or contracts to receive its stock) in exchange for notes. Thereafter, Enron booked the notes as assets on its balance sheet, increased shareholders' equity in like amount (contrary to accepted accounting principles), and recognized income by marking to market the value of its rights under the hedges.[61] The ability of the SPEs to make good on their hedges depended entirely on the value of Enron stock transferred. (See fig. 2–2.)

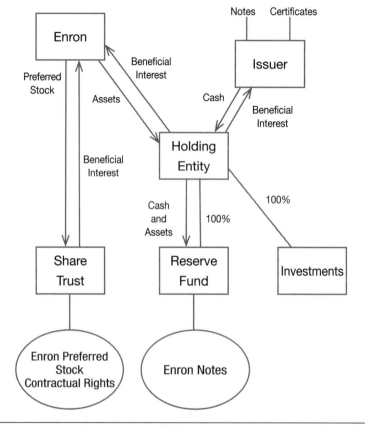

Figure 2–2. Simplified Diagram of Raptor I[62]   Source: *The Powers Report, (February 1, 2002), p.101.*

By November 2000, Enron had entered into hedge transactions with a notional value of more than $1.5 billion and had recognized a net gain of more than $500 million, equal to one-third of its earnings for 2000 (prior to restatement).[63] The Enron common stock used to capitalize the SPEs and support the swaps then began to decline in value, eventually leaving the SPEs insolvent. In the third quarter of 2001, Enron had to restate its financial statements, recording a $1.2 billion reduction in shareholder equity and a charge against income of $710 million.[64] For the 12-month period then ended, Enron's pretax earnings were $429 million, not $1.5 billion as previously

Physical Processing

Order Type: **NTAS**

Sel ID/Seq No:

136387

/14

Cust/Add: **17028000/02**   **LSSC**   **SIERRA COLLEGE LIBRARY**

Cust PO No.   **07-08**

BBS Order No: **C807226**   Ln: **204**   Del: **1**

Cust Ord Date: **12-Oct-2007**

BBS Ord Date: **12-Oct-2007**

1593700601-27632415

(9781593700607)

Sales Qty: **1**   #Vols: **001**

Energy companies and market reform

Subtitle: **energy companies and market reform wrong**   Stmt of Resp: **Jeremiah D. Lambert.**

HARDBACK   Pub Year: **2006**   Vol No.:   Edition:

Lambert, Jeremiah D.

Ser. Title:

Pennwell Publishing Company

Acc Mat:

Profiled   **PromptCat Barcode US   Mylar Dust Jacket (Clot**

Tech   **Barcode Label Applicati   Spine Label Protector U**

Services: **Barcode Label Protector   Spine Label PromptCat**

Base Charge Processing

Location:

Department:

Fund:

Stock Category:

Class #:   Cutter: Collection:

Order Line Notes:

Notes to Vendor:

Blackwell Book Services

151104

reported. The reversed transactions were not true economic hedges since Enron had borne almost all the risk and had entered into hedges with itself.[65]

Share trust transactions. Through share trust transactions, SPEs created by Enron raised $2.5 billion in off-balance-sheet financing supported by Enron preferred stock, notes, and related contractual obligations.[66] To implement a share trust transaction, Enron created a statutory business trust, the issuer, that sold notes or bonds and certificates of beneficial interest collateralized by Enron preferred stock to institutional investors, thereafter contributing the proceeds of sale to a holding entity. With the cash received (less a reserve fund), the holding entity purchased low-return assets from Enron, which reported the payment on its financial statements as "funds flow from assets sales and investments."[67] Enron also agreed to sell the preferred stock used as collateral to repay the issuer's notes or bonds when due, to issue additional stock, if necessary, to make up any shortfall, and to provide funds to repay the notes or bonds if the proceeds of stock sales were insufficient. Although Enron controlled the assets transferred, retained the related economic risks and rewards, and guaranteed the share trust transactions, both the issuer and the holding entity were treated as unconsolidated entities whose debt, incurred to finance the purchase of Enron's underperforming assets, would not appear on its balance sheet. (See fig. 2–3.)

Between 1999 and 2001, Whitewing and Osprey, the principal share trust SPEs, entered into 11 transactions with Enron to buy assets with a book value of more than $2 billion, collateralized by Enron preferred stock. Although the transactions were approved by the Enron board, the asset transfers were not true sales and should have been treated instead as loans.[69] Debt incurred by Whitewing and Osprey did not by its terms require funding until September 2002, unless accelerated by a decline in Enron's credit rating below investment grade. Triggered by other events, Enron's bankruptcy occurred in December 2001: "Before Whitewing could envelop Enron, the Raptors devoured the firm."[70]

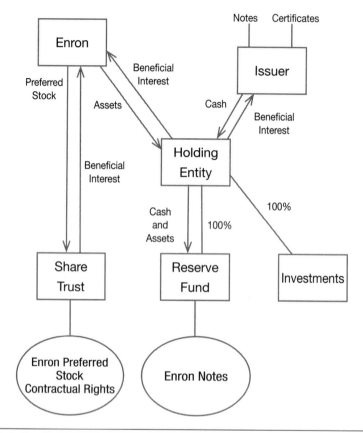

Figure 2–3. Simplified Diagram of a Typical Share Trust Transaction[68]

Source: Report of Permanent Subcommittee on Investigations, Committee on Governmental Affairs,
United States Senate (July 8, 2002) (hereinafter Subcommittee Report), p. 70

Prepay transactions. Enron used prepay transactions to maintain its investment-grade credit rating and tailored the amount of each transaction to the cash flow it needed to satisfy rating agencies in any given accounting period.[71] From 1992 through 2001, prepay transactions enabled Enron to raise $8.6 billion, $5 billion of which came from just 11 transactions with two banks, JPMorgan Chase and Citibank, consummated during the four-year period that ended in 2001. (See table 2–4.)

Table 2–4. Summary of Prepay Transactions, 1997–2001[72]

Name of Transaction	Date of Closing	Approximate Gross Proceeds Received by Enron Affiliate*	Date of Maturity
Chase VI	Dec. 18, 1997	$300 million	Dec. 2001
Chase VII	June 26, 1998	$250 million	June 2002
Chase VIII	Dec. 1, 1998	$250 million	Dec. 2002
Chase IX	June 28, 1999	$500 million	June 2004
Yosemite I	Dec. 22, 1999	$800 million	Oct. 2004
Yosemite II	Feb. 23, 2000	$331.8 million[134]	Jan. 2007
Chase X	June 28, 2000	$650 million	June 2005
Yosemite III	Aug. 25, 2000	$475 million	July 2005
Chase XI	Dec. 28, 2000	$330.4 million	Nov. 2005
Yosemite IV ($)	May 24, 2001	$475 million	Apr. 2006
Yosemite IV (£)	May 24, 2001	$154.4 million[135]	Apr. 2006
Yosemite IV (€)	May 24, 2001	$145.7 million[136]	Apr. 2006
Chase XII	Sep. 28, 2001	$350 million	Mar. 2002

* Note that these amounts do not reflect net increases in the prepay balances, as some later prepay transactions replaced earlier prepay transactions   *Source: Batson II, p. 60*

In a typical transaction, a financial institution prepaid a conduit entity for future delivery of an energy commodity. The conduit entity then transferred the amount prepaid to an Enron affiliate against its undertaking, guaranteed by Enron or a third-party letter of credit, to make future delivery of the same commodity to the conduit entity on identical terms. The financial institution in turn agreed to make future delivery of the same commodity to the Enron affiliate in exchange for its promise, similarly guaranteed, to repay the prepayment amount plus interest. On repayment, the circular delivery obligations of the parties cancelled out. No party assumed any material risk or captured an upside if the underlying commodity fluctuated in value. The financial institutions principally involved, JPMorgan Chase and Citibank, treated prepay transactions as unsecured loans even though each knew that Enron accounted for them as price management risk activities, not debt.[73] (See fig. 2–4.)

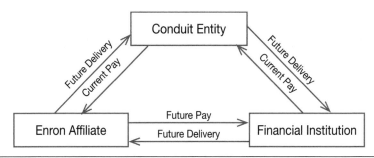

Figure 2–4. Basic Prepay Structure[74]   *Source: Batson II, p. 63*

Enron's prepay transactions produced virtually all its net cash flow from operations in 1999 and almost a third in 2000. Of $5 billion in prepay transactions as of June 30, 2001, Enron reflected less than $150 million as balance sheet debt.[75] If not for creative accounting, Enron's aggregate corporate indebtedness would have increased by 31% in 1999 and 39% in 2000. Its credit ratings would have declined accordingly.[76]

A bankruptcy examiner later determined that Enron's prepay obligations were effectively debt, hidden as commodity-related derivative deals by fraudulent bookkeeping. Through presentations made to the Finance Committee, board members knew of but did not question Enron's increasing reliance on prepay transactions and the resulting overstatement of its reported earnings and cash flow.[77]

Conflicts of interest

One commentator has described Enron's governance structure as *sui generis*:

> Other public corporations simply have not authorized their chief financial officer to run an independent entity that enters into billions of dollars of risky and volatile trading transactions with them; nor have they allowed their senior officers to profit from such self-dealing transactions without board supervision or even comprehension of the profits involved. Nor have other corporations incorporated thousands of subsidiaries and employed them in a complex web of off-balance sheet partnerships.[78]

Despite obvious conflicts of interest, the board several times waived a preexisting corporate code of conduct and allowed Enron's chief financial officer (Andrew Fastow) to establish and operate off-the-books entities for the purpose of doing business with Enron. Without debate or independent inquiry, the board approved code-of-conduct waivers enabling Fastow to establish three private equity funds in 1999–2000, known as LJM1, LJM2, and LJM3. The board did so knowing that the LJM partnerships were designed to transact business primarily with Enron, would be controlled and managed by Fastow, and would, as related parties, require effective controls and oversight to ensure that transactions with them were fair to Enron. Consequently, the board failed "to make sure the controls were effective, to monitor the fairness of the transactions, or to monitor Mr. Fastow's LJM-related compensation."[79]

Between 1999 and 2001, Enron entered into more than 20 transactions with the LJM partnerships that "defrauded Enron, its shareholders, the SEC, credit rating agencies, and others."[80] Doing such deals was nonetheless attractive to Enron, which wished to move poorly performing assets off its balance sheet, conceal anemic operating results, and manufacture earnings.

The first Enron-LJM transaction involved a $10 million Enron investment in the stock of Rhythms NetConnections, Inc. (Rhythms), an Internet service provider, and set the pattern for deals to follow.[81] Rhythms stock, purchased in March 1998 for $10 million, was soon worth $300 million, but could not be sold until the end of 1999. Accounting principles required Enron to mark the Rhythms stock and other portfolio investments to market. This meant that increases or decreases in value had to be reflected on Enron's income statement. Enron's management wanted to capture the increase in value of Rhythms stock already obtained while avoiding future income volatility. Enron also wanted to leverage the dramatic rise in the price of its own stock (as reflected in forward contracts with a financial counterparty).[82] Given the size and illiquidity of its Rhythms holdings, Enron could not find a counterparty to provide a commercial hedge.

Enron therefore looked to a vehicle of its own devising. Fastow proposed to create and serve as general partner of that vehicle (LJM1), a limited partnership that Enron would capitalize with appreciated stock, transferred in exchange for LJM1's promissory note. "The arrangement . . . permitted Enron's top financial officer—an individual with personal knowledge of Enron's assets, liabilities and profit margins—to set up his own company and sit on both sides of the table in negotiations between his business and his employer."[83] Using Enron's stock as collateral, LJM1 would thereafter enter into a swap with Enron to hedge Enron's position in Rhythms. However, the swap was not a true economic hedge, "which is obtained by paying a market price to a creditworthy counterparty who will take on the economic risk of loss."[84] Its viability depended instead on the value of the Enron stock transferred and could be compromised if the Rhythms and Enron stock declined together. (See fig. 2–5.)

On its face, LJM1 raised fundamental questions of fairness and legality: in serving concurrently as Enron's chief financial officer and LJM1's controlling person, Fastow had an obvious conflict of interest, since the proposed share-note exchange—not a true sale—would require that the note received be deducted from shareholder equity.[86] Fastow nonetheless presented the proposal to the Enron board, which approved it in June 1999 after minimal discussion and without prior review by Enron's Finance Committee.[87] The Rhythms transaction was unwound less than a year later, resulting in a windfall for LJM1, Fastow, and other Enron employees.[88] In November 2001, however, Enron could no longer avoid recognition that an LJM1 affiliate had not been properly capitalized using outside equity. With bankruptcy imminent, Enron restated its 1999 and 2000 financials, reducing its net income for those years by $95 million and $8 million, respectively.[89]

In October 1999, Fastow proposed creation of LJM2, a much larger equity fund, in which institutional investors were ultimately to make capital investments of $400 million. Because Fastow would also control LJM2, the board ratified a further waiver of Enron's code of conduct. It then approved LJM2 without substantive consideration. Enron's transactions with LJM2 were nominally subject to approval by senior officers and annual review by the Audit and Compliance Committee, conflict controls later described as "poorly designed and implemented."[90] Over two years, Enron entered into many transactions with LJM1 and LJM2, including asset sales and complex financial deals.

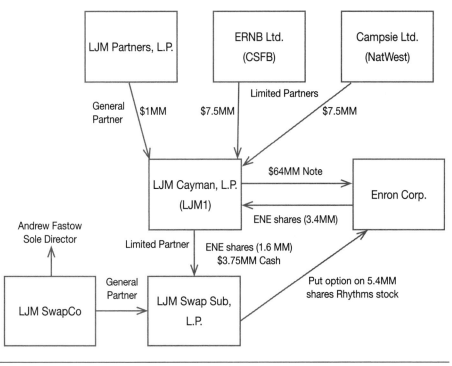

Figure 2–5. Diagram of Rhythms Transaction[85]   *Source: Subcommittee Report, p. 81*

LJM2 became an investor in and facilitator of Enron's transactions with four related SPEs called the Raptors, which served as counterparties for accounting hedges but had little or no economic substance.[91] With the Rhythms transaction as a blueprint, the Raptors served a similar purpose: enabling Enron to use the embedded value of its own equity to offset—and thus conceal from the market— almost $1 billion in losses in the value of portfolio investments.[92] In the fourth quarter of 1999 alone, LJM2 produced $2 billion of funds flow and $200 million in earnings for Enron. (See fig. 2–6.)

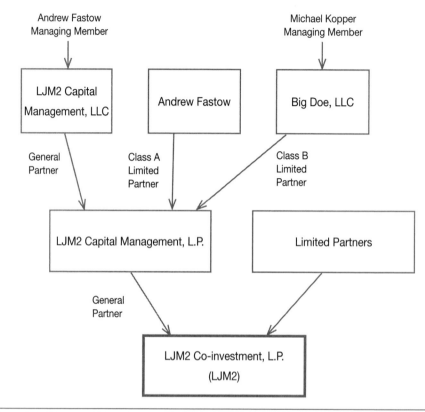

Figure 2–6. Diagram of LJM2 Structure[93] Source: Subcommittee Report, p. 74

The Raptors' financial ability to hedge depended on the sustained value of transferred Enron stock. The accounting hedges would work and the Raptors could offset Enron's portfolio losses only so long as Enron's stock price held or, if it declined, Enron issued additional stock, which Enron agreed to do pursuant to a "price swap derivative."[94] For a short time, Enron's dealings with LJM2 and the Raptors showed paper gains, allowing Enron to report increased funds flow, lower debt levels, and inflated earnings. By the third quarter of 2001, however, Enron's stock and its portfolio investments had each lost so much value that the Raptor transactions had to be unwound with disastrous financial consequences, noted earlier, that precipitated Enron's plunge into bankruptcy. Meanwhile, LJM2 and its principals earned extraordinary returns with minimal risk on projects collateralized with Enron stock.[95] All these consequences "flowed from the initial Board decision to ... allow Mr. Fastow to form, manage and profit from the LJM partnerships. . . . The Board cannot shift the responsibility for that decision to any other participant in the Enron tragedy."[96]

Inadequate public disclosure

In the decade preceding its bankruptcy, Enron submitted to the SEC annual and quarterly reports, annual proxy statements, registration statements for the sale of securities, and two filings in connection with proposed mergers.[97] Taken in their entirety, the filings were seriously deficient and concealed Enron's true financial condition by

- not fully disclosing the extent and nature of Enron's transactions with related parties, principally limited partnerships controlled by Enron's chief financial officer;

- improperly excluding the debt of certain SPEs from Enron's balance sheet;

- treating certain transactions as asset sales without actually transferring the risks of ownership, to remove underperforming assets from Enron's books;

- disguising loans as commodity trades and treating them as trading liabilities, rather than debt, and treating the cash received as cash flow from operations, rather than cash flow from financing;

- failing to disclose the full extent of contingent liabilities (i.e., debt that would become due if Enron stock or credit rating dropped below a specified level);

- accounting improperly for notes received in exchange for stock by deeming the note to be an asset that increased shareholder equity;

- treating uneconomic hedges as true hedges notwithstanding Enron's continued exposure to significant financial risk.[98]

The Powers Report described Enron's financial reporting as "fundamentally inadequate" and concluded that the Audit and Compliance Committee, among others, failed to provide "forceful or effective oversight of the disclosure process."[99] Enron's nondisclosures and improper accounting involved staggering amounts of money. Disguised loans accounted for $8 billion in liabilities treated as cash flow. Undisclosed contingent liabilities removed $4 billion in losses from Enron's financial statements. Improper hedging transactions, when reversed, led to a pretax charge against earnings of more than $700 million. Improper accounting of note-for-stock exchanges, when similarly reversed, resulted in a $1 billion reduction in shareholder equity.[100] Even after Enron restated its financials in November 2001, it acknowledged to its lending consortium that it had failed to reveal $25 billion in off-balance-sheet liabilities.[101] Triggered by these after-the-fact financial disclosures, Enron's bankruptcy soon followed, vaporizing shareholder equity once valued at $66 billion.

Enron's spectacular descent reflects, among other causal factors, a gross failure of corporate governance, subsequently addressed by Sarbanes-Oxley and similar remedial measures. Although arguably not complicit in Enron's fraud, the board was co-opted, toothless, and indifferent to its obligations. Board members signed Enron's annual SEC filings, and the Audit and Compliance Committee reviewed the related-party transactions described therein, all without visible prophylactic effect. Ultimately, the "board failed in its fiduciary duty to insure adequate public disclosure of Enron's off-the-books assets and liabilities,"[102] and those relying on the board to provide even a minimal safeguard against fraudulent financial reporting suffered huge losses as a result.

Royal Dutch Shell Group: Management by Committee

In January 2004, the Royal Dutch Shell Group (Shell) startled investors and the business world by announcing reclassification of 20% of its proved oil and gas reserves, primarily in Nigeria and Australia, equal to 3.9 billion barrels of oil equivalent (boe). The write-down cut Shell's reserve life from 13.4 years to 10.6 years, increased its worldwide five-year average reserve replacement cost from $5.49 to $12.57 per barrel (128% greater than the industry average of $5.51), increased its finding and development costs to $7.90 per barrel, and reduced its appraised net worth by $9.6 billion.[103]

Since over 70% of an oil and gas company's total market value is typically attributable to its proved reserves, investors' reaction was swift: following the announcement, shares of Shell Transport and Trading (Shell Transport), a member of the Shell Group, fell 6.84% on the London exchange and its American depositary receipts (ADRs) fell 6.96% on the New York Stock Exchange (NYSE), reducing its capitalization by almost £3 billion. Royal Dutch experienced a similar decline: its ordinary shares fell by 7.10% on the Amsterdam exchange, and its ADRs fell 7.87% on the NYSE.[104]

By May 2004, Shell's reclassification encompassed 23% of its proved reserves, equal to 4.47 million boe. Shell acknowledged that the reclassified reserves were not in fact proved reserves as defined by SEC Rule 4-10 (to which it was subject as a foreign issuer of stock registered with the SEC and traded on the NYSE).[105] In July 2004, Shell made an amended SEC filing, reducing its proved reserves and related future cash flows for the years 1999 through 2002.[106] For 2002 alone, the reclassification reduced Shell's future cash flows by $6.6 billion. (See table 2–5.) Reclassification of proved reserves also required Shell to reduce its reserves replacement ratio (RRR), a key industry metric and driver of company share price, for 1998 through 2002.

Table 2–5. Table Showing Reduction in Proved Reserves and Future Cash Flows[107]

Year	Reduction in "Proved" Reserves	% Reduction	Reduction in Standardized Measure	% Reduction
1997	3.13 boe	16%	N/A	N/A
1998	3.78 boe	18%	N/A	N/A
1999	4.58 boe	23%	$7.0 billion	11%
2000	4.84 boe	25%	$7.2 billion	10%
2001	4.53 boe	24%	$6.5 billion	13%
2002	4.47 boe	23%	$6.6 bilion	9%

Source: SEC Complaint in Civil Action H-04-3359, U.S.D.C., S.D. Houston (2004) (hereafter SEC Complaint)

Despite the economic impact of reclassification, Shell denied misconduct, arguing that the differences between its and the SEC's criteria for booking reserves were largely technical in nature. The investment community and regulators thought otherwise, however, and Shell's chairman, Sir Philip Watts, and its head of exploration, Walter van de Vijver, were compelled to resign on March 1, 2004.

The Davis, Polk & Wardwell Report

In February 2004, the Shell Group Audit Committee hired Davis, Polk & Wardwell (DPW) as independent counsel to investigate Shell's reclassification of reserves in Australia, Nigeria, Oman, and Brunei.[108] DPW focused on the knowledge and conduct of Shell's most senior management and the extent to which its internal guidelines on booking proved reserves were consistent with SEC regulations. (In 1998, to improve its industry-lagging RRR, Shell had adopted more aggressive internal guidelines just a few years before the SEC staff, in 2001, narrowed the definition of proved reserves contained in Rule 4-10. The SEC required that a product market must be shown to exist, with reasonable certainty, in conjunction with an economic method of extracting, treating, and transporting reserves produced from known reservoirs under existing economic and operating conditions.)[109]

At the time, Shell was wholly owned on a 60:40 basis by two holding companies: N.V. Koninklijke Nederlandsche Petroleum Maatschappij (Royal Dutch) and Shell Transport, respectively, which shared dividend and interest income and bore costs in the same ratio pursuant to an equalization agreement. Royal Dutch, the dominant partner, was managed by a self-perpetuating board of managers and supervisory board, and Shell Transport was managed by a unitary board, each of which comprised different individuals responsible to separate shareholder constituencies. Royal Dutch and Shell Transport in turn functioned through three intermediate holding companies, whose share capital and board seats were controlled by Royal Dutch. Under broad supervision of the Committee of Managing Directors (CMD) and the Conference (an informal gathering of the two parent company board members together with senior group executives), the intermediate holding companies enjoyed substantial autonomy and did business worldwide through operating subsidiaries.[110] (See fig. 2–7.)

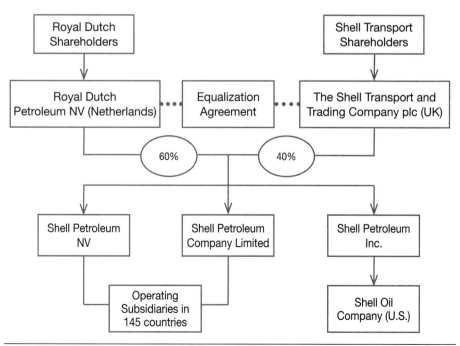

Figure 2–7. Royal Dutch/Shell Combined Group[111]   *Source: Knight, Shell Games, p. 70*

Figure 2–8 shows Royal Dutch/Shell corporate governance as it was before the resignations of Watts and van de Vijver in 2004.

In mid-2001, van de Vijver succeeded Watts as chief executive officer of Royal Dutch Petroleum, N.V., Shell's exploration arm, and Watts became chairman of the CMD and Shell Transport. According to the DPW Report, van de Vijver thereafter "engaged in a pointed dialogue" with Watts, expressing concern about reserves prematurely booked to meet external targets and reserve numbers that did not comply with the SEC's requirement of reasonable certainty. In February 2002, van de Vijver warned the CMD that Shell's proved reserves were "no longer aligned with the SEC rules" and could be overstated by as much as 2.3 billion boe.

In response, Watts directed van de Vijver to leave "no stone unturned" to achieve 100% RRR for 2002, a result facially inconsistent with de-booking. Van de Vijver's further presentation to the CMD in July 2002 therefore omitted his prior warning. The DPW Report saw this as evidence of Shell's intent to "'manage' the totality of the reserve position over time, with the hope that problematic reserve bookings could be rendered immaterial by project maturation, license extensions, exploration successes and/or strategic activity."[113]

Watts and van de Vijver were deemed "alert to the differences between the information concerning reserves that had been transmitted to the public, 'external,' and the information known to come members of management, 'internal.'"[114] In a September 2002 memorandum, van de Vijver confirmed that Shell's "reserves replacement and production growth were inflated," a warning he repeated to Watts several times during the next year.[115] In a culminating e-mail to Watts in November 2003, van de Vijver spoke of "lying about the extent of our reserves" and "far too aggressive/optimistic bookings."[116] Both knew that if its SEC filings overstated 2002 proved reserves, Shell would have to disclose the overstatement to all investors at the same time and without delay.[117]

	Royal Dutch Petroleum NV **Board of Managers** Jeroen van der Veer (President) Walter van de Vijver (CEO) Malcolm Brinded Rob Routs **Supervisory Board** Aad Jacobs (Chairman) Wim Kok Jonkheer Aarnout Louden Prof. Hubert Markl Prof. Joachim Milberg Lawrence Ricciardi Maarten van den Bergh (former Executive) Henny de Ruiter (former Executive)	The Shell Transport and Trading Company PLC **Board of Directors** Sir Philip Watts (Chairman and Managing Director) Judy Boynton (CFO) Sir Mark Moody-Stuart (Non Exec. and former Chair) Teymour Alireza (Non Exec.) Sir Peter Burt (Ind. Non Exec.) Dr. Eileen Buttle (Ind. Non Exec.) Luis Giusti (Ind. Non Exec.) Mary Henderson (Ind. Non Exec.) Sir Peter Job (Ind. Non Exec.) Sir John Kerr (Ind. Non Exec.) Lord Oxburgh (Ind. Senior Non Exec.)
TOP TIER COMPANIES		

Committee of Managing Directors

Sir Philip Watts (Chairman)
Jeroen van der Veer (Vice Chairman and CEO Chemicals)
Walter van de Vijver (MD and CEO Production & Exploration)
Judy Boynton (MD and CFO)
Malcolm Brinded (MD and CEO Gas & Power)
Rob Routs (MD and CEO Oil Products)

	Shell Petroleum NV **Board of Directors** Sir Philip Watts (Presidium) Jeroen van der Veer (Presidium) Walter van de Vijver (Presidium) Judy Boynton (Presidium) Malcolm Brinded (Presidium) Rob Routs (Presidium) Henny de Ruiter Sir Mark Moody-Stuart Maarten van den Bergh	Shell Petroleum Company Limited **Board of Directors** Sir Philip Watts Jeroen van der Veer Walter van de Vijver Judy Boynton Malcolm Brinded Rob Routs Henny de Ruiter Sir Mark Moody-Stuart Maarten van den Bergh	Shell Petroleum Inc. **Board of Directors** Robert F. Daniel Vilma S. Martinez Lynn Eisenhans Curtis R. Frasier Steven L. Miller Gorgon R. Sullivan M. Fran Keeth Raoul Restucci Sir Philip Watts
INTERMEDIATE TIER COMPANIES			

	Non U.S. Operating Companies	U.S. Operating Companies
OPERATING TIER		

Figure 2–8. Royal Dutch/Shell Corporate Governance[112]   *Source: Knight, Shell Games, p.77*

In late 2003, catalyzed by troublesome reserve audits in Australia, Nigeria, Oman, and Brunei, Shell commenced an internal review, followed by its decision to reclassify 20% of its reported proved reserves.[118] The DPW Report, made public on March 31, 2004, concluded that Shell management had for years managed, rather than de-booked, nonqualifying reserves, used ill-designed and out-of-date reserve guidelines, tolerated an inadequate internal audit staff who lacked instruction on regulatory requirements, and failed to present Shell's outside directors and the Group Audit Committee with information that would have allowed them to identify or address the issue.[119]

The Knight Vinke Institutional Partners Memorandum

Spurred by the reclassification announcement, a substantial investor in Shell shares, Knight Vinke Institutional Partners (KVIP), prepared a confidential memorandum attributing Shell's reserve problems to its flawed and idiosyncratic governance structure, evidenced by poor internal communications, inadequate controls, lack of accountability, and unclear reporting lines.[120] The KVIP Memorandum identified several underlying governance failures:

Management by committee. The CMD—composed of four Royal Dutch and two Shell Transport managing directors— determined policy and strategy for Shell's operating companies without independent review, while substantial power and autonomy remained with the chief executive officers of Shell's four main operating companies. None of those officers reported to the CMD or its chairman, and the CMD had no direct accountability to the boards or shareholders of Royal Dutch and Shell Transport:

The person presented as [Shell's] chief executive, the chairman of the CMD, apparently lacked either the authority or responsibilities or the accountability normally associated with a chief executive. He reported to two boards comprised of different individuals and so, effectively, to none.[121]

The KVIP Memorandum called this configuration management by committee.[122]

Management succession. The Royal Dutch Board of Managers and related Supervisory Board, which together controlled the majority shareholder in the Shell group, were effectively close-knit, self-perpetuating bodies. Through ownership or control of priority shares, they had "unfettered power" to nominate their members and reject nominations by shareholders, "shielded from shareholder intervention."[123]

Conflict at top-tier board level. The Royal Dutch and Shell Transport boards comprised two different groups of executive and nonexecutive/supervisory directors, each bound to consider the separate interests of their respective companies and shareholder constituencies.[124]

CMD's lack of transparency. As an internally appointed body, the CMD lacked transparency and accountability and had no defined lines of succession: "Fundamental decisions regarding overall strategy are seemingly taken without review from any independent body or representative."[125]

Lack of executive accountability. Shell's unique governance structure diluted and blurred lines of accountability of its operating company chief executives for the group's overall performance and management.[126]

The Financial Services Authority Final Notice

The Financial Services Authority (FSA), an independent body that regulates the financial services industry in the United Kingdom, enforces the Financial Services and Markets Act of 2000. In its Final Notice issued in August 2004, the FSA imposed a £17 million financial penalty on Shell Transport for Shell's "market abuse" in connection with "false and misleading" announcements of proved reserves and RRR from 1998 through 2003 made despite internal warnings.[127] The FSA determined that Shell had failed to put in place adequate systems and controls over reserves estimation and reporting.

Building on the DPW Report, the Final Notice traced Shell's reporting delinquency to revised guidelines issued in September 1998, citing an internal memorandum, "Creating Value through Entrepreneurial Management of Hydrocarbon Resource Values." The revised guidelines encouraged overstatement of proved reserves in Australia, Nigeria, Brunei, and Oman.[128] By mid-2000, the overstatement was well known within Shell, which nonetheless took "no further steps to assess the accuracy of its reported proved reserves."[129]

Following the SEC's guidance on Rule 4-10, however, an in-house audit committee urged Shell to revisit its aggressive internal guidelines. Memoranda prepared for management during 2002–3 recommended transparency in reporting, identified overstated reserves, and acknowledged that proved reserves were at risk. Despite this explicit guidance, Shell failed to de-book reserves that no longer qualified as proved while continuing to book proved reserves for projects that lacked necessary governmental approvals and deviated from Rule 4-10's technical requirements.[130]

In 2002, the chief executive officer of Shell's exploration company advised the CMD that its probabilistic reserve guidelines were "too aggressive," but did not recommend de-booking.[131] Later the Group Audit Committee was told that Shell's "potential exposure . . . is offset" by gas consumed on site or flared. Not until December 2003 did members of the Royal Dutch and Shell Transport boards finally accept that Shell had substantially overstated its proved reserves. Shell's reclassification—first announced to the public in January 2004—belatedly imposed a 23% haircut.[132]

The Final Notice emphasized Shell's failure to implement adequate guidelines and internal controls and heed numerous internal warnings. It singled out for special criticism the Group Audit Committee, whose petroleum engineer reported to Shell's exploration management, did not have an independent role, and lacked authority to enforce internal guidelines. To create and maintain the appearance of a strong RRR, the Final Notice concluded, Shell had reported proved reserves it knew or should have known were noncompliant with Rule 4-10.[133]

SEC enforcement

As the largest public company in the Netherlands, Royal Dutch was substantially owned by U.S. institutional investors, who held 20% of its stock in the form of ADRs traded on the NYSE, with a market value of approximately $25 billion.[134] Shell Transport's ADRs also traded on the NYSE. The stock of both companies was registered with the SEC, which commenced an enforcement action and filed a civil suit following Shell's reclassification announcement. The thrust of the SEC's case was consistent with the DPW Report and the FSA Final Notice: despite internal warnings, Shell had been led "to record and maintain proved reserves it knew, or was reckless in not knowing, did not satisfy applicable regulations and to report for certain years a stronger RRR than it had actually achieved."[135]

In August 2004, Shell settled with the SEC for $120 million and consented to a cease-and-desist order finding violations of the antifraud, internal controls, record-keeping, and reporting provisions of federal securities laws. Shell also committed $5 million to implement a comprehensive internal compliance program.[136] The investigations of both the SEC and the FSA continued following the settlement.

Epilogue

In November 2004, Shell announced, subject to shareholder vote, its prospective reorganization as a single company, Royal Dutch Shell, to be incorporated in the United Kingdom, headquartered in the Netherlands, and managed by a single board of directors consisting of 10 independent nonexecutive directors (six from Royal Dutch and four from Shell Transport) and five executive directors. Shell stated that the unified company would comply with the U.K. Combined Code and applicable provisions of the Sarbanes-Oxley Act. The reorganization also responded to a pension-fund shareholders derivative suit demanding that Shell install a single board to which management would be accountable.[137] In June 2005, federal prosecutors decided not to charge Royal Dutch Shell criminally for overstatement of its energy reserves, noting that it "has cooperated fully with the government's investigation, has implemented substantial remedial efforts to enhance its reserve reporting and compliance, and has paid a $120 million civil penalty to the SEC."[138]

Observations

The foregoing cases, when viewed from a board perspective, show the complex interaction between corporate strategy and regulatory requirements, particularly those related to financial disclosure and accounting. Although regulators may defer to companies on matters requiring business judgment, the managements of Northeast, Shell, and Enron exceeded the bandwidth of permissible corporate discretion as their respective boards stood by. More focused and timely government intervention could have prevented or mitigated the ensuing impact on markets, shareholders, and the public.

Notes

[1] See, e.g., *ACE Ltd. v. Capital Re Corp.*, 747 A.2d 95 (Del. Ch. 1999); *Aronson v. Lewis*, 473 A.2d 805 (Del. 1984), overruled in part on other grounds; *Brehm v. Eisner*, 746 A.2d 244 (Del. 2000). For a general discussion, see Eisenberg. "The Divergence of Standards of Conduct and Standards of Review." *Fordham Law Review*, 62: 437, 439 (1993) (hereafter *Eisenberg*); Drexler, Black, and Sparks. "The Proper Exercise of a Director's Responsibilities." In *Delaware Corporate Law and Practice*. Matthew Bender (2002).

[2] See, e.g., Baker and Hayes. "Reflecting Form over Substance: The Case of Enron Corp." *Critical Perspectives on Accounting*, 15: 767 (2004).

[3] See, e.g., Coffee. "What Caused Enron? A Capsule Social and Economic History of the 1990's." *Columbia Law and Economics Working Paper No. 214* (2003); Gordon. "Governance Failures of the Enron Board and the New Information Order of Sarbanes-Oxley." *Columbia Law and Economics Working Paper No. 216* (2003); Gordon. "What Enron Means for the Management of the Modern Business Corporation: Some Initial Reflections." *Columbia Law and Economics Working Paper No. 203* (2002); Coffee. "Understanding Enron: It's about the Gatekeepers, Stupid." *Columbia Law and Economics Working Paper No. 207* (2002) (hereafter *Coffee 2002*); Bratton. "Enron and the Dark Side of Shareholder Value," *Public Law and Legal Theory Working Paper No. 035.* The George Washington University Law School (2002) (hereafter *Bratton*); Partnoy. Testimony before the Committee on Governmental Affairs, U.S. Senate (January 24, 2002) (hereafter *Partnoy*); Strine. "Derivative Impact? Some Early Reflections on the Corporation Law Implications of the Enron Debacle." *Business Lawyer*, 57: 1371 (2003).

[4] See, e.g., Millstein. Prepared statement before the Committee on Banking, Housing, and Urban Affairs, U.S. Senate. Oversight Hearing on Accounting and Investor Protection Issues Raised by Enron and Other Public Companies (February 27, 2002).

[5] Financial reporting misrepresentation typically involves asset inflation, understatement of liabilities, false profits, and hidden losses. See *Report of Investigation by the Special Investigative Subcommittee of the Board of Directors of Enron Corp.* (February 1, 2002) (hereafter *The Powers Report*), pp. 22–26. See also *Partnoy*, p. 2.

[6] *In Re Caremark International Inc. Derivative Litigation,* 698 A. 2d 959 (Del. Ch. 1996). See also *McCall v. Scott,* 239 F.3d 808 (6th Cir. 2001).

[7] *Eisenberg,* p. 439 (1993).

[8] *In Re Caremark International Inc. Derivative Litigation,* 698 A. 2d 959, 962 (Del. Ch. 1996).

[9] Ibid. Accordingly, the duty to monitor, the duty of inquiry, and the duty to employ a reasonable decision-making process are arguably not protected by the business judgment rule and are subject instead to a gross-negligence standard of review, i.e., "a sustained or systematic failure of the board to exercise oversight" (p. 971). See also *Eisenberg,* p. 448.

[10] *In Re Caremark International Inc. Derivative Litigation,* 698 A.2d 959, 963 (Del. Ch. 1996).

[11] *Bratton,* p. 58. Cf. *Pereira v. Cogan,* 2001 U.S. Dist WL 243537 (S.D.N.Y. March 8, 2001). The protection afforded company directors by the business judgment rule is available only to those who can show that they fulfilled their fiduciary duties by acting on an informed basis, in good faith, and with the genuine conviction that they served the best interests of the company.

[12] Ibid.

[13] *The Role of the Board of Directors in Enron's Collapse.* Report of the Permanent Subcommittee on Investigations of the Committee on Governmental Affairs, U.S. Senate, Report 107-70 (July 8, 2002) (hereafter *Subcommittee Report*), p. 3. Members of the board also sold shares to the public at a time when false financial information was used to support the price of Enron stock.

[14] *Chao v. Enron,* Civil Action No. H-03-2257 (S.D. Tex.), and *Tittle v. Enron Corp. et al.,* Civil Action No. 01-3913 (S.D. Tex.) ($86.5 million settlement of Department of Labor and private class action litigation with respect to Enron's pension and employee stock ownership plans, including $1.5 million paid by directors from their own funds). Enron management froze employees' 401(k) accounts on October 17, 2001, the day Enron revealed a third-quarter loss of $638 million. Enron directors and senior management continued selling. Amalgamated Bank, the plaintiff in a lawsuit against Enron's officers and directors, alleged gross sales of $1 billion over a three-year period. *Bratton,* p. 17.

[15] *New York Times*, January 8, 2005, p. B1.

[16] This section is based on MacAvoy and Rosenthal. *Corporate Profit and Nuclear Safety*. Princeton University Press (2005) (hereafter *M&R*).

[17] Ibid., p. 10. Northeast's operating subsidiaries were Connecticut Light and Power, Western Massachusetts Electric Company, and Hartford Light Company. Ibid., p. 14.

[18] Ibid., p. 13.

[19] Northeast Utilities. *1988 Annual Report*, pp. 2–8; see also *M&R*, p. 12.

[20] *M&R*, pp. 18–26.

[21] Ibid., pp. 27–31.

[22] Ibid., p. 45.

[23] Ibid., p. 49.

[24] Ibid., pp. 54–55.

[25] Ibid., pp. 57–61.

[26] Northeast Utilities. *Annual Reports*, various years; see also *M&R*, pp. 81–82.

[27] *M&R*, pp. 61–63.

[28] Ibid., p. 84.

[29] Ibid., p. 72.

[30] Ibid., p. 78.

[31] Ibid., p. 103.

[32] Ibid., pp. 88, 101–2, 106–7.

[33] Ibid., p. 111.

[34] See *Subcommittee Report*, pp. 6–7.

[35] Bodurtha. *"Unfair Values"—Enron's Shell Game*. White paper (March 2003), The McDonough School of Business, Georgetown University (hereafter *Bodurtha*), p. 2.

[36] Gillan and Martin. *Financial Engineering, Corporate Governance, and the Collapse of Enron.* Working paper dated November 11, 2002, Center for Corporate Governance, University of Delaware (hereafter *Working Paper*), pp. 8–9.

[37] *Subcommittee Report*, p. 7

[38] *Bodurtha*, p. 3. Thus, more than $25 billion of additional debt was off balance sheet or classified as something other than debt. Approximately $14 billion of that amount had been incurred through structured finance transactions involving the use of special-purpose entities. Enron's presentation to its bankers divided the additional debt into eight categories: FAS 140 transactions, minority interest financings, commodity transactions with financial institutions, share trusts, equity forward contracts, structured assets, unconsolidated affiliates, and leases. See *Second Interim Report of Neal Batson, Court-Appointed Examiner, In Re Enron, et al.*, United States Bankruptcy Court, Southern District of New York, Case No. 01-16034 (AJG), January 21, 2003 (hereafter *Batson*), p. 10.

[39] *Securities and Exchange Commission v. Jeffrey K. Skilling and Richard Causey*, First Amended Complaint dated February 19, 2004, Civil Action No. H-04-0284, United States District Court for the Southern District of Texas, Houston Division (hereafter *SEC Enron Complaint*), ¶¶ 10–16, 18. In furtherance of the scheme, Skilling and Causey are alleged to have (i) used reserve accounts to mask volatility in Enron's wholesale energy trading earnings and to preserve such earnings for later application; (ii) manufactured earnings and improved Enron's balance sheet through overvaluation of Enron's merchant investment portfolio; (iii) concealed large losses and failures in Enron Energy Services and Enron Broadband Services by manipulating segment reporting, using reserved energy trading earnings, and manipulating expense accounting; (iv) represented earnings from increases in Enron's stock price as recurring earnings from energy operations; (v) used purportedly independent third-party investment entities to avoid booking losses, conceal debt, manage earnings, and enrich Enron executives; (vi) structured deals as energy transactions that were in fact unreported loans; and (vii) reported Enron's financial results in a false and misleading manner.

[40] Causey received more than $14 million from the sale of Enron stock and netted over $5 million.

[41] *Batson*, p. 17.

[42] *Bodurtha*, p. 16.

[43] Ibid., p. 16.

[44] *Subcommittee Report*, p. 8.

[45] *Batson*, p. 15.

[46] *Subcommittee Report*, p. 8.

[47] Ibid., p. 8.

[48] Ibid., p. 11.

[49] These ties encompassed consulting fees paid to directors, transactions with entities in which directors played a major role, and donations to groups with which directors were affiliated. *Working Paper*, p. 23. See also Strine. "Derivative Impact? Some Early Reflections on the Corporation Law Implications of the Enron Debacle." *Business Lawyer*, 57: 1371 (2002).

[50] *Working Paper*, p. 60.

[51] Special Investigative Committee of the Board of Directors of the Enron Corp. *Report of Investigation* (February 1, 2002) (hereafter *The Powers Report*), p. 22.

[52] *Batson*, p. 36. Enron was reluctant to issue equity for fear of an adverse effect on its stock price and to incur debt for fear of an adverse effect on its credit rating. Mark-to-market accounting created a large gap between net income and cash flow from operations. Enron therefore sought to raise cash while maintaining its credit rating without issuing equity or incurring debt.

[53] *Subcommittee Report*, pp. 15–16.

[54] Ibid., p. 17, 22.

[55] In addition to the transactions discussed in the text, Enron engaged in tax transactions to boost reported income by creating future tax deductions and recording in the current period the related projected benefits. See *Batson*, pp. 87–94. Enron also relied on financings to raise money classified on its balance sheet as minority interests, a category of financing treated by credit-rating agencies as hybrid equity, rather than debt. Typically, Enron would establish a majority-owned

subsidiary with a minority interest taken by another entity, financed by debt and equity in the proportions of 97% and 3%. The minority shareholder in the subsidiary was not consolidated with Enron for accounting purposes, and Enron's financing from this source was not counted as debt, with the result that its credit ratios were improved. See *Batson*, at pp. 79–85. Enron also used mark-to-market accounting to generate reported earnings by periodically revaluing complex, long-term contracts based on questionable valuation assumptions. Cornford. *Enron and Internationally Agreed Principles for Corporate Governance and the Financial Sector.* G-24 Discussion Paper Series No. 30. United Nations (June 2004).

[56] FAS 140 transactions are structured finance transactions intended to comply with either "Accounting for Transfers and Servicing of Financial Assets and Extinguishments of Liabilities," Statement of Accounting Standards No. 125, or its successor, "Accounting for Transfers and Servicing of Financial Assets and Extinguishments of Liabilities," Statement of Financial Accounting Standards No. 140. Enron first engaged in FAS 140 transactions in 1998. *Batson*, p. 107.

[57] *Batson*, p. 110.

[58] Ibid., pp. 37–39, 107–12.

[59] *Bratton*, p. 38. Enron's merchant investments arose through its expansion into international markets and its interest in growing domestic energy businesses. Merchant investments included Transportadora de Gas del Sur SA, Catalytica Energy Systems, Inc.; Azurix; Hanover Combustion; Avici Systems, Inc.; The New Power Company; Enron Oil & Gas; and EOTT Energy Partnership. Most merchant investments performed poorly and required additional support from Enron's stock. *Bodurtha*, pp. 34–35.

[60] *The Powers Report*, p. 97.

[61] *Bratton*, pp. 37, 39. See *EITF Issue No. 85-1*, "Classifying Notes Received for Capital"; SEC Staff Accounting Bulletin No. 40, Topic 4-E, "Receivables from Sale of Stock."

[62] *The Powers Report*, p. 101.

[63] The net gain recognized from this source during the first nine months of 2001 was $545 million. *The Powers Report*, pp. 119, 128; *Bratton*, n. 26, p. 39.

[64] *The Powers Report,* pp. 126, 128.

[65] Ibid., p. 97.

[66] *Batson,* p. 68. The principal vehicles were Whitewing Associates L.P. and related trusts (Osprey and Nighthawk).

[67] *Subcommittee Report,* p. 40. Enron reflected $1 billion in positive funds flow from this source on its 2000 balance sheet.

[68] Ibid., p. 70.

[69] *Batson,* p. 76.

[70] *Bodurtha,* p. 34.

[71] *Batson,* p. 62.

[72] Ibid., p. 60.

[73] Ibid., app. E, pp. 48–50. See also letter dated July 28, 2003, from Robert M. Morgenthau, District Attorney of the Borough of Manhattan, to the Board of Governors of the Federal Reserve System, Federal Reserve Bank of New York, Office of the Comptroller of the Currency, and New York State Banking Department, which states in part, "[JPMorgan Chase] and Citibank knowingly structured the prepaid transactions with Enron in a way that allowed Enron to engage in fraudulent accounting and to make its financial statements less transparent. The prepaids, ostensibly derivative transactions involving prepayment for volumes of crude oil or natural gas, created the appearance that three seemingly independent entities were engaged in legitimate arms-length commodities trading. In fact, the circular structure of the deals eliminated all conceivable market risk, and the transactions, even though they were handled by the derivatives departments, were really disguised loans. Enron should have recorded the prepaids as bank or credit financings and the cash received as cash flows from financings. It did neither. Instead it recorded the debt as liabilities from price risk management activities and the cash as cash flows from operating activities. As a result, Enron continued to function, even as billions of dollars worth of debt-like obligations from the prepaids accumulated on its books, hidden from the view of its investors, creditors and regulators alike."

[74] *Batson,* p. 63.

[75] Ibid., app. E, p. 3.

[76] *Batson,* p. 7.

[77] *Subcommittee Report,* pp. 21–22 and n. 48; *Batson,* p. 66.

[78] *Coffee 2002,* p. 3.

[79] *Subcommittee Report,* p. 24. Of the three LJM entities, only LJM1 and LJM2 became active. LJM1 was organized as a limited partnership in the Cayman Islands and refers to a company named LJM Cayman, L.P.; LJM2 was organized as a Delaware limited partnership and refers to a company named LJM2 Co-Investment, L.P. In each instance, the entity that served as the general partner of LJM1 or LJM2, responsible for running the equity fund on a day-to-day basis, was wholly owned by Fastow through intermediaries. Each of LJM1 and LJM2 was capitalized by limited partners, including banks, pension funds, and insurance companies. See also *The Powers Report,* pp. 68–74.

[80] *SEC Enron Complaint,* ¶ 35.

[81] For a general discussion, see *The Powers Report,* pp. 77–96.

[82] Enron entered into these contracts to hedge dilution resulting from its employee stock option programs. As the price of Enron stock rose, the contracts had become significantly more valuable. *The Powers Report,* p. 78.

[83] *Subcommittee Report,* p. 29.

[84] Ibid., p. 83.

[85] Ibid., p. 81.

[86] *Bodurtha,* p. 28., n. 59; *Bratton,* p. 37. As the note is paid, the reduction is amortized with a corresponding net increase to the shareholders' equity account.

[87] *Subcommittee Report,* p. 27.

[88] *The Powers Report,* pp. 90–91. The Powers Committee determined that the value LJM1 received in the unwinding was $70 million greater than the value Enron received, not including Enron shares still retained by LJM1 that had an undiscounted value of $251 million on April 28, 2000.

[89] Ibid., p. 84.

[90] *Subcommittee Report*, p. 29.

[91] Ibid., p. 44.

[92] Ibid., pp. 44, 70–73, 97–98. The strategy of using Enron's own stock to offset portfolio losses runs counter to a basic principle of accounting and financial reporting: except under limited circumstances, a company may not recognize gains on its income statement attributable to an increase in the value of its capital stock.

[93] Ibid., p. 74.

[94] *Partnoy*, p. 3, n. 26. Enron committed to issue additional stock if its counterparty's assets declined in value. The greater such decline, the more stock Enron had to issue. Enron's shareholders were therefore subject to substantial dilution, but Enron locked in gain on its portfolio stock and avoided future charges against income through an ostensible hedge.

[95] LJM2 was managed by Fastow and other Enron employees. It made an investment in each of the Raptors on which it was to receive an initial guaranteed return before any hedging or derivative transactions with Enron could take effect. The results were extremely favorable to LJM2. In October 2000, Fastow reported that the Raptors had realized internal rates of return of 193%, 278%, 2,500%, and 124%, respectively. *The Powers Report*, p. 128.

[96] *Subcommittee Report*, p. 38.

[97] "Financial Oversight of Enron: The SEC and Private-Sector Watchdogs." In *Report of the Staff to the Senate Committee on Governmental Affairs*, 107th Congress (October 8, 2002) (hereafter *Senate Staff Report*), p. 31. In addition, Enron had an ownership interest in 50 other companies that were required to file separately with the SEC. In half of those companies, Enron's ownership interest was 20% or greater.

[98] *Senate Staff Report*, pp. 24–25.

[99] *The Powers Report*, pp. 187, 202.

[100] Ibid., p. 26.

[101] *Bodurtha*, p. 44, n. 26.

[102] *Subcommittee Report,* p. 50.

[103] *Verteris Securities Class Action Directory,* http://www.securitiesassociation directory.com/casehome/2856 (February 14, 2005) (hereafter *Verteris*). Shell was not to be alone in this respect. In February 2004, El Paso Corporation announced that, as of January 1, 2003, it had overstated its natural gas reserves by 41%, equal to 3.64 trillion cubic feet, and would take a pretax charge against earnings of $1 billion. Following the announcement, the El Paso share price fell by 18%. See *Copland v. El Paso Corporation et al.,* civil action filed in U.S. District Court, Southern District of Texas, Houston Division, dated February 26, 2004.

[104] See Final Notice, dated August 24, 2004, of the Financial Services Authority (U.K.) (hereafter *Final Notice*), p. 2; see also *Verteris.* The 70% figure appears in Dharan. "Improving the Relevance and Reliability of Oil and Gas Reserves Disclosures." In *Shell Games: Corporate Governance and Accounting for Oil and Gas Reserves* (hereafter *Shell Games*), p. 32. Hearing before the Committee on Financial Services, U.S. House of Representatives, 108th Cong., 2d Sess., July 21, 2004. Royal Dutch is the largest listed company in the Netherlands, and Shell Transport is among the 10 largest in the United Kingdom.

[105] See complaint in Civil Action H-04-3359, *Securities and Exchange Commission v. Royal Dutch Petroleum Company and the "Shell" Transport and Trading Company,* P.L.C., U.S. District Court for the Southern District of Texas, Houston Division (hereafter *SEC Complaint*), p. 1. Proved reserves, as defined by SEC Rule 4-10 of Regulation S-X, 17 *Code of Federal Regulations* § 210.4-10, are "the estimated quantities of crude oil, natural gas, and natural gas liquids which geological and engineering data demonstrate with reasonable certainty to be recoverable in future years from known reservoirs under existing economic and operating conditions, i.e., prices and costs as of the date the estimate is made."

[106] Shell amended its original Form 20-F (Supplemental Information under Statement of Financial Accounting Standard No. 69) for 2002. FASB No. 69 requires extensive unaudited footnote disclosures related to a "standardized measure of discounted future net cash flows related to proved oil and gas reserve quantities" and annual changes therein.

[107] *SEC Complaint,* p. 4.

[108] *Report of Davis, Polk & Wardwell to The Shell Group Audit Committee,* dated March 31, 2004 (hereafter *DPW Report*), pp. 1–2. The Group Audit

Committee is responsible for reporting on financial and risk matters and is composed of six members, divided equally between representatives of Royal Dutch and Shell Transport, with each company's nominee holding the chairmanship alternately.

[109] *Final Notice*, p. 5.

[110] Knight. Testimony provided to the Committee on Financial Services, U.S. House of Representatives (July 21, 2004). (Eric Knight is the managing director of Knight Vinke Asset Management LLC.) See also *A Review of Corporate Governance at Royal Dutch/Shell and Proposals for Change.* Confidential memorandum of Knight Vinke Institutional Partners (hereafter, collectively, *Shell Games*), pp. 6–7, 64–70.

[111] *Shell Games*, p. 76.

[112] Ibid., p. 77.

[113] *DPW Report*, pp. 4–6.

[114] Ibid., p. 7.

[115] Ibid., p. 8.

[116] Ibid., p. 8.

[117] Ibid., p. 9.

[118] In Australia, as of December 31, 1997, Shell booked over 500 million boe of gas reserves based on an "expectation of availability of markets." In Nigeria, it booked substantial proved reserves that it knew in early 2000 could not be produced as originally projected within current license periods and sought to manage the problem by imposing a moratorium on new oil and gas additions. In Oman, it increased proved reserves in 2000 despite production declines from mature fields that failed to meet "aspirational" production targets. In Brunei, it booked proved reserves that were uneconomic to develop or in respect of which no final investment decision had been made. *DPW Report*, pp. 11–12.

[119] Ibid., pp. 12–14.

[120] *Shell Games*, pp. 56, 64.

[121] Ibid., pp. 6–7, 70.

[122] Ibid., p. 70.

[123] Ibid., pp. 7, 67.

[124] Ibid., p. 71.

[125] Ibid., p. 71.

[126] Ibid., p. 71.

[127] *Final Notice*, pp. 1–2.

[128] As revised in 1998, Shell's internal guidelines used probabilistic methods for estimating reserves in *immature* fields, but applied deterministic methods in *mature* fields and directed operating units to increase proved reserves to equal *expectation* volumes. *Expectation reserves* are the most likely estimate of hydrocarbon volumes remaining to be recovered from a project that is technically and commercially mature. Total production of a mature field under Shell's revised guidelines was typically greater than 30% of the field's expectation reserves. Nearly 40% of the total proved reserves Shell added in 1998 resulted from its guideline revision, as did 1.2 billion boe of reported proved reserves between 1998 and 2001. Before September 2003, Shell's guidelines with respect to frontier developments required neither a currently existing market for a field's hydrocarbons nor a commitment by Shell to develop the field or the infrastructure necessary to bring the hydrocarbons to market. *SEC Complaint*, pp. 6–7.

[129] *Final Notice*, p. 4.

[130] *SEC Complaint*, pp. 7–8.

[131] Ibid., p. 16.

[132] *Final Notice*, pp. 4–9.

[133] Ibid., pp. 11–15. See also *SEC Complaint*, pp. 9–10.

[134] *Shell Games*, p. 7.

[135] *SEC Complaint*, p. 5.

[136] *SEC Litigation Release No. 18844*, dated August 24, 2004.

[137] In June 2004, the National Retirement Fund of UNITE and Plumbers and Pipefitters National Pension Fund filed suit in Superior Court, Monmouth County, New Jersey, seeking this remedy.

[138] *The Wall Street Journal*, June 30, 2005, p. B2.

3 Corporate Self-Regulation:
The Accountant as Gatekeeper

Introduction

The collapse of Enron and similar corporate scandals have provoked a search for systemic causes. Beyond board delinquency, noted in the previous chapters, the quality of public companies' financial disclosure is a primary factor. Between 1997 and 2002, earnings restatements by public companies in the United States, often deemed a proxy for fraud, increased by 170%.[1] More than an exercise in retrospective accounting, restatements in those years cost shareholders $100 billion in lost market capitalization, shattered investors' confidence in financial reporting, and raised serious questions about accounting standards and accounting firms as corporate fiduciaries.[2] (See fig. 3–1.) Restatements follow well-recognized patterns and can be assigned to standard categories, as shown in table 3–1.

Auditors have long been regarded as guardians of financial disclosure—professional gatekeepers trusted by regulators and investors to assess, verify, and certify complex financial information—indispensable to the reporting process.[5] Federal securities laws require auditor certification of the financial statements of public companies in accordance with generally accepted accounting standards.[6] On certifying financial statements, "the independent auditor assumes a public responsibility transcending any employment relationship with the client . . . [and] owes ultimate allegiance to the corporation's creditors and stockholders, as well as to the investing public."[7] Deviation from this professional standard can be measured by the recent spike in earnings restatements, an index reflecting the extent of accounting firms' "[acquiescence] in aggressive earnings management."[8]

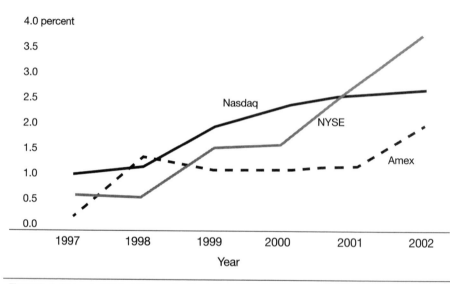

Figure 3–1. Percent of Listed Companies Restating, 1997–2002[3]
Note: The 2002 figures are estimated based on data collected through June 2002.

Source: GOA-03-138, October 2002, p.19

Table 3–1. GAO Financial Statement Restatement Database[4]

Category	Description
Acquisitions and mergers	Restatements of acquisitions or mergers that were improperly accounted for or not accounted for at all. These include instances in which the wrong accounting method was used or losses or gains related to the acquisition were understated or overstated. This category does not include in-process research and development or restatements for mergers, acquisitions, and discontinued operations when appropriate accounting methods were employed.
Cost or expense	Restatements due to improper cost accounting. This category includes instances of improperly recognizing costs or expenses, improperly capitalizing expenditures, or any other number of mistakes or improprieties that led to misreported costs. It also includes restatements due to improper treatment of tax liabilities, income tax reserves, and other tax-related items.
In-process research and development	Restatements resulting from instances in which improper accounting methodologies were used to value in-process research and development at the time of an acquisition.
Other	Any restatement not covered by the listed categories. Cases included in this category include restatements due to inadequate loan-loss reserves, delinquent loans, loan write-offs, improper accounting for bad loans and restatements due to fraud, and accounting irregularities that were left unspecified.
Reclassification	Restatements due to improperly classified accounting ietms. These include restatements due to improprieties such as debt payments being classified as investments.
Related-party transactions	Restatements due to inadequate disclosure or improper accounting of revenues, expenses, debts, or assets involving transactions or relationships with related parties. This category includes those involving special-purpose entities.
Restructuring, assets, or inventory	Restatements due to asset impairment, errors relating to accounting treatment of investments, timing of asset write-downs, goodwill, restructuring activity and inventory valuation, and inventory quantity issues.
Revenue recognition	Restatements due to improper revenue accounting. this category includes instances in which revenue was improperly recognized, questionable revenues were recognized, or any other number of mistakes or improprieties were made that led to misreported revenue.
Securities related	Restatements due to improper accounting for derivatives, warrants, stock options, and other convertible securities.

Note: Excluded are announcements involving stock splits and changes in accounting principles, as well as other financial statement restatements that were not made to correct mistakes in the application of accounting standards.

Source: GAO-03-395R, January 17, 2003, p. 6

Auditor acquiescence

Why did auditors go along with aggressive accounting policies favored by corporate management? One theory is that, during the 1990s, the risk of auditor liability declined while the benefits of acquiescence increased.[9] Liability declined because of judicial decisions that reduced time limitations applicable to securities fraud,[10] eliminated "aiding and abetting" as a cause of action in such cases,[11] and made it difficult to impute *scienter*, or knowledge, to an auditor without a direct financial interest in its client.[12] Also limiting auditors' potential exposure was legislation abolishing state court securities fraud class actions[13] while requiring that federal suits substitute proportionality for joint and several liability.[14] Not least, during the 1990s, the SEC brought very few fraud enforcement actions against the Big Five accounting firms.[15]

While exposure to liability declined, large accounting firms refashioned themselves as multidisciplinary providers and cross-sold increasingly valuable consulting services to audit clients. The audit function became a loss leader and portal of entry for nonaudit services. Accounting firms reduced audit fees, lowered the quality of audit services provided, and placed ever greater emphasis on consulting services.[16] In 2001, to cite but one example, Enron paid Andersen $27 million in consulting fees, $2 million more than its audit fees for the same period.[17] In that year, accountants' nonaudit revenues from large public companies exceeded $4 billion, while audit fees totaled less than half that amount.[18] As auditors grew more dependent on consulting income, they were more willing to risk reputational capital in pursuit of extraordinary returns.[19] Reciprocally, companies paying for such consulting services were more likely to engage in earnings management.[20] To protect the flow of consulting fees, auditors had a powerful economic incentive to approve aggressive accounting and questionable financial statements.

Generally accepted accounting principles and standards

The financial reporting system rests on generally accepted accounting principles (GAAP), which govern preparation of financial statements, and generally accepted accounting standards (GAAS), which provide a framework for the conduct of audits. Although both contain detailed bright-line rules, they are essentially principles-based normative systems concerned with the economic substance of transactions, rather than their form; that is, they prescribe minimum standards but presuppose the need for individual judgments based on principle in the preparation and audit of financial statements.[21]

The substance-form dichotomy may arise in the context of off-balance-sheet financing, revenue recognition, and financial statement disclosures. Whatever the mechanism employed, the auditor must determine whether a company is recording bogus revenue, boosting income through one-time gains, managing earnings through accruals or reserve accounts, or failing to record or disclose all liabilities.[22] Under GAAS, an audit of financial statements must be supported by evidence.[23] Where financial results depend on management estimates, the auditor must test and independently validate the process by which such estimates have been developed.[24]

If GAAP or GAAS are seen to contain ambiguities or invite self-serving interpretations, auditors may be pressured to take maximum advantage until adoption of correcting rules. Examples include:

- GAAP treatment of special purpose entities (used to remove assets and liabilities from a company's balance sheet, thereby improving leverage and financial ratios);

- mark-to-market accounting (used to report at fair value and thus permit recognition of income from financial instruments and long-term contracts based on estimates when quoted market prices are unavailable);

- footnote disclosures about transactions included in financial statements (used to obscure the true nature of derivative contracts, hedging activities, and related party transactions).[25]

The audit process

Beyond a company's outside accounting firm, the audit process involves the entire corporate governance infrastructure, including the company's board of directors, audit committee, and internal audit staff. Although the audit committee bears final responsibility for integrity of the audit process, GAAS require the outside accounting firm to assess common risk factors for financial reporting fraud, including:

- management compensation significantly dependent on bonuses, stock options, or other equity-based incentives, the value of which requires the company to achieve aggressive targets for operating results, financial position, or cash flow;

- inability of the company to generate cash flows from operations while reporting earnings and earnings growth;

- unusual or highly complex transactions presenting difficult form-over-substance issues;

- management efforts to influence audit results.[26]

If auditors detect possible material fraud, they are required to notify the company's senior management and the audit committee, which in turn is required to advise the SEC.[27] Too often in the energy business, however, as the following case histories illustrate, auditors have overlooked fraud in order to preserve client relationships.

CMS Energy Corp.:
Revenue Inflation through Round-Trip Trading

Background

CMS Energy Corp. (CMS) is an integrated energy company, built around old-line regulated electric and gas utilities serving retail customers in Michigan. During the 1990s, like many other traditional utilities, CMS diversified its operations to enter unregulated energy businesses, including wholesale trading of electricity and natural gas, and established a subsidiary, CMS Market Services & Trading (MST), for that purpose.

In November 1999, CMS appointed as MST's chief executive officer a former senior vice president of Reliant Energy (Reliant), the trading arm of a Texas utility. MST quickly became the primary engine of CMS's future growth and was transplanted from Michigan to Houston, the hub of domestic energy trading, where it proposed to sell electric power to cooperatives and municipalities under long-term contracts.

To enhance its credibility with prospective customers, MST needed to rank among the nation's top 20 energy companies in trading volume, a major leap from its position early in 2000. Round-trip trades were seen as a means to this end. As described by the SEC, round-trip trades are "massive pre-arranged transactions involving simultaneous purchases and sales of electric power or natural gas with the same counterparty for the same volume and at the same price, with no delivery contemplated and with neither party making any profit."[28] Since round-trip trades lacked economic substance, they had no effect on CMS's net income, earnings per share, or cash flows. However, they vastly increased its operating revenues, operating expenses, accounts receivable, accounts payable, and—most critically—reported trading volumes, thereby allowing MST to record a quantum leap in apparent trading activity.

MST's first round-trip trade took place, with Reliant as counterparty, in July 2000. It involved 10 million megawatt-hours and $380 million—1,000 times the size of a typical power transaction—and by itself lifted MST to a top 20 ranking. MST recorded revenues and expenses from the trade on a gross basis, reporting $380 million in revenues (for the purported sale) and the same amount in expenses (for the purported purchase). MST and Reliant settled their offsetting delivery obligations on a net basis with a book entry. No cash or power changed hands.[29]

Using the first round-trip trade as a template for further trades, MST recorded an additional $620 million in round-trip trading revenues during the fourth quarter of 2000, enabling CMS to overstate its revenues and expenses for the year on a consolidated basis by $1 billion (equal to 10% of its total annual revenue). During the first three quarters of 2001, CMS similarly overstated its revenues and expenses by $4.2 billion (equal to 36% of revenue) on the basis of MST's roundtrip trades, which inflated its reported trading volume by more than 70% in each year.[30]

To announce financial results for the first quarter of 2001, CMS issued a press release reporting that first-quarter operating revenue "totaled $4.13 billion, up 126 percent from $1.83 billion in the first quarter of 2000, due largely to significantly increased lower-margin energy and marketing transactions." SEC filings for the second and third quarters reflected operating revenue increases of 175% and 29%, respectively, compared to results for the same quarters of 2000. Reliant served as counterparty for 90% of CMS's round-trip transactions. In 2001, unregulated trading represented 45% of CMS's total revenue.[31] In that year, CMS reported total revenue of $11.6 billion (to which MST contributed $5.1 billion) but incurred a consolidated net loss of $545 million. (See table 3–2.)

Table 3–2. 2001 CMS Energy Financial Highlights[32]

	December 31	
	2001	**2000**
Revenue		
Electric utility	$ 2,683	$ 2,676
Gas utility	1,338	1,196
Independent power production[(a)]	935	1,171
Natural gas transmission[(a)]	1,290	1,053
Oil and gas exploration and production	212	136
Marketing, services and trading[(a)]	5,124	4,442
Other	22	28
Total Revenue[(a)]	$11,604	$10,702
Consolidated revenue	$ 9,597	$ 8,739
Net income before nonrecurring items[(b)]	$ 185	$ 246
Consolidated net income (loss)	$ (545)	$ 36
Per common share[(b)]		
Diluted earnings per average common share:		
Earnings per share before nonrecurring items	$ 1.41	$ 2.21
Earnings (loss) per share after nonrecurring items	$ (4.17)	$ 0.32
Dividends declared	$ 1.46	$ 1.46
Book value	$14.21	$19.48
Market value (year-end)	$24.03	$31.69

(a) Includes CMS Energy's share of unconsolidated revenue.
(b) Refer to Management's Discussion and Analysis for an explanation of the nonrecurring items.

Source: CMS Annual Report for 2001, p. 1

Auditor's guidance

In connection with CMS's financial statements for the third quarter of 2000, which recorded revenues and expenses from an initial round-trip trade on a gross basis, Andersen reviewed the accounting treatment with CMS's chief accounting officer. Treating the trade as a one-off transaction, Andersen offered no objection, and the inflated third-quarter financial statements were duly filed on Form 10-Q.[33]

CMS then booked over $600 million of round-trip trades in the fourth quarter of 2000. Andersen had not "approved, or even discussed with CMS, the recording of revenues and expenses associated with those roundtrip trades."[34] For the first quarter of 2001, CMS's Form 10-Q reflected $1.2 billion in round-trip trading revenue. Before filing, Andersen discussed with CMS the propriety of including that amount in its reported gross revenues and expenses. Andersen understood that the trades in question were simultaneous, with no physical delivery or margin, and lacked economic substance. Yet, according to the SEC, it did not object and contented itself with researching the appropriate accounting treatment.[35]

In May 2001, Andersen informed MST's controller that revenues and expenses from round-trip trades should be recorded on a net rather than gross basis, but failed to notify CMS of the recommended change in accounting.[36] During the second quarter of 2001, CMS entered into and recorded on a gross basis round-trip trades worth $2 billion. In October 2001, before CMS filed its third-quarter Form 10-Q, Andersen advised that round-trip trades could be recorded only if both parties to the trade bore credit and performance risk, if title to the subject commodity was transferred, and if checks were exchanged and cashed for the gross amount of the transaction.[37] Although MST's third-quarter trades involved no risk, transfer of title, or exchange of cash, CMS nonetheless recorded them on a gross basis, adding $1 billion to its revenues and expenses.

Restatement

In March 2002, Andersen advised CMS that its 2001 financial statements would have to be restated to record round-trip trades on a net basis. CMS's annual report on Form 10-K, filed shortly thereafter, eliminated $4.2 billion of previously reported revenue and expense for 2001 but failed to explain that the round-trip trades in question had been arranged with a single counterparty (Reliant), lacked economic substance, and were conducted for the sole purpose of inflating MST's trading volume.[38] Not until several months later, following an SEC inquiry and media attention, did CMS finally disclose the details underlying the reclassification and its failure to eliminate $1 billion of revenue and expenses from round-trip trades included in its 2000 financial statements, an omission attributed to "apparent oversight on the part of CMS and its auditor."[39]

In its second-quarter Form 10-Q, filed in August 2002, CMS acknowledged that MST had engaged in "simultaneous, prearranged commodity trading transactions" to increase "operating revenues, operating expenses, accounts receivable, accounts payable and reported trading volumes." CMS also stated its intent to eliminate $1 billion of revenue and expense from its 2000 financial statements. To respond to investigations launched by the SEC, FERC, and the CFTC, U.S. Attorney's Offices in the Southern District of New York and in Houston, and multiple shareholder class action lawsuits, CMS established a special committee of independent directors, assisted by outside counsel, to review round-trip trades and report by the third quarter of 2002. At the same time, Andersen resigned as auditor, withdrew its prior opinions, and could no longer give an opinion on CMS's restated financial statements. Ernst & Young was appointed as Andersen's successor.

Aftermath

In May 2002, CMS announced the resignation of the chief executive officer of MTS and, shortly thereafter, the resignation of William T. McCormick, its own chairman and chief executive officer; despite their forced resignations, these officers received severance payments of $2 million and $4 million, respectively. In June 2002, CMS announced a 25% workforce reduction and its exit from speculative energy trading. MST, renamed CMS Energy Resource Management, thereafter confined its business to buying fuel for CMS's independent power plants and selling their uncommitted power output.

Between May and September 2002, CMS's share price dropped by 50%, from $20 to $10, resulting in an aggregate equity loss of more than $1.3 billion. At the same time, rating services downgraded CMS's debt. A three-year snapshot, contained in CMS's 2003 annual report, reflects the extent of its self-inflicted financial damage. (See table 3–3.)

Table 3–3. CMS Energy Selected Financial Information, 2001–2003[40]

	2003	2002	2001
Operating revenue	$5,513	$8,673	$8,006
Earnings from equity method investees	164	92	172
Income (loss) from continuing operations	(43)	(394)	(327)
Cumulative effect of change in accounting	(24)	18	(4)
Consolidated net income	(44)	(650)	(459)
Income (loss) per average common share			
Basic and Diluted	(.30)	(4.68)	(3.51)
Cash from (used in) operations	(251)	614	372
Total assets	13,838	14,781	17,633
Long-term debt, excluding current maturities	6,020	5,357	5,842
Long-term debt, related parties (a)	684	–	–
Non-current portion of capital leases	58	116	71
Total preferred stock	305	44	44
Total Trust Preferred Securities	(a)	883	1,214
Cash dividends declared per common share	–	1.09	1.46
Market price of common stock at year-end	8.52	9.44	24.03
Book value of common share at year-end	9.84	7.48	14.98
Average common share outstanding (thousands)	150,434	139,047	130,758
Number of employees at year-end (full-time equivalents)	8,411	10,477	11,510
Electric Utility Statistics			
Sales (billions of KWH)	39	39	40
Customers (thousands)	1,754	1,734	1,712
Average sales rate (¢ per KWH)	6.91	6.88	6.65
Gas Utility Statistics			
Sales and transportation deliveries (bcf)	380	376	367
Customers (thousands) (b)	1,671	1,652	1,630
Average sales rate ($ per mcf)	6.72	5.67	5.34

(a) Effective December 31, 2001, Trust Preferred Securities are now included on the balance sheet as long-term debt-related parties

(b) Excludes off-system transportation customers

Source: CMS Annual Report, 2003

Table 3–3. (continued)

	millions of dollars, except as noted	
	2003	2002
Revenue		
Electric utility	$ 2,583	$ 2,644
Gas utility	1,845	1,519
Enterprises	1,085	4,508
Other	–	2
Consolidated Revenue	**$ 5,145**	**$ 8,673**
Consolidated net income (loss)	$ (44)	$ (650)
Ongoing net income[a]	122	117
Per common share		
Diluted earnings (loss)		
Reported earnings (loss)	$ (0.30)	$ (4.68)
Ongoing earnings[a]	(0.81)	(0.84)
Book value (year-end)	(9.84)	(7.48)
Market value (year-end)	8.52	(9.44)
Cash	532	351
Debt	6,171[b]	7,133[c]

(a) Ongoing net income differs from net income prepared in accordance with Generally Accepted Accounting Principles (GAAP) in that it excludes the effects of reconciling items, as shown in tables below.
(b) $6,855 million including Trust Preferred Securities
(c) $6,124 million excluding debt related to assets sold

	2003		2002	
Reconciliation of GAAP to Non-GAAP	**Net income (loss)**	**Per Share**	**Net income (loss)**	**Per Share**
Reported net income (loss) — GAAP basis	$(44)	$(.30)	$(650)	$(4.68)
Reconciling items				
Discontinued operations (income) loss	(23)	(.16)	(274)	1.97
Cumulative effect of accounting changes:				
EITF #02-03 MTM Accounting	23	0.15	–	–
SFAS No. 143 Asset Retirement Obligations	1	0.01	–	–
SFAS No. 133 Derivative Accounting	–	–	(18)	(0.13)
Net asset writedowns	79	0.52	458	3.29
Loss of tax benefits	–	–	54	0.39
Net asset (gain)/loss and other	86	0.59	(1)	–
Ongoing net income (loss) — non-GAAP basis	$122	$0.81	$117	$0.84

In 2004, CMS settled with the SEC and consented to entry of a cease-and-desist order alleging violations of antifraud, reporting, record-keeping, and internal controls regulations under federal securities laws.[41] Other companies that engaged in round-trip trades, including El Paso, Duke Energy, Dynegy, and Reliant, also confronted SEC investigations and class action lawsuits and suffered similar market losses. Reliant's power trades with CMS accounted for 20% of its total trading volume, inflated its revenues and expenses by $3.6 billion in 2001, and enabled CMS to leap from obscurity to a top 20 volume ranking among energy trading firms.[42] Like CMS, Reliant's parent was required to restate its financials by removing revenues from trades recorded on a gross basis.

Accounting rules

To place Andersen's accounting advice to CMS in context, it is necessary to consider the relevant standards set by the Financial Accounting Standards Board (FASB), the private-sector entity that promulgates GAAP under the SEC's oversight,[43] and the FASB's arm, the Emerging Issues Task Force (EITF), which addresses emerging issues on a more nearly real-time basis.[44] In 1998, in Issue No. 98-10, the EITF reached a consensus that energy trading contracts, such as those entered into by CMS and Reliant, should be marked to market—that is, measured at fair value determined as of the balance sheet date—and that gains and losses related to such contracts could be shown *either gross or net* in the income statement.[45]

EITF Issue No. 98-10 was responsive to comment letters from energy trading companies urging a gross presentation where settlement of trading contracts required physical delivery of the underlying commodity (instead of net cash settlement). Moreover, as the FASB staff had already learned from informal review of their financial statements, energy trading companies typically presented *all* contracts on a gross basis. "For some companies," the FASB staff acknowledged, "reporting on the gross method has resulted in substantial increases in revenues—in some instances the cumulative notional amounts of energy trading contracts are significantly larger than the company's physical capacity to deliver those quantities."[46]

EITF Issue No. 98-10 nonetheless permitted reporting of energy trading contracts on either a gross or net basis. Andersen, among other accounting firms, could therefore take a permissive view of revenue inflation attributable to round-trip trades without violating the applicable accounting rule. Arguably, however, it should have looked beyond technical compliance to inquire whether the transactions in question were reported "in accordance with their substance" and "presented fairly" CMS's financial condition, results of operations, and cash flows.[47]

Influenced by round-trip trading abuses, in June 2002, the EITF reversed its prior position, disallowed gross reporting of sales and cost of sales even on energy contracts settled through physical delivery, required all mark-to-market gains and losses (whether realized or unrealized) to be shown net on the income statement, and made the new rule applicable to all financial statements for periods ending after December 15, 2002.[48] Long overdue, the change nevertheless came too late to protect investors in CMS and its energy trading counterparties.

Enron: Mark-to-Market Accounting Writ Large

History

In June 1991, Enron's newly formed subsidiary, Enron Gas Services (EGS), approached the SEC's Office of Chief Accountant for authorization to use mark-to-market accounting to record natural gas trades.[49] Mark-to-market accounting would allow Enron to book the estimated present value of all future profits from a natural gas contract at its inception. Changes in contract value thereafter would be recorded as increases or decreases in revenue and reflected in Enron's income statement. Traditional accounting, in contrast, considered only historic cost and required revenue recognition over the life of the contract. Mark-to-market accounting was regarded as aggressive, particularly for long-term trading contracts unsupported by quoted market prices, since the value of such contracts had to be estimated by use of complex models containing problematic assumptions, including future gas prices, the pace of energy deregulation, and interest rate trends.

To apply mark-to-market accounting, Enron needed an SEC no-action letter. It characterized EGS as engaged in commodity trading, where mark-to-market accounting was the norm. In the face of initial resistance, Enron assured the SEC that mark-to-market earnings would not depend on subjective elements but would instead be based on known spreads and balanced positions. Enron's outside accounting firm, Andersen, supported the accounting change. In January 1992, the SEC issued the requested no-action letter.[50] Enron thereafter used mark-to-market accounting to report noncash earnings based on the estimated current market value of pending, speculative multiyear contracts. Enron computed an assumed profit, discounted to present value, and reported it in the current period.

A collateral development freed energy trading from CFTC regulation. In November 1992, Enron and other energy companies urged the CFTC to remove over-the-counter (OTC) energy futures contracts from regulatory oversight. Under the Futures Trading Practices Act of 1992,[51] the CFTC had newly acquired authority to exempt such contracts from regulation.[52] In a two-to-one order issued in January 1993, the CFTC granted Enron and others the exemption they had sought.[53] The order freed OTC energy futures contracts from government oversight, including exercise by the CFTC of its statutory authority to protect against contracts designed to defraud or mislead.[54] Wendy Gramm, CFTC chairwoman and a proponent of deregulation, voted in the majority, resigned from the CFTC on January 20, 1992, and joined Enron's board one month later.[55]

Accounting guidance

In May 1993, the FASB issued Statement of Financial Accounting Standard (SFAS) 115 to implement mark-to-market accounting for financial assets with readily determinable market values, such as stocks and traded futures. SFAS 115 defined three classes of securities— held to maturity (HTM),[56] available for sale (AFS),[57] and trading.[58] Companies are required to report unrealized gains and losses, net of taxes, according to asset classification: investments in marketable equity securities and all but HTM debt instruments are reported at fair market value, unrealized gains and losses from AFS securities are reported as a change in equity, and unrealized gains and losses from trading securities are recognized as income. HTM debt instruments are still reported on an amortized cost basis.

SFAS 115's fair-value accounting was strongly championed by the SEC, an unlikely advocate, since it had for decades consistently supported historical cost accounting. But the banking industry, heavily reliant on derivatives, opposed fair-value accounting as misleading and feared that fair-value estimates for the risk hedged in nontraded items would be based on "inconsistent and subjective factors."[59] In a letter to the FASB, Federal Reserve Chairman Greenspan concurred:

> Without reasonably specific, conservative standards for the estimation of market values, fair-value accounting for all financial instruments could inappropriately increase the reported volatility of earnings and equity measurements, reduce the reliability of financial statement values, and potentially permit abuses arising from potential overstatements.[60]

Chairman Greenspan's fears were not unwarranted. Under SFAS 115, long-term contracts for energy commodities not documented as normal sales and purchases could be carried on company balance sheets at estimated fair value and recognized in current earnings. Since such contracts are often uncertain, sparsely traded, and without readily ascertainable market values, however, fair-value accounting proved to be an invitation to manage earnings. Using theoretical models to describe value over time, energy companies could make self-serving assumptions about model variables (e.g., price curves and demand). Since mark-to-market gains predicated on such assumptions would not generate cash for years, if ever, such companies could report large accounting earnings without corresponding cash flows.[61]

In June 1998, after more than six years of intense deliberation, the FASB issued SFAS 133, which extended mark-to-market accounting to all financial derivatives, even those without traded market values.[62] Under SFAS 133, companies must carry all instruments meeting the definition of derivative (including energy trading contracts)[63] on their balance sheets at fair value and record any change in fair value in earnings unless there is an appropriate hedging relationship. Fair value is determined by estimating the price an entity would realize if it were to sell the asset in question or the price it would pay to relieve a liability in a current transaction between willing parties. Thus, SFAS 133 requires that derivatives be marked to market but allows hedge accounting under specific criteria. (See table 3–4.)

Table 3–4. Balance Sheet and Income Statement Impacts of Cash Flow and Fair Value Hedges[64]

Type of Derivative	Balance Sheet Impact	Income Statement Impact
Fair Value Hedge	Derivative (asset or liability) is reported at fair value. Hedged item is also reported at fair value.	Changes in fair value are reported as income/loss in income statement. Offsetting changes in fair value of hedged item are also reported as income/loss in income statement.
Cash Flow Hedge	Derivative (asset or liability) is reported at fair value. Changes in fair value of derivative are reported as components of Other Comprehensive Income (balance sheet).	No immediate income statement impact. Changes in fair value of derivative are reclassified into income statement (from Other Comprehensive Income in the balance sheet) when the expected (hedged) transaction affects the net income.
Speculative Transaction	Derivative (asset or liability) is reported at fair value.	Changes in fair value are reported as income/loss in income statment. (There will be no offsetting changes in the fair value of the hedged item.)

Source: Energy Information Administration, Derivative and Risk Management in the Petroleum, Natural Gas and Energy Markets, (October 2002), p. 58

From 1998 until promulgation of EITF Issue No. 02-03 in 2002, energy companies marked to market storage contracts, capacity contracts, firm power purchase agreements, firm fuel supply contracts, and weather derivatives. Thereafter nonderivatives, such as storage and capacity contracts, were subject to accrual rather than fair-value accounting.

Enron seizes the day

For long-term energy contracts that had no traded value, Enron used unverifiable cost and price assumptions to estimate market value, "including closing exchange and over-the-counter quotations, time value and volatility factors underlying the commitments."[65] Under mark-to-market accounting, Enron reported anticipated revenues from highly speculative, illiquid, and long-term agreements in current period income. Enron operating divisions that used mark-to-market accounting showed increasing paper profits; other divisions reported no profit.[66]

Enron also reported as revenue the entire value of EnronOnline trades, rather than just trading or brokerage fees. Enron's merchant model differed from the agency model adopted by traditional trading firms and grossly inflated its revenues and cost of goods sold, which were both duly reported in its income statement. Without such accounting enhancements, in 2000 Enron would have reported aggregate revenues of $6.3 billion, rather than $100.8 billion.[67]

Between 1996 and 2000, Enron's revenues increased by more than 750% and drove its stock price ever upward. Meanwhile, its return on equity and profit margins remained virtually the lowest among large energy companies. During the same period, Enron sustained massively negative free cash flows (i.e., cash not required for operations or reinvestment) that it attempted to offset, ultimately without success, through debt and equity financing.

Accounting rules and accounting firms

When it became clear that Enron had manipulated accounting rules to mislead investors, critics blamed the accounting system itself. GAAP, it was said, "has conditioned people to look not at whether the information presented to the market is a true and fair characterization of the condition of the company, but at whether it [complies] with the rules."[68] Enron's misuse of mark-to-market accounting, with Andersen's concurrence, provided an egregious case in point, since Enron (and its trading peers) seldom entered into verifiable exchange-traded transactions. For long-term, speculative transactions, Enron instead determined its own forward price curves. Although such projections were subject to a reasonableness test, Andersen deferred to Enron's bonus-driven management to protect a valuable client relationship and the continued flow of huge fees. Enron's reported earnings were therefore simply a matter of opinion, apparently plausible but grossly inaccurate. In a mark-to-market regime, cash flow remained the only indisputable fact.

In opining that Enron's financial statements "fairly presented" its financial position, Andersen could not disclaim close familiarity with Enron's business and had every reason to know that its financial reporting violated basic accounting precepts of reliability, completeness, and conservative assessment of risk, falsely represented Enron's financial position, and violated GAAP and GAAS.[69] Andersen nonetheless consented to incorporation of its reports in Enron's Forms 10-K and numerous prospectuses used by Enron for registered offerings of stock and debt securities.

Observations

In reaction to accounting derelictions, the Sarbanes-Oxley Act of 2002 (and related SEC and NYSE initiatives) implemented a radical shift in regulatory philosophy concerning corporate governance and disclosure. The previous market-based approach was displaced by one that is strongly prescriptive. Company executive officers must now certify annual and quarterly filings with the SEC and report on a company's required disclosure controls and procedures and internal control over financial reporting. Non-GAAP financial measures are now regulated, and real-time disclosure of specific corporate events is required. Boards and audit committees are subject to rigorous independence requirements. The latter have sole authority to hire and fire independent auditors, must preapprove all accounting services provided, and must approve critical accounting policies and practices. Auditors are prohibited from providing most nonaudit services to audit clients. Public companies must disclose whether they have adopted a code of ethics applicable to senior management and, if so, whether they have granted waivers on behalf of company officers.[70] These and other related remedial rules significantly raise the bar for corporate compliance but do not ensure that self-regulation will necessarily be an effective prophylactic against corporate fraud.

Notes

[1] Coffee. "What Caused Enron? A Capsule Social and Economic History of the 1990's." *Columbia Law and Economics Working Paper No. 214* (2003) (hereafter *Coffee 2003*), p. 8; *Financial Statement Restatements.* United States General Accounting Office Report, GAO-03-138 (October 2002) (hereafter *GAO Report*), p. 4. The number of restatements rose from 92 in 1997 to 225 in 2001.

[2] *GAO Report*, pp. 5–6. See also Bratton. "Shareholder Value and Auditor Independence." *Duke Law Journal*, 53: 439, 487 (2003) (restatements attributed to strategic noncompliance in conflict with the stated interpretation of the regulator).

[3] *GAO Report*, p. 19.

[4] *Financial Statement Restatement Database.* United States Government Accounting Office, GAO-03-395R (January 17, 2003), p. 6.

[5] Debt-rating agencies, securities analysts, and investment bankers have also been identified as gatekeepers. *Coffee 2003*, p. 5. See also Cox. *The Oligopolistic Gatekeeper: The U.S. Accounting Profession.* Duke University (2004) (hereafter *Oligopolistic Gatekeeper*).

[6] Securities Act of 1933, 15 *U.S. Code* § 77aa(25)(26); Securities Exchange Act, 15 *U.S. Code* § 78m(a)(2); 17 *Code of Federal Regulations* 210.1-02(d) (2004).

[7] *United States v. Arthur Young*, 465 U.S. 805, 814 (1984).

[8] *Coffee 2003*, p. 9.

[9] Ibid., p. 12, 25–26.

[10] *Lampf Pleva, Lipkind & Petigrow v. Gilbertson*, 501 U.S. 350, 359–61 (1991).

[11] *Central Bank of Denver, N.A. v. First Interstate of Denver, N.A.*, 511 U.S. 164 (1994).

[12] See, e.g., *DiLeo v. Ernst & Young*, 901 F.2d 624, 629 (7th Cir. 1990). The prevailing definition of *scienter* contemplates "an extreme departure from the standards of ordinary care... which presents a danger of misleading buyers that is either known to the defendant or so obvious

that the actor must have been aware of it." *Sunstrand Corp. v. Sun Chem. Corp.*, 553 F.2d 1033, 1045 (7th Cir. 1987).

[13] Securities Litigation Uniform Standards Act of 1998, Public Law No. 105-353, 112 Stat. 3227.

[14] Private Securities Litigation Reform Act of 1995 (PSLR), Public Law No. 104-67, 202 Stat. 737 (1995).

[15] Coffee. "Understanding Enron: It's about the Gatekeepers, Stupid," *Columbia Law and Economics Working Paper No. 207* (2002) (hereafter *Coffee 2002*), p. 26 and n. 54.

[16] Sunder. *Collapse of Accounting: Causes and Cures*, http://www.som.yale.edu/faculty/sunder/research.html (April 13, 2005).

[17] *Coffee 2002*, p. 27; Bratton. "Enron and the Dark Side of Shareholder Value," *Public Law and Legal Theory Working Paper No. 035*. The George Washington University Law School (2002), p. 68; Coffee. Testimony before the Committee on Commerce, Science, and Transportation, U.S. Senate. In *The Enron Debacle and Gatekeeper Liability: Why Would the Gatekeepers Remain Silent?* (December 18, 2001) (intransigence by an audit partner with regard to aggressive accounting treatment proposed by the client could expose the accounting firm to loss of greater nonaudit revenues, which the client could elect to purchase elsewhere).

[18] *Oligopolistic Gatekeeper*, p. 23 (citing a 2002 study of 1,224 large public companies by the Investor Responsibility Research Center).

[19] *Coffee 2002*, p. 34.

[20] Frankel, Johnson, and Nelson. "The Relation between Auditors' Fees for Non-Audit Services and Earnings Quality." *MIT Sloan Working Paper No. 4330-02* (2002) (available from Social Sciences Research Network, http://www.ssrn.com/ [at id = 296557]).

[21] See, e.g., St. Denis. "Cooking the Books: Tricks of the Trade in Financial Fraud." *United States Attorneys' Bulletin* (May 2003) (hereafter *St. Denis*), p. 19. "Generally accepted accounting principles recognize the importance of reporting transactions and events in accordance with their substance. The auditor should consider whether the substance of transactions or events differs materially from their form." *Statement on Auditing Standards No. 69*, AU § 411.06. American Institute of Certified Public Accountants (1992), SAS 69. See also *Statement of Financial*

Accounting Concepts No. 2, FASB (1980), app. B, ¶ 160: "The quality of reliability, and, in particular of representational faithfulness, leaves no room for accounting representations that subordinate substance to form."

[22] Schillit. *Financial Shenanigans* (1993), p. x.

[23] See *Evidential Matter, Statement on Auditing Standards No. 31,* AU § 326.01. American Institute of Certified Public Accountants (1980), SAS 31.

[24] See *Auditing Accounting Estimates, Statement of Auditing Standards No. 57,* AU § 342.10. American Institute of Certified Public Accountants (1989).

[25] Baker and Hayes. "Reflecting Form over Substance: The Case of Enron Corp." *Critical Perspectives on Accounting,* 15: 767, 771–82 (2004).

[26] *St. Denis,* p. 22.

[27] See *Statement on Audit Standards No. 82,* AU § 316.17. American Institute of Certified Public Accountants (1997); 15 *U.S. Code* § 78b [§ 10A(b)].

[28] *In the Matter of CMS Energy Corp., Securities Act Release No. 8403* (March 17, 2004) (hereafter *Securities Act Release No. 8403*), p 2.

[29] Ibid., n. 5.

[30] Ibid., p. 2.

[31] Public Citizen. *The Public Utility Holding Company Act and the Protection of Energy Consumers: An Examination of the Corporate Records of the Top Companies Pushing for PUHCA Repeal* (September 2002), p. 11.

[32] CMS annual report (2001), p. 1.

[33] *Securities Act Release No. 8403,* p. 5.

[34] Ibid., p. 5.

[35] Ibid.

[36] Ibid.

[37] Ibid., pp. 5–6.

[38] Ibid., p. 6.

[39] Ibid., p. *3*.

[40] CMS annual report (2003).

[41] *Securities Act Release No. 8403.* In 2003, CMS also reached a settlement with the CFTC, including a $16 million fine, for reporting false natural gas price and volume information in an attempt to manipulate prices in violation of the Commodity Exchange Act (CEA). See *In the Matter of CMS Marketing Services and Trading Company and CMS Filed Services, Inc.,* CFTC Docket No. 04-05 (November 25, 2003).

[42] *In the Matter of Reliant Resources, Inc. and Reliant Energy, Inc., Securities Act Release No. 8232* (May 12, 2003), p. 5.

[43] FASB is an operating unit of the Financial Accounting Foundation, a not-for-profit entity, whose trustees select FASB board members on the basis of their technical expertise in financial accounting and reporting.

[44] See Nazareth. Testimony concerning transparent financial reporting for structured finance transactions, before the Permanent Subcommittee on Investigations, Committee on Governmental Affairs, U.S. Senate (December 11, 2002), pp. 9–10.

[45] EITF Issue No. 98-10, *Accounting for Contracts Involved in Energy Trading and Risk Management Activities*; EITF Issue No. 00-17, *Measuring the Fair Value of Energy-Related Contracts in Applying Issues No. 98-10*; and EITF Topic No. D-105, *Accounting in Consolidation for Energy Trading Contracts between Affiliated Entities When the Activities of One but Not Both Affiliates Are within the Scope of Issue No. 98-10.* Issue 98-10 defined fair value, with respect to a specific contract, as "the amount at which that contract could be bought or sold in a current transaction between willing parties." The task force noted that "valuation models, including option-pricing models, should be used only when market transactions are not available to evidence fair values."

[46] *June 19–20 2002 EITF Meeting Summary.* Deloitte & Touche, p. 73.

[47] *Statement on Accounting Standard No. 69, The Meaning of Present Fairly in Conformity with Generally Accepted Accounting Principles.*

[48] EITF Issue No. 02-3, *Issues Involved in Accounting for Derivative Contracts Held for Trading Purposes and Contracts Involved in Energy Trading and Risk Management Activities.* As a result, certain energy trading contracts—those not considered to be derivatives under SFAS No. 133—were subject to accrual rather than fair-value accounting, with

revenue and expense recognized at the time of contract performance, settlement, or termination.

[49] "Financial Oversight of Enron: The SEC and Private-Sector Watchdogs" In *Report of the Staff to the Senate Committee on Governmental Affairs* (October 8, 2002) (hereafter *Watchdog Report*), p.40. Enron Gas Services (whose CEO was Jeffrey Skilling) later became Enron Capital and Trade Resources Corp. and eventually Enron North America.

[50] *Watchdog Report,* pp. 41–42.

[51] Public Law No. 1-2-546, 106 Stat. 3590.

[52] Pursuant to amendments enacted in 1974, the CEA subjects contracts for the sale of a commodity for future delivery to the exclusive jurisdiction of the CFTC. 7 *U.S. Code* § 2(i). In addition to a finding that an exemption from regulation is in the public interest, the CFTC must determine that the exempted transactions will be entered into only by appropriate persons and will not impede the CFTC from fulfilling its duties under the CEA. 7 *U.S. Code* § 6(c).

[53] *Exemption for Certain Contracts Involving Energy Products,* 58 *Federal Register* 21286-02 (April 20, 1993).

[54] 7 *U.S. Code* § 6(b).

[55] See *How Lax Regulation and Inadequate Oversight Contributed to the Enron Collapse.* Minority Committee on Government Reform, U.S. House of Representatives (February 7, 2002).

[56] HTM securities (debt only) are those in respect of which the acquirer has the ability and intent to hold until maturity. No changes in market value are reported in the income statement. The investment is carried at historical cost in the balance sheet.

[57] AFS securities are all debt securities not held for trading that an institution does not have the positive intent and ability to hold until maturity and equity securities with readily determinable fair values not held for trading. AFS securities are reported at fair value with unrealized gains or losses (i.e., the amount by which fair value exceeds or falls below amortized cost) reported, net of tax, directly in a component of common stockholders' equity.

[58] Trading securities (debt and equity) are those acquired for short-term profit potential. Changes in market value are reported in the income statement, net of taxes. The investment is marked to market in the balance sheet.

[59] Roberts. Prepared testimony before the Securities Subcommittee of the Banking, Housing and Urban Affairs Committee, U.S. Senate. Oversight Hearing on the Financial Accounting Standards Board and Its Proposed Derivatives Accounting Standard (October 9, 1997), p. 6.

[60] Ibid., p. 8. Volatility attributable to SFAS 115 proved to be significant. In 1999, e.g., JPMorgan Chase reported unrealized gains on equity investments of $1.46 billion, of which $962 million occurred in the fourth quarter, and unrealized losses of $1.05 billion in 2000.

[61] *Derivatives and Risk Management in the Petroleum, Natural Gas, and Electricity Markets.* Energy Information Administration (October 2002), p. 40.

[62] SFAS 133 became effective for fiscal years that began after June 15, 2000, but adoption as early as the third quarter of 1998 was allowed.

[63] SFAS 133 establishes the following definitional characteristics of a derivative: (i) its cash flow or fair value must fluctuate and vary based on the changes in one or more underlying variables; (ii) the contract must be based on one or more notional amounts or payment provisions or both, even though title to such amount(s) never changes hands; (iii) the contract requires no initial net investment or an insignificant initial net investment relative to the value of the underlying item; and (iv) the contract can be readily settled by a net cash payment or with an asset readily convertible to cash. Accordingly, SFAS 133 defines a derivative by generic properties and does not identify qualifying contracts. At the same time, however, SFAS 133 does specify certain contracts (mostly of a purely financial type, e.g., traditional life insurance) that are not to be accounted for as derivatives even though otherwise qualifying under the definition. Included among such contracts, relevant for energy transactions, are those with respect to the normal purchase and sale of commodities for which net settlement is not intended, delivery is probable, and the commodity is expected to be used or sold in the ordinary course of business. See *Derivatives and Risk Management in the Petroleum, Natural Gas, and Electricity Markets.* Energy Information Administration (October 2002), pp. 55–56.

[64] Ibid., p. 58.

[65] Herdman. Testimony concerning recent events relating to Enron Corporation, before the Subcommittee on Capital Markets, Insurance and Government Sponsored Enterprises and Subcommittee on Oversight and Investigation, Committee on Financial Services, U.S. House of Representatives (December 12, 2001), p. 9.

[66] Dharan and Bufkins. *Red Flags in Enron's Reporting of Revenues and Key Financial Measures.* White paper (March 2003) (hereafter *Dharan and Bufkins*), pp. 8–10.

[67] *Dharan and Bufkins*, p. 17.

[68] Bassett and Storie. "Accounting at Energy Firms after Enron. Is the 'Cure' Worse than the 'Disease'?" *Policy Analysis*, 469: 1–17 (February 12, 2003), p. 4.

[69] FASB Statement of Concepts No. 2, ¶¶ 58–59, 79, 95, 97. See also *Relationship between Registrants and Independent Accountants.* SEC Accounting Series Release No. 2961 (August 20, 1981).

[70] For a general discussion, see Bostelman. *The Sarbanes-Oxley Deskbook.* Practising Law Institute (2005).

4 FERC's Shortfall as Market Regulator

Background

For many years, FERC (and its predecessor, the Federal Power Commission) regulated electric utilities and natural gas companies as monopolies and controlled their participation, prices, and profits in wholesale markets.[1] Beginning around 1980, driven by economic and technological developments, FERC recognized a need to reduce the scope of heavy-handed price regulation by encouraging competitive gas and electricity markets with the expectation that competition would lead to lower costs and, ultimately, lower prices for consumers. In moving to a market-based approach, however, FERC did not fully understand or adequately define market power, particularly as it appeared in the electricity industry. In addition, FERC failed to assure the justness and reasonableness of market-based prices and permitted growing industry concentration through utility mergers and acquisitions.

After the NGPA established and then eventually removed federal wellhead price ceilings for various categories of natural gas, FERC issued Orders 436 and 636 to open interstate pipeline transportation systems on equal, nondiscriminatory terms to producers, suppliers, and users. In doing so, FERC required interstate pipeline companies to unbundle storage, sales, and transportation services and relinquish traditional merchant functions. Thereafter, it decoupled the purchase and sale of natural gas from transportation, encouraged primary and secondary markets in pipeline capacity, and treated natural gas as a commodity, tradable by consumers, brokers, and resellers at competitively determined prices pursuant to contract or in wholesale spot markets at distribution hubs and city gates. In 1990, futures contracts for natural gas delivered at Henry Hub were first traded on the New York Mercantile Exchange (NYMEX). The Wellhead Decontrol Act removed all first sales from FERC's Natural Gas Act jurisdiction as of January 1, 1993.[2]

Electricity markets were slower to emerge. When the Federal Power Act became law in 1935, the predominant industry vehicle was a vertically integrated electric utility that owned generation, transmission, and distribution facilities, sold electricity as a bundled service to wholesale and retail customers within an exclusive service area, and built its own power plants and transmission lines, entering into interconnection agreements with neighboring utilities only if required. Most electricity markets were confined within state boundaries, and almost all generation was sited at or near load centers. All segments of the industry—generation, transmission, and local distribution—were presumed to be natural monopolies.

As entities with an obligation to serve the public, utilities were (and in certain respects still are) subject to cost-based rate regulation at both the wholesale and the retail levels—a regime that continued relatively unaffected until the late 1970s, when enactment of PURPA required that utilities purchase power from qualifying nonutility generators at long-run avoided cost. PURPA spurred competition by allowing such generators to enter wholesale markets previously dominated by incumbent utilities. FERC provided further encouragement by authorizing power sales at market-based rates on a case-by-case basis. The Energy Policy Act of 1992, a subsequent milestone, authorized FERC to require utilities to grant wholesale buyers and sellers access to their transmission lines and created exempt wholesale generators as an additional competitive nonutility power source, removed from the strictures of PUHCA.[3] FERC also conditioned its approval of utility mergers on applicants' compliance with open-access transmission requirements and adoption of market-based power rates.

FERC increasingly relied on market forces to contain wholesale prices and, commencing in the 1980s, approved more than 850 applications submitted by companies wishing to sell power competitively in wholesale markets.[4] Electric power marketers, including independent market intermediaries and utility affiliates, were authorized to trade electricity at market-based rates if the seller and its affiliates did not have, or had adequately mitigated, market power in generation and transmission and were unable to erect other barriers to entry.[5] For affiliated power marketers, FERC also required the related utility to have on file an open-access transmission tariff. For unaffiliated suppliers without state-regulated retail load obligations, however, market-based rate authorization effectively removed most remaining regulatory constraints.

The economic rationale advanced by FERC for market-based rates differed fundamentally from that underlying cost-based regulation. The latter addressed market power by controlling profits, not by fostering efficiency. A growing chorus of critics argued that it failed to encourage innovation, risk taking, and lowest costs.[6] Over time, to promote competition, FERC shifted its focus from setting cost-based rates for each jurisdictional seller to establishing market rules of general applicability.

In 1996, FERC issued Orders 888 and 889, under which transmission owners were required to open their high-voltage power lines to all qualified wholesale buyers and sellers of electricity on a nondiscriminatory basis; functionally unbundle transmission and generation services; and voluntarily transfer operating control (but not ownership) of their transmission facilities to an ISO. Order 2000, issued in 1999, requested that utilities voluntarily place their transmission facilities under the control of regional transmission organizations (RTOs) to succeed the ISOs created under Order 888, including those operating centralized, bid-based power markets.

Given the sweeping nature of the changes involved, FERC had undertaken an ambitious program to restructure the electric power industry, even though, at the time, it lacked legislative authority over electricity generation, construction of transmission lines, intrastate transmission, or retail sales, all of which fell under state or local jurisdiction. FERC also lacked direct authority over system reliability, which remained largely the province of electric utilities and the North American Electric Reliability Council. The Energy Policy Act of 2005, discussed in the following sections, has plugged several of these legislative gaps, granting FERC new authority to mandate reliability standards and site transmission lines, but the ultimate effect of these changes remains to be determined.

FERC's Legal Mandate

The Federal Power Act grants FERC exclusive jurisdiction over interstate rates for the transmission and sale of wholesale electricity.[7] FERC's primary responsibility is to "guard the consumer against excessive rates,"[8] which must be "just and reasonable"[9] and applied in a nondiscriminatory manner.[10] FERC has exclusive authority to determine whether wholesale rates meet this statutory standard[11] and the correlative duty to reform rates that do not or that, stated differently, fall outside a "zone of reasonableness" within which rates are high enough to be compensatory to the utility but not excessive to the consumer.[12] Prior to the Energy Policy Act, FERC had limited authority to order refunds and disgorgement of profits where rates exceeded this threshold.[13]

The just and reasonable standard does not require a prescribed pricing formula. FERC therefore enjoys "broad rate-making authority"[14] and may rely on market-based rates in lieu of traditional cost-of-service regulation, but only where the relevant market is in fact competitive.[15] As one court of review has explained,

> In a competitive market, where neither buyer nor seller has significant market power, it is rational to assume that the terms of their voluntary exchange are reasonable, and specifically to infer that the price is close to marginal cost, such that the seller makes only a normal return on its investment.[16]

In authorizing market-based rates, FERC must first make a finding that the relevant market is "sufficiently competitive to preclude [the seller] from exercising significant market power"—that is, from raising "its price without losing substantial business to rival sellers"[17]—and thereafter must assure the continued validity of the initial finding by requiring the seller to file periodic reports on transactions as a condition of its authorization.[18] So long as a seller lacks market power and buyers have alternatives, market-based rates are presumed to meet the just and reasonable standard, notwithstanding likely fluctuations.[19]

Since spot wholesale electricity markets are uniquely vulnerable to the exercise of market power, however, FERC may not simply accept prevailing prices as evidence of competition.[20] Nor can it rely on a single market snapshot. Power systems are dynamic and subject to wide load variations. Electricity travels in real time over a common transmission grid subject to line constraints that may limit the number of generators able to sell power into congested regions. Unless caps or other administrative constraints apply, congestion can cause steep price increases if competitive suppliers in peak load periods are unable or unwilling to sell into the market. Because demand for electricity is insensitive to its hourly wholesale price, a few pivotal generators can unilaterally impose higher prices without forgoing sales.[21] An accurate, ongoing assessment of market power requires that FERC take such system characteristics into account.

To do so, FERC focused on wholesale markets. Unlike the SEC and the CFTC, however, prior to the Energy Policy Act of 2005, FERC did not have statutory authority to intervene in market operations—including authority equivalent to the SEC's under Rule 10b-5 to define and deal with market manipulation,[22] for which there was no analogue in federal electricity law.[23] FERC therefore undertook market-based regulation with legislative authority from a bygone cost-of-service era, compounded by absence of a go-forward legislative mandate.[24]

Inadequate enforcement capability also constrained FERC's response to market rigging. Prior to the Energy Policy Act of 2005, FERC had no power to impose civil penalties for most violations of the Federal Power Act[25]—a severe handicap in addressing market rules, merger authorization, and disposition of jurisdictional facilities. Such civil penalties as it could impose were negligible in comparison to those under the Securities Exchange Act or the Commodity Exchange Act.[26] FERC's criminal authority was similarly limited and inadequate. Prior to the Energy Policy Act of 2005, criminal penalties under the Federal Power Act had not changed since 1935.[27]

The Filed-Rate Doctrine

For many decades, as already noted, FERC relied on cost-of-service methodology that permitted recovery of operating costs plus a reasonable profit. Utilities in the wholesale power market typically entered into long-term, fixed-rate contracts and filed those contracts at FERC, which then determined whether the rates charged were just and reasonable.

Under long-standing judicial precedent (the filed-rate doctrine), a rate on file with and approved by an administrative agency is the only legal rate and binds buyers and sellers with the "force of law."[28] A filed rate is also binding on the courts,[29] which treat the obligation to charge only that rate as "essential to preventing price discrimination."[30] Unless and until FERC authorizes prospective changes through its official procedures, the filed rate controls.[31]

Aggrieved energy consumers may therefore seek redress only at FERC, which has no statutory authority to compel payment of damages or reparations if a filed rate is found to be unjust, unreasonable, or otherwise contrary to public policy. In that event, FERC may set a new rate going forward and order a refund for the amount charged in excess of the just and reasonable rate following the refund effective date, that is, 60 days after a complaint is filed with FERC or after it issues notice of an investigation.[32]

Until the Ninth Circuit Court of Appeals decision in *California v. FERC* (see "FERC's Legal Mandate"), FERC proceeded on the premise that it could not provide a retroactive remedy to market participants who had paid unjust and unreasonable rates before the refund effective date, a legal posture that effectively immunized all past sales and barred billions in potential refunds. Section 5 of the Natural Gas Act provides FERC with even less latitude, since there is no provision for a refund effective date. FERC may therefore change an existing rate prospectively only after finding it to be unjust and unreasonable.[33]

As reliance on competitive market forces displaced company-specific cost-of-service rate making, the filed-rate doctrine was seen to be a legal anachronism:

> The market-based regime employed by FERC fundamentally changes the relationship of the regulatory agency to the commodity, and sweeps away the underpinnings of the filed rate doctrine. FERC no longer brings its unique expertise to bear on rate setting: the *market,* not the agency, sets the rate. In such a system, courts no longer need to defer to the agency's expertise.[34]

Under market-based regulation, sellers of electricity at wholesale no longer post proposed prices or related cost support but instead file generic market-based tariffs, which typically state that rates will be determined by agreement of the parties. To obtain market-based rate authority, a seller must first demonstrate that it lacks market power in the relevant market or has mitigated any market power it may have. A seller with market-based authority must also file quarterly after-the-fact reports listing transaction-specific information (e.g., priced sales and purchases in the preceding three-month period), so that FERC can monitor the seller's exercise of market power over time and determine whether its rates are just and reasonable.[35]

Market-based regulation therefore depends critically on the empirical validity of the initial assessment that a seller lacks market power and on the impact of subsequent transaction information provided by the seller. If the initial assessment is flawed or periodic information is not supplied, then a seller with market power may be effectively removed from regulatory oversight while also being insulated from legal liability by the filed-rate doctrine.[36] Unfortunately, FERC's enthusiasm for market-based regulation has not been matched by equivalent analytical rigor. In the words of one well-regarded regulatory economist,

> FERC does not appear to have a clear definition of market power, has not identified the empirical indicia it will use to measure the presence and extent of market power, does not routinely collect or analyze the data necessary to draw conclusions about market power, has not defined how much market power is too much market power to satisfy its obligations to ensure that wholesale electricity prices are just and reasonable, and it does not appear to have a well developed set of mitigation measures that it can choose from if it indeed finds that there is a significant market power problem.[37]

Economic theory suggests that a power generator's incentive to withhold output does not require a large share of the market, a finding that contradicts antitrust law's linkage of market concentration and anticompetitive harm. Thus, a withholding strategy can be viable if profit lost on capacity withheld is more than compensated by profit earned on sales at supra-competitive prices. When supply is tight, a profit-maximizing firm can produce a significant price increase by withdrawing only a small amount of marginal capacity. FERC's first-generation market-based rate policy used a market share threshold that was too high (20%) and failed to account adequately for transmission constraints.[38]

Hub-and-Spoke System

Until quite recently, in determining whether a seller had market power in generation, FERC employed hub-and-spoke methodology to measure two aspects of market share—installed and uncommitted capacity—against a time-averaged threshold of 20% within a seller's service area and in first-tier interconnected markets.[39] If market share were less then 20%, the seller would not be deemed to dominate the market, that is, to have the ability to raise the market price above a competitive level.[40] FERC developed and applied hub-and-spoke methodology over a 10-year period, beginning with independent power marketers and proceeding to traditional investor-owned utilities and their affiliates. Although the methodology addressed supply concentration, it entirely ignored demand-side response and the inelasticity of electricity supply at full output, factors permitting pivotal suppliers to set prices and exercise market power.[41]

Hub-and-spoke methodology also ignored the impact of import limitations and transmission constraints—that is, how the regulated transmission network is operated, how access to it is priced, and how scarce transmission capacity is allocated.[42] As a result, it did not produce accurate definitions of geographic markets. By addressing only *ex ante* market share, hub-and-spoke methodology failed to recognize that competitive electricity markets depend on transmission operations, especially congestion management and system response to emergencies, and that bidding, scheduling, and operating protocols play a crucial role in determining whether market power can be exploited.[43]

Given its inherent limitations, hub-and-spoke methodology yielded market power determinations that were detached from economic reality:

> The process FERC uses to determine whether a firm is eligible to receive market-based prices is fatally flawed. First, the dichotomy implicit in the FERC process that a firm either possesses market power or does not possess market power is factually false. Depending on conditions in the transmission network and the operating decisions of all market participants, almost any firm can possess substantial market power in the sense of being able to impact significantly the market price through its unilateral actions. Second, it is also extremely difficult, if not impossible, to determine on a prospective basis the frequency that a firm possesses substantial market power given the tremendous uncertainty about system conditions and the incentives they create for the behavior of other firms in the market. Finally, the methodology used by the FERC to make a determination of whether a firm has the ability to exercise market power uses analytical techniques long acknowledged by the economics profession as grossly inadequate.[44]

In short, FERC did not properly measure the extent of market power, failed to collect and analyze relevant data beyond its *ex ante* hub-and-spoke assessment, and ignored such market power variables as peak loads, transmission reliability margins, maintenance outages, congestion, and ancillary power sources. As a result, FERC lacked a meaningful analytical tool to ensure just and reasonable rates. FERC also failed to develop and impose adequate mitigation measures when market power was found to exist.[45]

Electric Industry Mergers

Mergers during the period 1993–2003 totaled $190 billion, were concentrated in the Midwest and Northeast, and posed significant market power issues—horizontally, by combining generation capacity, and vertically, by combining transmission and generation capacity or generation capacity and fuel supply assets.[46] Even in the relatively permissive regulatory environment of the past decade, several major utility mergers attracted the opposition of FERC, the Department of Justice (DOJ), and the Federal Trade Commission (FTC). (See table 4–1.)

Electricity mergers are subject to regulatory review by the DOJ and the FTC under Section 7 of the Clayton Act, which makes illegal mergers or acquisitions that "substantially . . . lessen competition or . . . tend to create a monopoly."[48] By contrast, FERC employed a public interest standard under Section 203 of the Federal Power Act with review limited to dispositions of jurisdictional facilities,[49] while the antitrust agencies were free to challenge any electricity merger. In markets within the purview of the Federal Power Act, however, FERC has exclusive jurisdiction over pricing and refunds,[50] and antitrust remedies have generally not applied.[51] Traditionally, FERC has imposed behavioral remedies, such as conditioning mergers on open-access transmission, while antitrust agencies have required structural remedies, such as divestiture.[52]

In 1996, FERC issued a merger policy statement (MPS) to clarify its interpretation of the public interest standard by considering a merger's effect on competition, ratepayer protection, and regulation.[53] The MPS adopted the DOJ/FTC Horizontal Merger Guidelines and established a process for screening proposed mergers for anticompetitive effects. Its methodology involves a three-part analysis:

1. Identifying relevant products and services (e.g., nonfirm energy, firm energy, reactive power, peak and off-peak power, and long-term capacity)

2. Determining the scope of the geographic market for each product

3. Estimating a merger's price impact with reference to concentration of suppliers in each geographic market

Table 4–1. Mergers Conditionally Approved by FERC or Challenged by DOJ/FTC[47]

Merging Parties	Date, Type and Location	Agency Taking Action	Competitive Issues and Remedy
Ohio Edison/ Centerior	1997 Electric–Electric Midwest	FERC	Issues: Transmission foreclosure Remedy: Transmission priority, transmission capacity allocation, and price cap requirements, "expectations" that the merged company would relinquish control of its transmission to an Independent System Operator
Pacific Enterprises/ Enova Corp.	1998 Electric–Gas West	FERC and DOJ	Issues: Gas transportation foreclosure, deterrence of generation entry Remedy: Same-time pipeline capacity disclosure requirements (FERC) and divestiture of two gas-fired generators (DOJ)
PacifiCorp/Energy Group PLC (Peabody Coal)[a]	1998 Electric–Coal West	FTC	Issues: Raising rival's costs, deterrence of generation entry Remedy: Divestiture of coal mining properties, prohibitions on inter-affiliate transfer of non-public coal customers' information
CMS Energy/ Panhandle Eastern	1999 Electric–Gas Midwest	FTC	Issues: Gas transportation foreclosure Remedy: Pipeline-to-pipeline interconnection requirement
Dominion Resources/ CNG	2000 Electric–Gas Mid-Atlantic	FTC	Issues: Gas transportation foreclosure, detterence of generation entry Remedy: Divestiture of gas distribution assets
American Electric Power/Central and SouthWest	2000 Electric–Electric Midwest	FERC	Issues: Transmission foreclosure Remedy: Market monitoring, obligation to join an RTO, accepted parties offer to divest generation
DTE Energy/ MCN Energy	2001 Electric–Gas Midwest	FTC	Issues: Lessening of competition between centrally supplied electricty and self-generation Remedy: Easement over portion of gas distribution capacity
Koch Industries/ Entergy	2001 Electric–Gas South	FTC	Issues: Regulatory evasion Remedy: Transparency requirements for gas procurement

(a) The merger was not consummated—another firm eventually purchased Peabody Coal.

Source: Moss AIA (2005), p. 29

Merger review under the MPS employs structural analysis to define geographic and product markets and assess concentration in those markets. Because the volatility of electricity demand creates numerous time-differentiated products, relevant geographic markets are framed by such factors as generation price differentials, transmission losses, transmission constraints, and spot prices—each a moving target. Market definition therefore depends on complex models, significant data input, and sensitivity analysis using different assumptions.[54]

Not surprisingly, market definition has proved the most contentious feature of merger cases at FERC. The MPS methodology identifies a destination market of relevant consumers and applies a delivered price test to determine potential suppliers, that is, those capable of delivering power to a destination market at a cost no greater than 5% above the price that would obtain if there were no merger. The delivered price test relies on transmission prices, potential suppliers' generation costs, competitive market prices, economic capacity, and other capacity-related factors.[55] However, as the MPS notes,

> The amount and price of transmission available for suppliers to reach wholesale buyers at different locations throughout the network can vary substantially over time. If this is the case, the analysis should treat these narrower periods separately and separate geographic markets should be defined for each period.[56]

Of the 70 consummated mergers involving investor-owned utilities between 1993 and 2003, several presented particularly difficult market definition problems attributable to transmission availability and time-differentiated products.[57]

A threshold concern, according to industry analysts, is that the delivered price test fails to address the implications of transmission congestion:

> In electricity, limits on transmission capacity, combined with the lack of economic storage, create circumstances in which there may be no additional competitive supply *at any price*. Such circumstances, in which a single supplier is *pivotal* (*i.e.*, monopolizes a portion of the market demand) result in periodic extreme price increases rather than smaller increases sustained continuously over longer periods of time. Ironically, the focus on the ability to sustain small increases sometimes overlooks the more serious problem. In some cases an electricity supplier may not find it profitable to raise prices by 5%, but would find it profitable to raise prices by 500%. . . . Clearly if transmission capacity limits power flow into a region, those limits also define the scope of the market. However, capacity limits only bind some of the time, and it is difficult to predict just how often they will be relevant. The physical properties of electricity transmission greatly complicate this task. Power is injected and withdrawn from an integrated network, rather than "shipped" from one point to another, as in a railroad network. The actual path taken by power flows is determined by the physical characteristics of the network rather than by commercial transportation arrangements.[58]

Even before implosion of the California power market, the Midwest price spike of June 1998—when spot electricity prices reached $7,500 per megawatt-hour, or 100 times the average energy price—lent credence to this observation.

Although the greatest concern about mergers is their impact on prices, FERC has historically relied on a market concentration screen (the Herfindahl-Hirschmann index), derived from the DOJ/FTC Horizontal Merger Guidelines, to measure potential market power.[59] A market concentration screen presupposes a relationship between a firm's market share and its ability to raise offer prices unilaterally or withhold output as a means to the same end. However, as applied by FERC, a market concentration screen does not take into account several essential features of electricity markets: tight markets created by short-term limits on both generation and transmission capacity, absence of price-responsive demand, and significant variability in spot prices from hour to hour.[60] To capture these effects, a market concentration screen must define electricity sales during off-peak and on-peak hours, for example, or even from hour to hour, as separate product markets, each of which may have a different geographic market associated with it. Information on product differentiation is thus essential to the evaluation of competitive effects.[61]

For most mergers reviewed between 1993 and 2003, FERC relied primarily on the merging parties' self-serving analysis of their own pending merger. In contrast, the DOJ and the FTC performed an independent analysis based on review of confidential data. Applicant-filed analysis at FERC predictably took advantage of MPS's broad and subjective standards to manipulate data, methodology, and modeling. This led to significant variation in concentration findings for the same or contiguous markets in sequential cases and undercut the analytical consistency, predictability, and credibility of FERC's merger decisions.[62]

In addition, the theoretical market concentration model used by FERC did not work well. In the real world of electricity, firms that have short-term control over both transmission and generation can indirectly leverage that control to reach more output than they own, especially where transmission capacity is constrained. In the California market meltdown of 2000–2001, to cite but one illustration, no single producer held more than an 11% share of the generation supply within the state.[63] Market analysis considerations have become even more significant with the repeal of the Energy Policy Act of 2005 by PUHCA, implicit encouragement of industry consolidation, and assignment to FERC of increased responsibilities in reviewing utility mergers.

Observations

FERC decoupled electricity generation and transmission and required open-access nondiscriminatory transmission to promote industry competition, efforts that paralleled those it had undertaken for natural gas. FERC also favored bid-based power markets, using the PJM as a model, but placed too much reliance on their self-executing nature while according too little recognition to systemic factors that militated against competition. Pro-competitive philosophic principles controlled and, for a time, left a regulatory void. Opportunistic market players planned accordingly and took advantage of this void, inflicting massive damage on consumers, companies, investors, and markets in the process.

Notes

[1] This and the immediately following paragraphs draw on *Energy Markets: Concerted Actions Needed by FERC to Confront Challenges That Impede Effective Oversight.* United States General Accounting Office, GAO-02-656 (June 2002) (hereafter *GAO-02-656*), pp. 19–25.

[2] First sales include all sales other than those by interstate or intrastate pipelines, local distribution companies, or their affiliates. The only sales over which FERC retains regulatory jurisdiction are those for the resale of domestic gas by pipelines, local distribution companies, or their affiliates.

[3] Energy Policy Act of 1992, Public Law No. 102-486, 106 Stat. 2776 (1992). PUHCA, repealed by the Energy Policy Act of 2005, regulated interstate holding companies engaged, through subsidiaries, in the electric utility business or in the retail distribution of natural or manufactured gas. Such holding companies were subject to regulation by the SEC with respect to the structure of their utility systems, transactions among companies that were part of the holding company system, acquisitions, business combinations, issuance and sale of securities, and financing transactions. See Public Utility Holding Company Act of 1935, §§ 1–36, 15 *U.S. Code* §§ 79a-79 (2000).

[4] See, e.g., *Entergy Servs., Inc.*, 58 FERC ¶ 61,234, 61,753 (1992) (competitive markets provide greater efficiencies than traditional cost-based regulation in electric generation and supply).

[5] See, e.g., *Progress Power Marketing, Inc.*, 76 FERC ¶ 61,155, at 61,919 (1996); *Northwest Power Marketing Co., L.L.C.*, 75 FERC ¶ 61,281, at 61,899 (1996); *Heartland Energy Services, Inc.*, 68 FERC ¶ 61,223, at 62,062–63 (1994).

[6] Kelliher. "Market Manipulation, Market Power, and the Authority of the Federal Energy Regulatory Commission." *Energy Law Journal*, 26 (1) (2005) (hereafter *Kelliher*), p. 10.

[7] See, e.g., *Nantahala Power and Light Co. v. Thornburg*, 476 U.S. 953, 956 (1986).

[8] *City of Detroit v. FPA*, 230 F.2d 810, 817 (D.C. Cir. 1956).

[9] 16 *U.S. Code* §§ 824d, 824e.

[10] 16 *U.S. Code* § 824d(b); *Entergy Louisiana, Inc. v. Louisiana Public Service Com'n,* 539 U.S. 239, 41 (2003).

[11] *Mississippi Power & Light Co. v. Mississippi,* 487 U.S. 354, 371 (1988).

[12] *FPC v. Hope Natural Gas Co.,* 320 U.S. 591, 602–03, 610–12 (1944).

[13] See, e.g., *The Washington Water Power Co.,* 83 FERC ¶ 61,282 (1998).

[14] *Mobil Oil Exploration & Producing Southeast Inc. v. United Distribution Co.,* 498 U.S. 211, 224 (1991).

[15] *Elizabethtown Gas Company v. FERC,* 10 F.3d 866, 870 (D.C. Cir. 1993). See also *Louisiana Energy and Power Auth. v. FERC,* 141 F.3d 364 (D.C. Cir. 1998).

[16] *Tejas Power Corp. v. FERC,* 908 F.2d 998, 1004 (D.C. Cir. 1990).

[17] *Elizabethtown Gas Company v. FERC,* 871.

[18] *California v. FERC,* 383 F.3d 1006, 1013 (9th Cir. 2004).

[19] *State of California, ex rel. Bill Lockyer, Att'y Gen. of Cal. v. British Columbia Power Exch. Corp.,* 99 FERC ¶ 61,247, 62,062 (May 31, 2002).

[20] *FPC v. Texaco,* 417 U.S. 380, 397 (1974).

[21] Wolak. Statement before the Committee on Governmental Affairs, U.S. Senate (June 13, 2001) (hereafter *Wolak 6-13-01*), pp. 2–3.

[22] McDiarmid. *Taking Stock: The Successes and Limitations of Open Access.* White paper presented to National Rural Electric Cooperative Association (January 11, 2005) (hereafter *McDiarmid*), pp. 19–22.

[23] *Kelliher,* p. 16. For general background, see Federal Power Act §§ 201–14, 16 *U.S. Code* §§ 824-824m.

[24] *GAO-02-056,* p. 47.

[25] Prior to its amendment by the Energy Policy Act of 2005, Section 316A of the Federal Power Act limited civil penalties to those in respect of provisions added or amended by the Energy Policy Act of 1992, namely, Sections 211–14. FERC had no legal authority to impose civil penalties for other violations of the Federal Power Act, including those under Sections 205 and 206. See *Kelliher,* pp. 22–23.

[26] Prior to its amendment by the Energy Policy Act of 2005, Section 316A limited civil penalties to not more than $10,000 per day per violation. By contrast, the Commodity Exchange Act provides for civil penalties capped at the higher of $100,000 or triple the monetary gain, and the Securities Exchange Act of 1934 provides for civil penalties of up to the greater of $100,000 for an individual and $500,000 for a company, or the "gross amount of pecuniary gain." *Kelliher*, p. 23.

[27] Prior to the Energy Policy Act of 2005, a knowing and willful violation was subject to a maximum penalty of $5,000 and imprisonment for up to two years, with an additional $500 per day for continuing violations. Federal Power Act § 316, 16 *U.S. Code* § 825o (2000).

[28] See *Keogh v. Chicago & Northwestern Rwy. Co.*, 260 U.S. 156 (1922); *Lowden v. Simon-Shields Lonsdale Grain Co.*, 306 U.S. 516, 520 (1939).

[29] See, e.g., *Montana-Dakota Utils. Co. v. Northwestern Pub. Serv. Co.*, 341 U.S. 246, 251–52 (1951).

[30] *Maislin Indus., U.S., Inc. v. Primary Steel*, 497 U.S. 116 (1990).

[31] *Arkansas Louisiana Gas Co. v. Hall*, 453 U.S. 571, 577 (1981). See also *Conservation of Power and Water Resources*, 18 *Code of Federal Regulations*, pt. 35.1(a), (e) (2005).

[32] Federal Power Act, 16 *U.S. Code* § 824d. Cf. *California v. FERC*, No. 02-73093 (9th Cir. September 9, 2004).

[33] *GAO-02-656*, p. 48.

[34] *Attorney General's Energy White Paper* (State of California) (April 2004) (hereafter *AG White Paper*), p. 40.

[35] *California v. FERC*, No. 02-73093 (9th Cir. September 9, 2004), p. 13,133. See Federal Power Act, 16 *U.S. Code* § 824d(c).

[36] *California v. FERC*, No. 02-73093 (9th Cir. September 9, 2004), p. 13,135.

[37] Joskow. Statement before the Committee on Governmental Affairs, U.S. Senate (June 13, 2001), p. 7.

[38] Moss. *Electricity and Market Power: Current Issues for Restructuring Markets.* American Antitrust Institute Working Paper No. 05-01 (2004) (hereafter *Moss Restructuring*), p. 7.

[39] See, e.g., *New York State Electric & Gas Corp.*, 78 FERC ¶ 61,309 (1997). A seller is required to compare its controlled generating capacity to the sum of (i) that capacity, (ii) any alternative generating capacity in the service area, and (iii) all generating capacity in first-tier utilities.

[40] See, e.g., *Order Conditionally Accepting Market-Based Tariff, Huntington Beach Development, L.L.C.*, 96 FERC ¶ 61,212 (2001). Pursuant to hub-and-spoke methodology, an applicant for market-based rates must perform a separate analysis of installed and uncommitted capacity with respect to each utility that is directly interconnected with the applicant (i.e., with respect to first-tier utilities) and must compare the applicant's capacity to the sum of capacity controlled by the applicant, by the first-tier utility, and by utilities interconnected with the first-tier utility either directly or through the applicant. See *New York State Electric & Gas*, 78 FERC ¶ 61,309, at 62,327–28 (1997).

[41] Stoft. *An Analysis of FERC's Hub-and-Spoke Market-Power Screen.* California Electric Oversight Board (September 2001) (hereafter *Stoft*), p. 2. For a general discussion, see Joskow. *The Difficult Transition to Competitive Electricity Markets.* Prepared for the conference Electricity Deregulation: Where from Here?) (May 2003) (hereafter *Joskow 5-03*).

[42] *Joskow 5-03*, p. 11.

[43] *Wolak 6-13-01*, p. 5.

[44] Wolak. Statement before the Committee on Governmental Affairs, U.S. Senate (November 12, 2002), p. 9.

[45] Joskow. Statement before the Committee on Governmental Affairs, U.S. Senate (November 12, 2002), p. 7.

[46] Moss. *Electricity Mergers, Economic Analysis, and Consistency: Why FERC Needs to Change Its Approach.* American Antitrust Institute (January 13, 2005) (hereafter *Moss Mergers*), p. 8.

[47] *Moss Restructuring*, p. 29.

[48] 15 *U.S. Code* § 45 (2000). The FTC additionally enforces Section 5 of the Federal Trade Commission Act.

[49] Federal Power Act § 203(a), 16 *U.S. Code* § 824(b)(2000). These involve the sale, lease, or disposition of public utility facilities used in transmission and the sale of energy at wholesale in interstate commerce. The Energy Policy Act of 2005 expanded the scope of FERC's authority under Section 203.

[50] See, e.g., *Pub. Utility Dist. No. 1 of Grays Harbor County Washington v. Idacorp, Inc.*, 379 F.3d 641 (9th Cir. 2004).

[51] See, e.g., *Montana-Dakota Utilities Co. v. Northwestern Public Service Co.*, 341 U.S. 246 (1951); *California v. Dynegy, Inc.*, 375 F.3d 831, 85053 (9th Cir. 2004).

[52] *Moss Restructuring*, pp. 27–28.

[53] *Inquiry Concerning the Commission's Merger Policy under the Federal Power Act: Policy Statement*. Order No. 592, 61 F.R. 68,595 (December 30, 1996) (hereafter *Order 592*). FERC screens vertical mergers using the same data and criteria that it uses to assess horizontal mergers. Vertical market power would exist if a firm had a significant share of both transmission and generation capacity in a particular area, enabling it to deny transmission capacity to its generation competitors and increase the price of its generation.

[54] *Moss Mergers*, pp. 11–12.

[55] Economic capacity means generation the variable costs of which permit delivery of electric power to a relevant market after paying necessary transmission and ancillary service costs at a price close to the competitive price in the relevant market. See *Order 592*, pp. 69–75.

[56] *Order 592*, p. 75.

[57] *Moss Mergers*, p. 13.

[58] Bushnell. *Looking for Trouble: Competition Policy in the U.S. Electricity Industry*. Center for the Study of Energy Markets, University of California Energy Institute (April 2003) (hereafter *Bushnell*), p. 7.

[59] *Order 592*, pp. 75–79.

[60] *Bushnell*, p. 11.

[61] *Comment of the Staff of the Bureau of Economics of the Federal Trade Commission*, FERC Docket No. RM98-4-000 (September 11, 1998). A merger between firms in markets for differentiated products may diminish competition by enabling the merged firm to profit by unilaterally raising the price of one or both products above the pre-merger level if the resulting sales loss can be offset by sales of the product of the merger partner. Ibid., p. 6.

[62] *Moss Mergers*, p. 3.

[63] *McDiarmid*, p. 9.

5 The Deregulated Gas Supply Market

Since removal of wellhead price controls, the gas supply market has evolved from a collection of regulated monopolies to a national system of producers, pipeline, storage, and local distribution companies, marketers, and consumers (see table 5–1).

Table 5–1. The U.S. Natural Gas Industry at a Glance[1]

	Participants	Miles of Pipe	Regulatory Regime in 2001
Producers	8,000 Independents 24 Majors	0	Phased price deregulation Begun in 1979, completed in 1989
Pipelines	160	259,000	Federal Energy Regulatory Commission (FERC)
Natural Gas Marketers	260	0	Unregulated
Local Gas Utilities	1,500	1,139,000	State Utility Commissions
End Users Residential Commercial Industrial	56 million 5 million 200 thousand	0	Unregulated
Electric Utilities	500	0	Interstate – FERC Intrastate – State Commissions

Source: Dept. of Energy, Energy Information Administration, AGA

In the 1980s and 1990s, FERC issued a series of directives, including Orders 436 and 636, that granted end users nondiscriminatory pipeline access to competitive gas suppliers and opened pipeline transportation to producers, suppliers, and users on equal terms.[2] Industrial and commercial users, among others, could then buy gas directly from producers and marketers for shipment on interstate pipelines. Pipeline companies eventually unbundled their transportation, storage, and sales services, and shippers created a secondary capacity market by releasing to other shippers unneeded pipeline transportation capacity, on either a temporary or a permanent basis.[3]

As a result of these initiatives, producers today sell natural gas at wholesale to consumers, market intermediaries, and resellers free of federal government price control pursuant to contract or on the spot market at a specific location for the price prevailing at that time and place. Wholesale prices are set by supply and demand in the marketplace, subject only to FERC review to ensure that the prices are just and reasonable. Buyers and sellers also arrange to transport gas to market, with the buyer typically paying the pipeline for transportation and any required ancillary services en route, such as storage.[4]

A pipeline may deliver gas directly to consumers located along its right-of-way or at the city gate to a local distribution company, regulated as an intrastate utility, which redelivers the gas to residential, commercial, and industrial users. In the case of residential customers, the local distribution company purchases gas for resale. For commercial and industrial customers, however, it usually delivers gas they have purchased directly from remote producers and acts as a transporter only.[5]

Deregulation of the wholesale gas industry has led to proliferation of market centers or distribution hubs, associated geographically with central pipeline interconnections, where individuals and companies come together to buy and sell natural gas on the spot market. In 1990, as a further market adaptation, futures contracts for natural gas delivered at the Henry Hub, a distribution center in Louisiana, were first traded on NYMEX. Since then, NYMEX has also created contracts for trading natural gas at other hubs, with prices determined at the Henry Hub.[6]

Natural gas prices are therefore set in two markets, each traded with reference to a particular market hub: a spot market, for natural gas bought and sold that day, and a futures market, for gas to be sold from 1 to 36 months in advance. Market participants are able to trade natural gas as a physical commodity while also using derivatives, including natural gas futures and options, to speculate or hedge against price risk. Derivatives trade over the counter (OTC) and on NYMEX without federal regulation at prices that typically move in parallel with those in the actual physical or cash market.[7]

NYMEX files the terms and conditions of traded contracts with the CFTC, which requires daily reporting of market information, including position size, trading volume, open interest, and prices. NYMEX participants are subject to the CFTC's antifraud rules, must meet minimum financial requirements, and are largely protected against counterparty credit risk. OTC markets, in contrast, are not subject to CFTC regulation and allow trading of natural gas derivatives on negotiable terms with regard to maturity dates, quantities, and delivery points, either multilaterally or principal-to-principal through an electronic trading facility.[8]

Emerging Problems

Deregulation of the natural gas supply market has not been free of problems. When FERC required that natural gas pipelines unbundle their merchant and transportation functions, it did so functionally, by corporate separation, not by compelling physical divestiture. Pipeline companies were still allowed to have marketing affiliates, subject to rules of nondiscrimination that precluded according an affiliate's gas an advantage over that of third parties in the competition for pipeline space or granting price discounts to an affiliate not available to third parties. Although well intentioned, FERC's standards of conduct for pipeline operations prior to the Energy Policy Act of 2005 were inadequate to prevent anticompetitive practices and affiliate abuse by large, diversified energy companies in deregulated markets.[9] As originally issued, its affiliate regulations also failed to control nonmarketing affiliates, local distribution companies, or affiliated producers and gatherers.[10]

With the emergence of spot markets, natural gas price indexes established by the trade press became indispensable for disseminating market price information, valuing assets, and pricing financial and physical transactions. Contracts for the sale of physical natural gas are typically tied to the reported daily spot and bid week market index prices published by *Gas Daily, Inside FERC, Natural Gas Intelligence (NGI)*, and *Natural Gas Week*. Index prices are also used for settling many financial derivatives, such as swaps, options, forwards, and basin-to-border price transactions.[11] Notwithstanding their critical importance to the natural gas market and collateral impact on the cost of electricity produced by gas-fired generation, gas price indexes were compiled without adequate safeguards or controls, could not be independently verified, and were subject to widespread manipulation.[12]

Internet-based trading systems (e.g., EnronOnline) that provided one-to-many trading platforms for physical energy products and energy derivatives gained a large share of the world's natural gas trading volumes, traded gas at prices unrelated to the actual costs of supply, invited widespread market manipulation, and were only belatedly addressed by FERC.[13]

Deregulation of the gas supply market led to increased price volatility, including price spikes (see fig. 5–1). Price volatility presented a formidable challenge to FERC, which was slow to react to market manipulation, to the CFTC, which lacks general regulatory authority over trading in the OTC derivatives markets, and to the Energy Information Administration, which attempted to fulfill its mission with an outdated natural gas data collection system. The Energy Policy Act of 2005 has, in response, addressed enforcement and information issues.

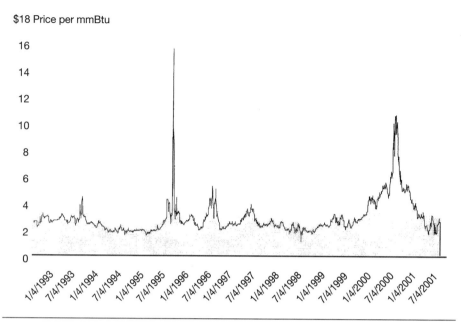

$18 Price per mmBtu

Figure 5–1. Natural Gas Wholesale Prices per mmBtu, Adjusted to 2001 Dollars[14]

Source: GAO-03-46, December 2002, p.2

El Paso: Affiliate Abuse and Market Manipulation

El Paso Corporation (El Paso), a holding company, sits at the apex of a complex group of related companies engaged in natural gas production, transportation, trading, and other businesses (see fig. 5–2). Originally a regional natural gas pipeline company serving the western United States, El Paso expanded dramatically between 1996 and 2001, largely by merger and acquisition, to become an international energy company with diverse interests in natural gas production, gas transportation, power generation, and petroleum. Its assets grew in five years from $2.5 billion to over $44 billion following a merger with the Coastal Corporation in 2001. To finance its expansion, El Paso incurred large amounts of debt.[15]

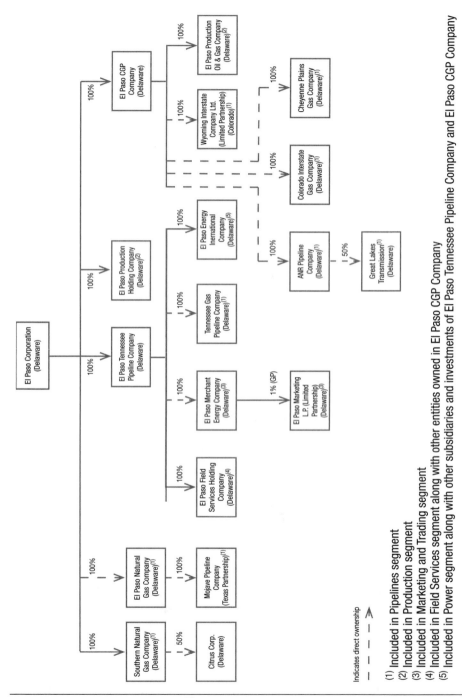

Figure 5–2. El Paso Organization Chart[16]   *Source: El Paso Annual Report, Form 10-KA, March 23, 2005, p. 1.*

El Paso conducts regulated and nonregulated operations through five business segments, several of which it is exiting:

- The largest interstate natural gas pipeline system in the United States connecting the nation's principal gas supply regions to the six largest consuming regions (56,000 miles of pipeline and 420 billion cubic feet of storage capacity, including eight wholly owned and four partially owned interstate transmission systems and five underground gas storage entities)

- Oil and gas production (3.6 million net developed and undeveloped acres and 2.2 trillion cubic feet of gas equivalent [Tcfe] of proved natural gas and oil reserves worldwide)

- Marketing and trading (in liquidation)

- Power production (10,400 MW of gross generating capacity in 16 countries)

- Processing and gathering services, primarily in southern Louisiana

El Paso's wholly owned interstate transmission systems are described in further detail in figure 5–3 and table 5–2.

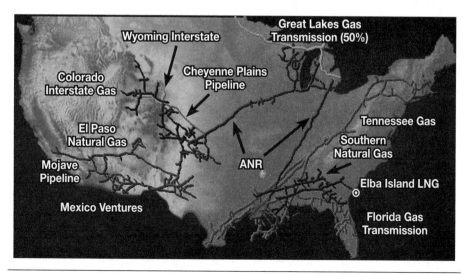

Figure 5–3. Map of El Paso's Wholly Owned Transmission System

Source: El Paso Form 10-K, 2004, March 23, 2005, p.4

Table 5–2. El Paso's Wholly Owned Transmission Systems (companion table to figure 5–3)[16]

Transmission System	Supply and Market Region	As of December 31, 2004			Average Throughput[1]		
		Miles of Pipeline	Design Capacity (MMcf/d)	Storage Capacity (Bcf)	2004	2003 (BBtu/d)	2002
Tennessee Gas Pipeline (TGP)	Extends from Louisiana, the Gulf of Mexico, and south Texas to the northeast section of the U.S., including the metropolitan areas of New York City and Boston	14,200	6,876	90	4,469	4,710	4,596
ANR Pipeline (ANR)	Extends from Louisiana, Oklahoma, Texas and the Gulf of Mexico to the midwestern and northeastern regions of the U.S., including the metropolitan areas of Detroit, Chicago and Milwaukee	10,500	6,620	192	4,067	4,232	4,130
El Paso Natural Gas (EPNG)	Extends from the San Juan, Permian, and Anadarko basins to California, its single largest market, as well as markets in Arizona, Nevada, New Mexico, Oklahoma, Texas, and northern Mexico	11,000	5,650[2]	—	4,074	3,874	3,799
Southern Natural Gas (SNG)	Extends from Texas, Louisiana, Mississippi, Alabama, and the Gulf of Mexico to Louisiana, Mississippi, Alabama, Florida, Georgia, South Carolina and Tennessee, including the metropolitan areas of Atlanta and Birmingham.	8,000	3,437	60	2,163	2,101	2,151
Colorado Interstate Gas (CIG)	Extends from most production areas in the Rocky Mountain region and the Anadarko Basin to the front range of the Rocky Mountains and multiple interconnects with pipeline systems transporting gas to the Midwest, the Southwest, California, and the Pacific Northwest	4,000	3,000	29	1,744	1,685	1,687
Wyoming Interstate (WIC)	Extends from western Wyoming and the Powder River Basin to various pipeline interconnections near Cheyenne, Wyoming	600	1,997	—	1,201	1,213	1,194
Mojave Pipeline (MPC)	Connects with the EPNG and Transwestern transmission systems at Topock, Arizona, and the Kern River Gas Transmission Company transmission system in California, and extends to customers in the vicinity of Bakersfield, California	400	400	—	161	192	266
Cheyenne Plains Gas Pipeline (CPG)	Extends from the Cheyenne hub in Colorado to various pipeline interconnects near Greensburg, Kansas	400	396[3]	—	89	—	—

(1) Includes throughput transported on behalf of affiliates

(2) This capacity reflects winter-sustainable west-flow capacity and 800 MMcf/d of east-end delivery capacity

(3) This capacity was placed in service on December 1, 2004. Compression was added and placed in service on January 31, 2005, which increased the design capacity to 576 MMcf/d

Source: El Paso Form 10-K, 2004, March 23, 2005, p. 4,5

Manipulation of the California energy market

Over 80% of the natural gas consumed in California is imported from out of state.[18] During 2000–2001, California experienced sharply higher gas prices, driven in part by increased demand from gas-fired power units and transportation constraints. Within a single year, however, natural gas spot prices for California residential customers almost doubled, an increase that reflected a radical decoupling of border prices and those at the Henry Hub. California consumers paid $6.6 billion for natural gas in 1999 and $12.3 billion the following year.[19] Higher prices were accompanied by unprecedented volatility. Under normal circumstances, the price differential between production basin and border prices is measured only by transportation costs. From November 2000 to June 2001, California customers often paid two to three times the Henry Hub price, an increase that bore no relationship to transportation costs. (See fig. 5–4.)

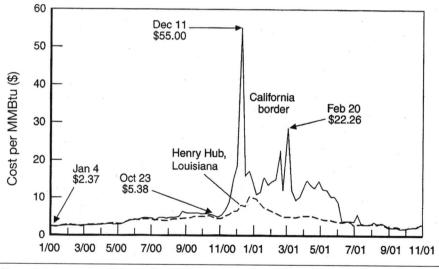

Figure 5–4. Comparison Between Henry Hub and California Gas Prices[20]

Source: Enerfax Daily (2001)

In April 2000, the Public Utilities Commission of the State of California (CPUC) filed a complaint at FERC against El Paso Natural Gas Company (El Paso Pipeline) and El Paso Merchant Energy-Gas

LP and El Paso Merchant Energy Company (collectively referred to as El Paso Merchant) under Section 5 of the Natural Gas Act, alleging affiliate abuse and anticompetitive collusion impacting the delivered price of natural gas. CPUC asked FERC to terminate three transportation contracts between El Paso Pipeline and El Paso Merchant or to compel El Paso Merchant to release unused transportation capacity to replacement shippers.[21] The complaint triggered a lengthy proceeding at FERC.

El Paso Merchant's acquisition of 1,220 MMBTU per day of capacity on El Paso Pipeline, an affiliated entity, gave El Paso Merchant more than 35% of the Southern California gas transportation market, enabled it to realize huge profits, and lay at the core of the case. CPUC, Southern California Edison, and Pacific Gas & Electric contended that El Paso Merchant had acquired firm capacity on El Paso Pipeline at an undisclosed discount and then intentionally withheld 500–700 MMBTU per day from March to November 2000, keeping prices artificially high and indirectly imposing $3.7 billion in unnecessary power purchase costs on California electricity consumers. FERC regulations require a pipeline to fully schedule its system, transport volumes up to certificated capacity, and offer all available capacity to the market. A pipeline is not permitted to withhold capacity if it receives requests for service that it can fulfill.[22]

The presiding administrative law judge (ALJ) at FERC viewed the undisclosed discount as evidence of "blatant collusion" between El Paso Merchant and El Paso Pipeline in violation of applicable affiliate regulations; concluded that El Paso Corporation had failed to maintain the required firewall between its regulated and unregulated businesses; and found that El Paso Merchant's bid for capacity had been approved by El Paso Corporation's CEO, William Wise, who knew that the capacity would enable El Paso Merchant "to influence the physical market" and increase its "physical spreads." The ALJ also found that the El Paso affiliates had the ability to exercise market power although he initially declined to conclude that they had in fact done so.[23]

In a later phase of the same proceeding, however, newly presented evidence led the ALJ to conclude that El Paso Pipeline had "withheld extremely large amounts of capacity that it could have flowed to its California delivery points," thereby "substantially [tightening] the supply of natural gas at the California border [and] significantly broadening the basis differential." The ALJ recommended that FERC institute penalty procedures for the unlawful exercise of market power and violation of its Standards of Conduct for Pipelines with Marketing Affiliates.[24] Immediately following the ALJ's decision, El Paso Corporation's stock dropped more than $4 per share, a decline of over 35%.

In June 2003, the California attorney general filed suit against El Paso. The suit alleged that

- El Paso Pipeline had withheld substantial amounts of transportation capacity under its control, in part by running its facilities at less than maximum approved operating pressure, in violation of FERC rules;

- El Paso Pipeline had diverted available pipeline capacity away from the Southern California border in order to raise gas prices;

- El Paso Merchant had systematically restricted natural gas transportation capacity to the Southern California border by refusing to release capacity for use by other shippers seeking to move gas to California;

- El Paso Pipeline and El Paso Merchant had coordinated their activities, under senior management's oversight, to widen the spread between the price of gas at the border and the market price of gas in producing basins;

- As of November 2000, El Paso Merchant's dominant position in the market for critical supplies of natural gas delivered at the Southern California border had permitted it to charge very high, supra-competitive prices, imposing additional costs on gas-fired generators in the state, increasing the price of electricity in California, and contributing to rolling blackouts and interruptions in electricity service.[25]

Settlement and aftermath

In June 2003, the El Paso entities entered into an omnibus settlement involving four states (California, Washington, Oregon, and Nevada) and multiple California parties. Under the settlement, El Paso agreed to pay almost $1.7 billion, to be used for ratepayer relief, consisting of $600 million payable initially and $900 million payable over 20 years ($386 million in cash and the balance as a price reduction under a power supply contract, both collateralized by oil and gas properties). El Paso Pipeline also agreed to extensive structural relief to preclude further manipulation of gas supplies in California, including a commitment to make available 3.29 billion cubic feet per day of capacity with California delivery points, construction of a pipeline expansion project, and a bar against any affiliated entity's obtaining additional firm capacity on its facilities for five years from the effective date of the settlement (June 2004).[26]

During 2002 and 2003, El Paso recorded pretax charges of $1 billion related to the settlement. In June 2004, when the settlement became effective, over $600 million was released to the settling parties, reflected as a current reduction of El Paso's cash flows from operations. By February 2004, El Paso's stock had suffered a 90% decline, and it was the defendant in 17 shareholder class action lawsuits, a shareholders derivative lawsuit, an Employee Retirement Income Security Act (ERISA) class action lawsuit, and natural gas commodities lawsuits (not all related to natural gas price manipulation).[27] In 2003, dissident shareholders launched a proxy contest that nearly succeeded in replacing El Paso's board of directors and forced the resignation of its chief executive officer (who nonetheless received severance compensation of $24 million).[28]

In a recent proceeding that raises core El Paso issues in a different context, the Alaska Gasline Port Authority commenced a federal antitrust suit against BP and Exxon Mobil Corp., alleging that BP's refusal to ship natural gas from Alaska and Exxon Mobil's failure to develop its gas fields in that state amount to warehousing, in an effort to drive up prices in the U.S. gas market, which the companies supply with 1.7 trillion cubic feet annually, equal to 9% of the domestic total.[29]

EnronOnline:
Trading Platform as Manipulation Tool

In November 1999, Enron launched an Internet-based trading platform, EnronOnline (EOL), that provided pricing information for hundreds of commodities, including electricity and natural gas. Enron's natural gas trading volume increased by 80% in the following year, when it captured almost 16% of the market, having a notional value of $2.8 billion per day. (See table 5–3.)

Enron claimed significant advantages for EOL, including "dynamic real-time pricing, informed price competition, transaction efficiency and timeliness."[31] Trading on EOL replaced transactions previously conducted by telephone and fax and reflected a fundamental shift to online platforms, which in 2001 accounted for almost 40% of all natural gas trading nationwide.[32]

Unlike other commodity trading exchanges (including NYMEX, the Chicago Mercantile Exchange, and the Chicago Board of Trade)—many-to-many exchanges matching buyers and sellers— EOL was a one-to-many platform that required buyers and sellers to deal directly with Enron as the only principal on the other side of each trade. During trading hours, EOL offered two-way bid and ask Internet quotes, executable by entities with an EOL trading account, and showed the total volume of product available for purchase or sale at indicated price levels (known as the *stack*). To buy or sell on EOL, a trader simply clicked on the offer or bid price. As an unregulated, bilateral trading platform, EOL established the bid and asked prices, enabled Enron to profit from the spread between the two, and posted, executed, settled, and cleared every trade.[33]

Table 5–3. Top 20 North American Gas Marketers Ranked by 2000 Sales Volume*[30]

2000 Rank	Company[1]	2000	1999	2000 Share (%)**	1999 Share (%)**
1	Enron (1)	23.8	13.3	15.9	10.4
2	Duke (2)	11.9	10.5	7.9	8.2
3	Aquila (3)	10.5	10.4	7.0	8.1
4	Coral (4)	10.2	9.8	6.8	7.7
5	Dynegy (5)	9.7	8.8	6.5	6.9
6	Sempra (11)	8.9	5.8	5.9	4.5
7	Reliant (7)	8.7	6.8	5.8	5.3
8	BP Amoco (12)	8.4	5.4	5.6	4.2
9	El Paso (8)	6.9	6.7	4.6	5.2
10	Mirant[2] (12)	6.9	5.4	4.6	4.2
11	Axia[3] (10)	6.5	6.5	4.3	5.1
12	TransCanada (9)	6.4	6.6	4.3	5.2
13	PG&E (6)	5.0	8.4	3.3	6.6
14	Williams (14)	4.3	4.2	2.9	3.3
15	Texaco (16)	3.9	3.4	2.6	2.7
16	AEP (21)	3.8	2.7	2.5	2.1
17	ExxonMobil (15)	3.7	3.6	2.5	2.8
18	Chevron (17)	3.4	3.2	2.3	2.5
	Conoco (17)	3.4	3.2	2.3	2.5
	TXU (19)	3.4	3.0	2.3	2.3
	Total	149.7	127.7		

*Volumes represent North American physical natural gas sales and exclude financial transactions. Sales volumes are provided by company officials.
**Share of 20 largest marketers.
[1] Number in ( ) indicates 1999 ranking.
[2] Formerly Southern Energy, Inc.
[3] Formerly Koch Energy Trading and Entergy Power Marketing Co.

Source: FERC Staff Report, August 16, 2001, p. 6

By posting bid and asked prices for a particular location at a given price, an Enron trader could effectively determine the index price at that location. In its Final Report on price manipulation in Western markets, FERC staff concluded,

> On EOL, Enron had access to trading histories, limit orders, and volumes of trades, and therefore understood the liquidity of the market. In contrast, an unaffiliated trader on EOL was only able to see the activity that was posted electronically on the EOL screen. More significantly, when bid and asked prices were changed, the trader was unable to know if it was due to a legitimate trade or if prices were being manipulated. . . . This lack of transparency prevented the trader from knowing with whom he was competing. Moreover, because the EOL platform was wholly controlled by Enron, there were no fixed rules. The EOL operator had an infinite ability to manipulate what was posted. . . . Simply put, the use of EOL enabled Enron to post any price it wanted.[34]

EOL soon became the dominant trading platform for natural gas transactions tied to prices indexed at Topock on the California border and the primary source of price discovery in California's gas markets during 2000 and 2001. Marketers in California used EOL to trade Topock natural gas, both for spot and next-day delivery and for derivatives based on trade press indexes.[35]

FERC staff's initial inquiry

In May 2001 FERC's general counsel initiated a staff-level inquiry into EOL and electronic energy trading (e-trading) that culminated in a report prepared in August 2001, just months before Enron's collapse. The report effectively gave EOL a pass, and the staff of the Senate Governmental Affairs Committee later found that "FERC's review was too cursory, settled for incomplete answers, [and] drew the wrong conclusions."[36]

The report nonetheless flagged certain concerns:

- EOL screens do not show prices or volumes of completed transactions, nor does EOL indicate when a deal has been made. EOL displays changes in bids and offers, but traders outside of Enron do not know whether those changes reflect a completed transaction or whether the changes have been initiated by Enron unilaterally. Enron alone has information about the actual volumes and prices transacted on its trading platform. EOL therefore operates as a proprietary extension of Enron's trading units, with an Enron trader acting as either buyer or seller in every transaction.

- In a one-to-many trading system such as EOL's, the risk of default is borne by the party making the market. Credit risk is not dispersed among all market participants as it is in a many-to-many exchange. If the one-to-many market maker does not carefully control exposure to risk, its financial stability may be compromised by overextending credit.

- Natural gas and power indexes reported to the press are typically anecdotal and lack transparency. There is no way to verify that reported prices and volumes represent actual trades. Certain reporting services (*NGI* and *Gas Daily*) publish gas price indexes based on e-trading, including weighted average prices supplied by Enron. Since EOL does not make transaction prices and volumes public, however, there is no way to determine whether an index based on EOL trading data reflects manipulation by Enron.

- EOL provides Enron with competitive advantages, including better market access, lower transaction costs, and better information. If Enron and EOL continue to grow at their current pace, competitive problems could develop.[37]

Despite these findings, the report did not accurately assess the potential for market abuse inherent in Enron's dominant position or forecast the implications of Enron's financial instability. Nor was the report distributed to FERC commissioners to inform their decision making before Enron's collapse. FERC also failed to establish a formal process for monitoring EOL's market impact and clarify jurisdictional boundaries between itself and CFTC for that purpose.[38]

Final report

While FERC staff were reaching essentially benign conclusions in its initial inquiry, traders using EOL and other electronic platforms were engaged in anticompetitive conduct—contributing to artificially high natural gas spot prices at the California border and, given the linkage between the natural gas and electricity markets, with impact on the electric power market as well.

Between December 2000 and May 2001, the price of natural gas at the California border increased over tenfold, reaching $55 per MMBTU. Inflated spot prices for natural gas also determined clearing prices paid by wholesale buyers of spot electric power. The cost of gas-fired electricity spiked accordingly.[39] During this period of extreme volatility, traders were buying and selling natural gas on EOL at spot prices unrelated to actual cost and without having to make physical delivery. Financial positions were settled for cash, not product. Financial transactions therefore created ostensible demand (financial plus physical) that far exceeded the available supply of gas at the Topock gate and exacerbated the effects of physical shortage.[40]

In February 2002, FERC staff launched a fact-finding investigation into manipulation of natural gas and electricity markets in California and other Western states. Staff found, among other things, that EOL was a key enabler of churn trading and that, with proprietary knowledge of market conditions, Enron had during 2000 and 2001 manipulated thinly traded physical gas markets while realizing almost $600 million in speculative, derivative-based profits.[41] Enron market makers were not simply passive suppliers of liquidity, profiting from the bid-asked spread, but were instead active speculators who used the information advantage gained from their central position in the physical markets in associated financial markets (e.g., futures, options, and swaps).[42] (See table 5–4.)

Enron traders thus manipulated the price of natural gas to profit from positions taken in the OTC financial derivatives markets in transactions that fell within FERC's jurisdiction and were authorized by a blanket certificate.

Table 5–4. Profits to Enron from EOL Market-Making: Trades for Physical Delivery of Gas at Henry Hub, Louisiana[43]

	Trading Profit	Gain on Inventory	Total Profit	Profit per Trade	Profit as Percent of Trading	Total Dollars Transacted	Number of Trades
All Trades	−3.8	−2.0	−5.8	−0.1	−0.09	6,606.1	52,828
By Contract Term							
Long-term	0	0	0	0	0	0	0
Medium-term	−1.8	0.4	−1.5	−0.4	−0.08	1,819.5	3,524
Short-term	−1.9	−2.4	−4.3	−0.1	−0.09	4,786.6	49,304
By Calendar Month							
January 2000	0.0	0.0	0.0	0.0	−0.20	0.3	14
February 2000	0.0	−0.1	−0.1	−0.2	−0.53	13.0	328
March 2000	0.0	0.0	0.0	0.0	0.04	36.9	570
April 2000	0.0	−0.1	−0.1	−0.1	−0.15	48.4	750
May 2000	−0.1	−0.2	−0.2	−0.2	−0.12	209.4	1,050
June 2000	−0.4	0.0	−0.4	−0.2	−0.09	432.1	1,864
July 2000	−0.1	−0.1	−0.2	−0.2	−0.12	209.8	1,237
August 2000	0.1	−0.1	0.0	0.0	−0.01	309.5	1,546
September 2000	0.0	−0.2	−0.2	−0.1	−0.08	242.2	1,225
October 2000	−0.1	−0.2	−0.4	−0.2	0.11	336.4	1,972
November 2000	−0.3	0.6	0.3	0.1	0.04	742.2	3,309
December 2000	−1.6	0.6	−1.0	−0.4	−0.20	474.3	2,327
January 2001	0.0	−0.6	−0.5	−0.2	−0.14	374.0	2,328
February 2001	0.3	−0.2	0.2	0.1	0.04	393.4	2,579
March 2001	−0.3	0.0	−0.3	−0.1	−0.07	414.5	3,386
April 2001	−0.2	−0.3	−0.5	−0.1	−0.13	394.6	3,477
May 2001	−0.2	−0.2	−0.4	−0.1	−0.10	396.7	3,540
June 2001	−0.5	−0.4	−0.9	−0.2	−0.17	568.7	4,579
July 2001	−0.1	0.0	−0.1	0.0	−0.04	290.6	3,855
August 2001	−0.5	−0.2	−0.7	−0.2	−0.26	267.8	3,625
September 2001	0.0	0.1	0.2	0.1	0.13	132.0	2,603
October 2001	0.2	−0.1	0.1	0.0	0.04	245.3	4,698
November 2001	−0.1	−0.3	−0.4	−0.2	−0.57	75.2	1,966
December 2001	0	0	0	0	0	0	0

Trading profit reflects the excess of the average Enron sell price over the average Enron buy price times the quantity of matched EOL trading. Gain on inventory reflects profits on the net EOL order imbalance, measured by the differential between the final EOL price for the contract and the average inventory acquisition price. Total profit is the sum of trading profit and gain on inventory. Total dollars transacted is the sum of total purchases and total sales on EOL. Profit as a percent of trading is total profit relative to total dollars transacted. Dollar amounts are in millions except for profit per trade, which is in thousands. Short-term contracts involve delivery periods of three days or less. Medium-term contracts involve delivery periods of four to 31 days. Long-term contracts involve delivery periods over 31 days.

Source: FERC Report, Manipulation in Western Markets, Docket No. PA02-2-000, 203, p. 14

FERC staff also focused on anomalous trading patterns at Topock and identified *churning* as the principal driver—that is, the repeated buying and selling of substantial physical quantities of spot gas on EOL in a short period of time that increased prices, price volatility, and price uncertainty in the entire Southern California gas market.[44] Reliant, a principal Enron counterparty and trader of physical spot market gas at the California-Arizona border, typically bought and sold large quantities of gas within a 90-minute trading day, finishing with a net position much smaller than gross volume.

On January 31, 2001, for example, Reliant bought 1,010,000 MMBTU and sold 730,000 MMBTU for a net purchase of 280,000 MMBTU. To achieve this result, Reliant entered into serial transactions at the rate of one every 10 seconds over the course of 30 minutes, producing sharp price movements on EOL that all traders could see without knowing the cause. By contrast, bilateral gas trades not transacted on EOL would not have affected the prices at which Enron offered to buy or sell and would not have been perceived as new market prices.[45] Reliant and Enron also entered into a netting arrangement under which all of Reliant's purchases from Enron, taken together, formed a volume-weighted average price. The parties netted sales and purchases and settled the balance at the average price. When Reliant was a net buyer, it had a financial incentive to churn.[46]

Since virtually every gas trader had an EOL screen, EOL became a primary source of price discovery. Enron always posted a two-way price, that is, a price at which it was willing to buy and a price at which it was willing to sell. As Reliant's churn trading changed bid-asked prices posted on EOL, the entire market saw the rapid, pronounced price movements, but only Enron and Reliant knew why prices were moving. Enron could also compare Reliant's activity with every other trader's transactions for its own speculative purposes. In effect, EOL provided Enron with a continuous option to access liquidity through orders provided by its clients.[47]

In the Final Report, FERC staff concluded that

- There was a clear, robust, and statistically significant relationship between Reliant's churning and rising gas prices;

- Gas prices in Southern California were, on average, almost $9 per MMBTU higher than they would have been without Reliant's EOL trading activity;

- As an active trader of financial gas derivative products in Southern California, Reliant made significant profits from financial trades based on its churning activities ($18 million in December 2000 alone);

- Since EOL served as the primary source for price discovery, its prices were incorporated in gas indexes published in *Gas Daily* and other trade press outlets, with the result that Reliant's churning moved the entire market.[48]

Notwithstanding these conclusions, Reliant's rapid-fire trades were, remarkably, not found to violate FERC's market-based regulations, since prior to the Energy Policy Act of 2005, those regulations "contain[ed] no explicit guidelines or prohibitions for trading gas."[49]

Manipulation of Published Natural Gas Price Indexes

Price indexes, compiled and published by the energy trade press, track forward and spot prices in gas and electric markets. Indexes commonly determine price terms in energy contracts and are also used to hedge transportation costs, settle imbalances and determine penalties under pipeline tariffs, and provide benchmarks to regulators reviewing the prudence of gas and electricity purchases. Index publishers rely on price information voluntarily provided by market participants and derived from trades occurring at specified locations. Given their widespread impact on energy transactions, indexes must be accurate, transparent, and reliable if markets are to function efficiently.[50]

Accordingly, the Final Report by FERC staff focused attention on energy price indexes, which were thought to be susceptible to manipulation by market participants.[51] However, the Final Report addressed more than price manipulation by a single gas pipeline. It raised, with justification, the sobering thought that natural gas and electricity contracts worth billions had been priced in reliance on indexes reflecting deliberately overstated or false information.[52] After issuing an initial report in August 2002, FERC staff saw its broad apprehensions come vividly to life as five companies (Dynegy, American Electric Power [AEP], Williams, CMS, and El Paso), in quick succession, admitted to having manipulated energy price indexes. Ultimately, many other companies were also involved.

The Final Report catalogued an array of manipulative practices, including reporting data according to a company's book bias (i.e., reporting high prices if the company had a long position and low prices if it had a short position), reporting inflated volumes, coordinating with another company's trader to report offsetting trades, attempting to lower or raise the price at a trading point by reporting only certain trades, reporting trades seen on EOL or other trading platforms, and reporting nonexistent trades.[53]

Dynegy

In September 2002, Dynegy announced that for several years its trading desks had systematically reported false data to the trade press, including both monthly (*Inside FERC* and *NGI*) and daily (*Gas Daily*) index compilers, by fabricating trades to reach a predetermined average and inflating volumes. In the absence of fixed-price trades at certain locations, Dynegy traders had also submitted bogus data, on trades that never occurred. In December 2002, the CFTC announced a $5 million settlement with Dynegy and West Coast Power, based on its finding that Dynegy had "knowingly submitted false information to the reporting firms in an attempt to skew those indexes to [its marketing affiliate's] financial benefit."[54]

AEP

In September 2003, the CFTC filed a complaint against that American Electric Power Company and its subsidiary, AEP Energy Services, Inc., in federal district court. The CFTC alleged that AEP had engaged in a "pervasive and widespread scheme," in violation of the Commodity Exchange Act (CEA), to deliver false and misleading information about gas trades to index compilers such as *Platts* and within two years had realized a $63.5 million trading profit on 3,600 purported natural gas trades, almost 80% of which were knowingly inaccurate. The CFTC's complaint followed AEP's admission, in October 2002, that its employees had engaged in inaccurate reporting to index compilers.[55] Eventually AEP paid $30 million to settle the CFTC suit: $30 million to the Department of Justice to avoid prosecution and end an ongoing investigation and $21 million to FERC as a fine for according affiliates preferential treatment in gas storage.[56]

Williams

In July 2003, the CFTC issued an order settling charges of manipulation and false reporting against the Williams Companies, Inc. and their subsidiary, Williams Energy Marketing and Trading (collectively referred to as Williams), which paid a civil penalty of $20 million for having violated the CEA. Based on an investigation by the Corporate Fraud Task Force, the order found that the respondents had "knowingly submitted false information to [publishers of natural gas indexes] in an attempt to skew those indexes for [their] financial benefit."[57] The order followed Williams' public acknowledgement in October 2002 that its natural gas trading business had provided "inaccurate information to an energy industry publication that compiles and reports index prices."[58]

The dry terminology of official pronouncements does not convey the dynamics or essential details of Williams' manipulative activities. These are set forth, however, in a plea agreement, between a Williams' basis trader and the United States that was filed in federal district court.[59]

The Williams natural gas group dealt with both physical and financial trades. Physical trades included next-day gas (to flow the next day), baseload gas (to flow throughout the next month), and term gas (to flow for any designated length of time beyond 30 days). In financial trades, transacted on NYMEX or off exchange (directly between companies), neither party intended to take delivery. Financial trades enabled Williams to speculate and hedge against price risk in the physical markets.

Regardless of the nature of the transaction, contract prices were often tied to index prices published by *Inside FERC* and *NGI's Bidweek Survey*, among others, on the first day of each business month, reflecting transactions at locations throughout the United States where natural gas is purchased and sold. Monthly index prices were determined by data collected from natural gas traders during the last week of the month, known as bid week. The index price at any given location represented a volume-weighted average price for baseload gas bought and sold at that location at a fixed price during the most recent bid week.

Williams basis traders bought and sold natural gas products to arbitrage the difference between the price of a physical natural gas contract at a given location and the price of a standard contract traded on NYMEX. Basis traders were also responsible for reporting prices to index publishers. For the four years ending on June 30, 2002, Williams traders conspired to report "fictitious trades to *Inside FERC* and *NGI* for the purpose of manipulating the published index prices to increase the value or profitability of Williams' natural gas positions."[60] To the extent that false trades were included in the index calculations, the published index prices did not reflect the legitimate forces of supply and demand.

As described by the Williams basis trader in the plea agreement,

> To achieve the goals of the conspiracy, most of the trades I reported were deliberately fabricated. At the end of each week, the physical traders would orally inform me of their actual fixed price, baseload trades and I would list these trades in an Excel spreadsheet. Then I would add fictitious trades to the spreadsheet to achieve the desired weighted average price at each location for which I reported to the index publications. My supervisor taught me how to arrange the collection of false trades on this spreadsheet to look like a random sampling that would appear credible to the index publications. . . . For the false trades I included in the spreadsheet, the reported prices and volumes did not represent any actual trades executed by Williams during the relevant bid week.[61]

El Paso

In November 2002, El Paso Merchant Energy (El Paso) announced that it had found evidence of "misreported trade data" and "systematic price manipulation" by its Northeast, Mid-Continent, and Gulf trading desks for the period between July 2000 and December 2001. The data involved almost 650 million MMBTU of fixed-price physical gas and showed that El Paso had misreported 99% of the prices on trades worth over $2 billion.[62] In March 2003, El Paso paid a civil fine of $20 million to settle CFTC charges of attempted manipulation and false reporting. The CFTC settlement order found that El Paso had "knowingly submitted false information" to skew price indexes for its financial benefit.[63]

Other companies

In 2003–2004, the CFTC settled cases alleging false reporting and attempted manipulation against CMS Marketing Services and Trading Company ($16 million civil penalty); Reliant Energy Services, Inc. ($18 million civil penalty); Aquila Merchant Services, Inc. ($26.5 million civil penalty); e prime, Inc. ($16 million civil penalty); Western Gas Resources, Inc. ($7 million civil penalty); Coral

Energy Resources, Inc. ($30 million civil penalty); Entergy-Koch Trading, LP ($3 million civil penalty); ONEOK Energy Marketing and Trading Company, LP ($3 million civil penalty); and Calpine Energy Services, LP ($1.5 million civil penalty).[64]

Epilogue

In June 2003, FERC implemented the Final Report's recommendations on price manipulation in California and Western markets by requiring sellers of natural gas or electricity at market-based rates to abide by a code of conduct. FERC issued final market behavior rules in November. The rules require blanket certificates to contain prophylactic provisions addressing market manipulation, reporting, and record retention. Under the rules, FERC can require disgorgement of profits and revocation of a seller's license.[65] The Energy Policy Act of 2005 enhances civil and criminal penalties for statutory violations and FERC's enforcement powers.

Observations

Markets for gas and electricity are intertwined. Manipulation of gas prices, whether through withholding or trading abuses, therefore has an impact on two basic commodities. Given huge derivative markets, manipulation of the physical product can be further leveraged financially, often beyond purview of regulators. Where a single company has significant concurrent interests in both gas and electricity, the opportunity for market manipulation expands exponentially.

Notes

[1] Lewis. *FERC Regulation of Interstate Gas Transportation: The Natural Gas Act, Open Access, and Unbundling.* Law Seminars International (March 17, 2005) (hereafter *Lewis*), p. 2.

[2] Order 436, issued in 1985, established a voluntary framework under which interstate pipelines could offer nondiscriminatory, open-access transportation to customers at competitive rates on a first-come, first-serve basis, enabling pipelines to act solely as transporters of gas rather than as both transporters and sellers. In 1992, Order 636 made pipeline unbundling mandatory, requiring that the marketing and transportation functions of interstate pipeline companies be housed separately within arm's-length affiliates. Thereafter, the marketing affiliate had to compete on equal price, volume, and timing terms with third parties. Interstate pipelines were required to establish electronic bulletin boards to post available and released capacity, accessible to all customers on an equal basis.

[3] *Energy Markets: Concerted Actions Needed by FERC to Confront Challenges That Impede Effective Oversight.* United States Government Accounting Office, GAO-02-656 (June 2002) (hereafter *GAO-02-656*), p. 20.

[4] Ibid., pp. 20–21.

[5] Ibid., p. 21.

[6] Ibid., p. 21.

[7] The Commodity Exchange Act excludes certain types of derivatives entirely from the CFTC's jurisdiction, such as off-exchange swaps between certain qualifying parties (called eligible contract participants) that are based on broad economic measures like interest rates or stock indexes beyond the control of the parties. The Commodity Exchange Act also exempts other derivatives from much, if not all, of the CFTC's jurisdiction, such as electronically executed multilateral transactions in energy or metals commodities among qualifying commercial enterprises, over which the CFTC retains antifraud and antimanipulation authority. See *Natural Gas: Analysis of Changes in Market Price.* United States Government Accounting Office, GAO-03-46 (December 2002) (hereafter *GAO-03-46*), pp. 3–4, 31. A futures contract is an agreement to buy or sell a commodity for delivery in the

future at a price, or according to a pricing formula, that is determined at the inception of the contract. An obligation under a futures contract may be fulfilled without actual delivery of the commodity by an offsetting transaction or cash settlement. An option gives the buyer the right, but not the obligation, to buy or sell a commodity at a specific price on or before a specific date. Ibid., p. 4, n. 1.

[8] *GAO-03-46*, pp. 31–32.

[9] Standards of Conduct, 18 *Code of Federal Regulations* § 161.3. See Weaver. "Can Energy Markets Be Trusted? The Effect of the Rise and Fall of Enron on Energy Markets." *Houston Business and Tax Law Journal*, 1 (4): 17 (2004) (hereafter *Weaver*), p. 52.

[10] *GAO-03-46*, p. 30.

[11] Bernstein. *The Rise and Fall of Enron's One-to-Many Trading Platform.* White paper (2004) (hereafter *Bernstein*), p. 2.

[12] *Final Report on Price Manipulation in Western Markets*, FERC Docket No. PA02-2-000 (March 2003) (hereafter *Final Report*), p. ES-3.

[13] *Bernstein*, pp. 2–3.

[14] *GAO-03-46*, p. 2.

[15] El Paso Corporation, SEC Form 10-K/A for 2004 (March 23, 2005), p. 1.

[16] Ibid., p. 1

[17] Ibid., pp. 4–5.

[18] *Final Report*, p. I-4, n. 7

[19] Kahn and Gerth. "Energy Industry Raises Production at Record Pace." *New York Times*, May 13, 2001.

[20] Weare. *The California Electricity Crisis: Causes and Policy Options.* Public Policy Institute of California (2003), p. 29.

[21] Initial Decision, *Public Utilities Commission of the State of California v. El Paso Natural Gas Company et al.*, 97 FERC ¶ 63,004 (October 9, 2001) (hereafter *Initial Decision*).

[22] 18 *Code of Federal Regulations* § 284.7(a) and 284.9(a)(1) (2001); Order 637A, FERC Stats. & Regs., Regulation Preambles July 1996–December 2000, ¶ 31,099, at 31,564 (2000).

[23] *Initial Decision,* passim, 100 FERC ¶ 63,041 (2002). See 18 *Code of Federal Regulations,* pt. 161 (2001).

[24] *Initial Decision* (phase II) (September 23, 2002).

[25] *People v. El Paso Natural Gas Co.,* No. 03-4565 (C. D. Cal. filed June 26, 2003).

[26] *Attorney General's Energy White Paper.* State of California (April 2004), p. 61; *El Paso Form 10-Q* (third quarter 2004), pp. 23–24.

[27] *El Paso Form 10-Q* (third quarter 2004), pp. 23–24. Plaintiffs have alleged misuse of off-balance-sheet financing, excessive borrowing, egregious executive compensation, use of mark-to-market accounting to inflate reported earnings, manipulation of natural gas price indexes, and false reporting of natural gas reserves.

[28] *El Paso Proxy Fight Looming,* SRI Media (June 3, 2003).

[29] *The Wall Street Journal,* December 20, 2005, p. A3.

[30] *FERC Staff Report* (August 16, 2001) (hereafter *FERC Staff Report*), p. 6.

[31] Comments of Enron Corporation regarding B2B electronic marketplaces submitted to the Federal Trade Commission. Quoted in *Bernstein,* p. 2.

[32] Berick. Testimony before the Committee on Governmental Affairs, U.S. Senate . In *Asleep at the Switch: FERC's Oversight of Enron Corporation* (November 12, 2002) (hereafter *Berick*).

[33] *Final Report,* p. IX-25. The Commodity Exchange Act, as amended in 2000 by the Commodity Futures Modernization Act, exempted electronic trading facilities, energy swaps, OTC derivatives, and energy spot market transactions from regulation. *Bernstein,* p. 9, n. 19.

[34] *Final Report,* p. VII-14.

[35] *Bernstein,* pp. 1–3, 6; *Final Report,* p. III-34.

[36] *Berick,* p. 5.

[37] *FERC Staff Report,* pp. 14–16.

[38] Letter dated May 14, 2002, from Senator Joseph I. Lieberman to the chairman of FERC.

[39] *Final Report*, p. ES-4; *Bernstein*, pp. 5–7. Each 10-cent increase in the price of natural gas resulted in a $34 million increase in the cost of electricity to Southern California's customers alone.

[40] *Bernstein*, p. 7.

[41] *Final Report*, p. ES-2.

[42] Ibid., p. VII-14.

[43] Ibid., p. VIII-14

[44] Ibid., pp. II-2–5.

[45] Ibid., pp. II-4–5.

[46] Ibid., p. II-7.

[47] Ibid., p. IX-30.

[48] Ibid., pp. II-8–9, II-59.

[49] Ibid., pp. II-60–61. Section 284.402 of FERC's regulations authorizes any person who is not an interstate pipeline to sell gas for resale in interstate commerce at negotiated rates. 18 *Code of Federal Regulations* § 284.402 (2002).

[50] *Policy Statement on Natural Gas and Electric Price Indices*, 104 FERC ¶ 61,121 (July 24, 2003), p. 2.

[51] *Final Report*, p. III-1.

[52] *Weaver*, pp. 57–58.

[53] For a summary, see Moody. *Natural Gas Price Issues: An Update.* APPA (November 2004), p. 16.

[54] *Final Report*, p. III-7.

[55] *U.S. Commodity Futures Trading Commission v. American Electric Power, Inc. et al.*, Civil Action No. 02 03 091, filed September 30, 2003, in United States District Court for the Southern District of Ohio.

[56] Ayres. "AEP to Pay $81 Million Penalties for Natural Gas Violations." *Financial Crime News*, February 22, 2005.

[57] *CFTC Release No. 4824-03* (July 29, 2003).

[58] *Final Report*, p. III-9.

[59] *Plea Agreement* (No. CR 04-0404 SI) filed in United States District Court for the Northern District of California (San Francisco Division) by Thomas J. Pool.

[60] Ibid., p. 4.

[61] Ibid., p. 4.

[62] *Final Report*, p. III-13.

[63] *CFTC Release No. 4765-03* (March 26, 2003).

[64] *CFTC Annual Report* (2004), pp. 22–23.

[65] See FERC Docket No. RM03-10-000.

6 Implosion of the California Electricity Market—Part I

California's energy crisis of 2000–2001 was an epic economic and operational disaster. Amid rolling power blackouts, wholesale energy costs increased almost 400% in a single year (rising from $7.4 billion to $27.1 billion) and remained elevated for the following year until the crisis abated. California's largest utility, Pacific Gas and Electric (PG&E), went bankrupt. The state floated an $11.9 billion bond issue to finance long-term, high-cost forward power purchase contracts signed with energy suppliers as a last resort under economic duress. Taking advantage of the state's dysfunctional power market, merchant generators and traders captured unprecedented windfall profits, overcharging California consumers $9 billion and driving prices far above competitive levels in the process.[1] Manipulation of the California market continued until FERC mandated a regionwide must-offer requirement and price cap in June 2001.[2] Failure of the California energy market precipitated long-term regulatory, economic, and political fallout, not least the abatement or reversal of initiatives to restructure electricity markets nationwide.

Background

California's electric power system is part of a single synchronized network encompassing 1.8 million square miles in 14 Western states, two Canadian provinces, and a portion of Baja California Norte, in Mexico. The network is supervised by the Western Electricity Coordinating Council (WECC), one of 10 regional councils comprising the North American Electric Reliability Council (NERC). Transactions in any part of the WECC system affect flows elsewhere in the system.

Before its restructuring, the California electricity market was served by vertically integrated investor-owned utilities (or publicly owned counterparts) that generated or contracted to acquire power for sale, owned and operated the transmission system, and distributed electricity to captive end-use customers. The California Public Utility Commission (CPUC) determined how much utilities could charge retail customers for service and what investments in generation, transmission, and distribution facilities were recoverable through regulated rates. As the interstate transmission system expanded, utilities also traded surplus energy, priced between the seller's and buyer's respective marginal generation costs, to take advantage of differing system peak periods.[3]

After passage of the Northwest Power Act of 1980, the Bonneville Power Administration began to sell excess power to other utilities and marketers at cost. To take advantage of this new source of low-cost power, utilities established a multistate bulk-marketing consortium, the Western Systems Power Pool (WSSP), which became a platform for negotiated short-term transactions and eventually for transactions with standardized terms for sales and swaps of energy and capacity.[4] WSSP contracts encouraged development of a competitive forward market in the West among electric utilities and government entities as a means of leveling seasonal differences in load demand and supplementing baseload capacity. Contracts covered month-ahead, day-ahead, hour-ahead, and real-time energy supplies. At first, WSSP operated through bulletin board price postings, fax notifications, term contracts, and telephone inquiries, but larger utilities and marketers soon developed trading floors and more sophisticated information systems.

In the early 1990s, despite the evolving bulk-power market, California consumers experienced commodity prices 25–50% higher than the national average, driven by the sunk costs of local nuclear power projects and expensive long-term contracts that qualifying facilities had imposed on utilities under federal law. To drive prices lower, commercial and industrial consumers needed to acquire cheap power from third-party generators using incumbent utilities' transmission and distribution systems. At the same time, incumbent utilities needed to ensure recovery of sunk generating costs that would otherwise be stranded if large-scale users could freely import competitively priced power over the utilities' wires.

After years of contentious debate and negotiation, the CPUC adopted a restructuring plan, codified in Assembly Bill 1890 (AB 1890), enacted by the California legislature in September 1996. AB 1890 presented several then-novel features patterned after European electricity-restructuring regimes:

- Through energy service providers, retail customers could buy power in the wholesale market from third-party suppliers, bypassing incumbent utilities (PG&E, Southern California Edison [SCE], and San Diego Gas & Electric [SDG&E]), which would then deliver purchased power to customers over their transmission and distribution facilities through energy service providers. Any customer who did not choose an energy service provider would by default continue to receive generation service from their utility provider.

- An ISO, organized with FERC approval, would control real-time dispatch and balancing of electrical flows on incumbent utilities' combined transmission network and ensure all market participants equal access to the network.

- A nonprofit power exchange (PX) would be organized, again with FERC approval, to operate forward markets (initially day-ahead and hour-ahead) open to all participants. Incumbent utilities would be required to effect all purchase and sale transactions through the PX (the buy-sell requirement).

- Incumbent utilities would be strongly encouraged to sell off their in-state fossil-fuel power plants and would have up to four years within which to recover their stranded costs (i.e., sunk costs not likely to be recoverable with the advent of competitive wholesale market prices) through a competitive transition charge.

- Residential and small commercial customers would enjoy a 10% rate reduction, but all retail rates would be frozen at levels high enough to permit utilities' recovery of stranded costs by taking advantage of the difference between the expected lower market price of power and the mandated retail rate. The rate freeze would end in March 2002 or when the incumbent utilities had recovered their stranded costs, whichever came first. Once they had recovered their stranded costs, the market would set retail prices, presumably below the rate-freeze level.[5]

- The California Electricity Oversight Board (Oversight Board), a newly created panel with members appointed by the Governor and the legislature, would provide additional oversight at the state level.

In April 1996, the incumbent utilities filed at FERC for approval of the restructuring plan, including the proposed transfer to the ISO of control over their transmission facilities and authorization to sell power at market-based rates through the PX. In a series of orders, FERC largely accepted the filings but rejected, for jurisdictional reasons, a permanent role for the Oversight Board in overseeing the ISO's governance or operations.[6]

AB 1890 protected customers from market risks through a rate freeze but required incumbent utilities to divest in-house generating capacity and purchase power on the spot market. In so doing, AB 1890 laid the groundwork for the ensuing energy crisis.[7]

The Calm Before the Storm

As planned, the incumbent utilities sold their fossil fuel plants (retaining nuclear, hydroelectric, and other generating assets) to several wholesale merchant energy companies, including Duke, Mirant, Dynegy/NRG, AES/Williams, and Reliant, and relinquished control of their high-voltage transmission lines to the ISO. Each company acquired approximately 20% of the utilities' aggregate thermal capacity but had no obligation to sell back power under long-term fixed price contracts. After divestiture, the utilities produced less than 50% of their customers' power needs and purchased the additional power required through the PX. The ISO and the PX started operations in 1998 as nonprofit entities overseen by stakeholder boards that included representatives of generators and their trade associations.

The ISO managed day-to-day operations of the electricity grid, purchasing limited amounts of power and capacity to balance system fluctuations as they arose. To do this, the ISO ran a real-time balancing market—that is, a spot market for immediate delivery of electricity—that enabled market participants to match, on a last-hour basis, their forward purchases with customers' actual electricity loads. Market participants implemented forward trades in the real-time market through scheduling coordinators, who submitted balanced schedules to the ISO for each hour one day before delivery (adjusted in real time to accommodate errors in load forecasting, plant outages, and uninstructed deviations). Each schedule identified specific generating units as sources of supply and distribution points required in order to meet customer demands.[8] If the schedules initially submitted were not deemed feasible (i.e., could not work without causing blackouts, congestion, or other reliability risks), the ISO requested modifications and then relieved congestion so as to be at least cost consistent with balanced schedules.

Keeping the system in equilibrium during each hour thus required that the ISO purchase capacity (ancillary services) in forward markets and operate a real-time energy market.[9] The ISO purchased capacity or energy only to maintain system balance, not for its own account. It passed all charges or credits (for imbalance energy) or uplift charges (for capacity) through the scheduling coordinators, who provided bids specifying the amounts they would accept or pay to increase or decrease production from scheduled generating units. The ISO then used those bids to construct a supply curve with which to control the real-time flow of system power and minimize congestion in the day-ahead and hour-ahead markets.[10]

The PX ran day-ahead and hour-ahead electricity auctions open to all participants. The day-ahead auction matched cumulative demand bids and supply offers to create a single balanced portfolio and day-ahead market clearing price for each hour of the next trading day. Each hour therefore constituted a new market. Market participants submitted proposed supplies of and demands for electricity expressed as supply and demand curves, which the PX aggregated to determine the market-clearing price. All supply offers below and load bids above the market-clearing price were then accepted or charged at that price, and each participant whose offer or bid was accepted or charged provided a detailed schedule. As coordinator for all trades, the PX submitted balanced schedules for each hour of the next day to the ISO.[11] (See fig. 6–1.)

Energy Markets

PX Forward Market	PX Day-ahead Market	PX Day-of Market	ISO Real-time Market

ISO Ancillary Services Markets

Regulation Up/Down	Spinning Reserve	Non-Spinning Reserve	Replacement Reserve

Figure 6–1. California's deregulated markets (1998–2001)[12]

For four years after restructuring, the incumbent utilities had to buy and sell electricity through the PX's day-ahead market. Although the PX was not intended as the only source for forward electricity purchases, the utilities' divestiture of long-term generating capacity forced dependence on the day-ahead market. At the same time, the buy-sell requirement meant that utilities could not use a mix of long- and short-term forward contracts to minimize price risks. In 1999, SCE asked the CPUC for authority to serve one-third of its minimum load though PX block-forward contracts. The CPUC agreed but provided no guarantees that the related costs would be recoverable.[13]

It soon became clear that merchant generators, using the utilities' divested generation assets, could largely control the price of power in the day-ahead market outside the purview of state regulation. Unburdened by forward contract obligations, generators had no incentive to bid competitively and could instead set prices far in excess of marginal cost by withholding output and jamming overloaded transmission lines at critical locations. Since the PX operated under FERC jurisdiction, moreover, restructuring implied, among other things, a massive state-to-federal shift in regulatory authority.[14]

As a condition of divestiture, FERC determined whether each merchant generator would be able to exercise market power (improper control over price or supply) by using a formula that established 20% of the California electricity supply market as the maximum permissible market share.[15] But FERC did not consider a generator's ability to increase prices during peak load periods when increased demand, coupled with transmission constraints, would predictably allow it to exercise market power, nor did FERC require generators to offer long-term power sales contracts to the divesting utilities as a hedge against price risks.

Instead, on the basis of the 20% market share formula, FERC routinely certified that the seller and its affiliates do not have, or have adequately mitigated market power in generation and transmission and cannot erect barriers to entry. With that sweeping certification in hand, merchant generators could thereafter charge virtually any price the market would bear, free of retroactive challenge.[16] Having received official authorization to charge market-based rates, they could also contend that FERC had created a filed rate beyond collateral attack in an antitrust or unfair competition enforcement action.[17]

In granting certification, FERC assumed that the market would discipline prices more efficiently than cost of service regulation, clear at or close to short-run marginal cost, and allow no seller sufficient market power to set prices. FERC based its assumptions on a theoretical auction market model that ignored predictable real-world concerns such as congestion, parallel bidding, withholding, and gaming. The justification FERC offered for market-based authority thus rested on a flimsy analysis, shaped in part by its desire to facilitate CPUC's divestiture requirement.[18] At bottom, FERC lacked a clear definition of market power, did not identify the facts necessary to measure its presence and extent, failed to collect and analyze supporting data, and did not have well-developed mitigation measures in place to address market power abuses if they occurred.[19]

Recognizing market power abuse as a potential problem, however, the PX and the ISO each adopted a market monitoring and information protocol (MMIP), incorporated in tariffs filed with FERC. Although the MMIP does not expressly prohibit specific behavior, it identified *gaming* and *anomalous market behavior* as prohibited practices subject to scrutiny and, potentially, disgorgement of unjust profits. Gaming means taking unfair advantage of market rules, transmission constraints, and generation availability, such as loop flow, facility outages, and seasonal limits on energy imports. Anomalous market behavior is behavior not commonly found in competitive markets, such as physical withholding of generation capacity and pricing inconsistent with prevailing supply and demand conditions. While the ISO could seek to correct such misconduct through sanctions and penalties, FERC was the "court of last resort."[20]

The stage was thus set for the California energy crisis. As will be seen, FERC initially failed to enforce its statutory just and reasonable rate standard. The CPUC, for its part, refused to increase retail electricity rates sufficiently to allow utilities to pass through wholesale power costs. It also prevented them from entering into long-term contracts, thus compelling reliance on volatile spot markets for energy supplies. Merchant generators, smelling blood in the water, manipulated the state's energy markets to extract enormous profits at the expense of system reliability, incumbent utilities, and consumers.

Crisis Onset

California's restructured electricity markets opened in March 1998 and functioned reasonably well for the first two years, although FERC had to impose price caps on several occasions.[21] Energy prices in 1998–99 averaged around $30 per megawatt-hour (MWh). Relatively low wholesale prices allowed incumbent utilities to recover a portion of their stranded costs and retire $17 billion in debt.[22]

Market dynamics changed radically in 2000. In June of that year, average PX prices for wholesale power reached the previously unthinkable level of $166 per MWh and stayed at, near, or above that level for a year. Electricity costs for 2000 totaled approximately $27 billion, compared to $7 billion in 1999. The CPUC estimated that, during the June–September period alone, generators received $4 billion in excess of competitive baseline price revenues. Higher prices were accompanied by declining reliability. In 2000, the ISO declared more than 50 system emergencies, compared to one-fifth that number in 1998–99.[23] From May 2000 until June 2001, the California electricity market experienced emergency alerts, rolling blackouts, and huge price spikes. (See table 6–1.)

Market observers and regulators at first attributed the price surge to a convergence of factors: increased demand driven by hot weather, insufficient rainfall for hydropower supply from the Northwest, frozen retail rates, the buy-sell requirement, a spike in natural gas prices, and a shortfall in installed California generating capacity.[25] Soon, however, it became clear that merchant suppliers' market power, including both physical and economic withholding, enabled them to drive electricity prices far above competitive levels. Desperate to avoid blackouts and system outages, the ISO had no choice but to procure power in the short-term market at almost any price. In 2001, for example, it accepted a real-time energy bid from Duke Energy at $3,380 per MWh. This bid generated revenues of $11 million for a single trade and was later described as an "abuse of market power."[26]

Table 6–1. Annual Costs for Energy and Ancillary Services for CAISO Control Area, 1998–2001[24]

	1998	1999	2000	2001
ISO Load (GWh)	169,239	227,533	237,543	227,024
System Costs (Million $)				
PX Energy	$ 4,148	$ 5,866	$ 18,842	N/A
Bilateral Energy	$ 556	$ 982	$ 4,046	$ 21,194
Real Time Energy	$ 209	$ 180	$ 2,877	$ 4,162
Ancillary Services	$ 638	$ 404	$ 1,720	$ 1,346
Total	$ 5,551	$ 7,432	$ 27,485	$ 26,702
Average Costs ($/MWh of Load)	$ 33	$ 33	$ 116	118

Note: 1998 data are for the last three quarters of the year. Bilateral energy costs for 2001 (labeled "Forward Energy" in the source document) include costs of DWR purchases.

Source: CAISO-DMA (2001a) and CAISO-DMA (2002a)

Profits soared for merchant generators that had acquired fossil assets from incumbent utilities and now owned 40% of California's electric power capacity. For the third quarter of 2000 alone, the following increases in net income were reported:

- Dynegy—up 83%
- Reliant—up 37% overall; wholesale energy division up 642%
- Duke—up 74%
- AES—up 131%
- NRG—up 221%
- Southern Energy—up 59%[27]

Although it had no plants in California, Enron reported a 34% increase in fourth-quarter 2000 profits from the California wholesale power market, where its traders, accounting for one-quarter of all trades, manipulated market rules and used false information.[28] Through cookie jar reserves, Enron kept $1.5 billion in crisis-related trading profits off its books to avoid political exposure. It also mounted a highly successful public relations campaign to characterize the crisis as a self-inflicted supply-and-demand imbalance, urged an end to the retail price freeze, and fought imposition of wholesale price caps. High unregulated prices, Enron contended, would signal scarcity and induce new entrants to build plants or transmission lines, thereby easing the supply shortage.[29]

As day-ahead energy prices rose stratospherically and the rate freeze continued, SCE and PG&E incurred massive wholesale power costs they could not recover from retail customers. In late 2000, they sought emergency relief. The CPUC granted a 40% increase in retail rates, finding that "SCE's and PG&E's continued financial viability and ability to serve their customers has been seriously compromised by the dramatic escalation in wholesale prices."[30] The utilities also asked for authorization to enter into long-term bilateral power contracts outside the PX markets. The CPUC consented but would not set reasonableness standards for forward purchases or approve specific long-term contracts submitted for review, leaving recovery of contract-related costs open to later attack.

Without effective relief from the CPUC, PG&E and SCE lacked the revenues needed to repay the billions in debt they had incurred to purchase power in the spot market.[31] In December 2000, the Secretary of Energy, acting under Section 202(c) of the Federal Power Act, ordered certain suppliers to provide electricity to California utilities on the ISO's certification of inadequate supply. Although well-intentioned, the Secretary's intervention did nothing to relieve the utilities' price or pass-through concerns. In January 2001, major rating services downgraded their bonded indebtedness to near-junk status.[32]

The utilities' financial distress raised the specter of massive blackouts and devolved on the California Department of Water Resources (CDWR) an unprecedented power procurement responsibility. In January 2001, Governor Davis authorized CDWR to buy power for PG&E and SCE with $400 million appropriated from the state's General Fund.[33] Shortly thereafter, the legislature passed Assembly Bill 1X granting CDWR expanded authority to purchase energy on behalf of the state's retail customers. It also amended AB 1890 to place the utilities' retained generating assets under cost-based regulation by the CPUC.[34]

CDWR immediately commenced buying power to make up the shortfall left by PG&E and SCE, that is, the gap between power produced by the utilities' retained generation and total customer demand. Lacking an in-place portfolio of short- and long-term contracts, CDWR still had to purchase six million MWh of power per month (equal to 8,000 MWh every hour of every day) in markets subject to rotating outages and "infused with the abuse of market power."[35] As an emergency entrant, CDWR was unable to neutralize sellers' leverage through strategic forward purchases—which was considered the "single most important element for disciplining longer term transactions."[36] Merchant generators were quick to extract inflated spot market prices, embedded in and amortized over the duration of long-term contracts.

In April 2001, PG&E filed for Chapter 11 bankruptcy protection, asserting that the energy crisis and retail rate freeze had prevented it from recovering approximately $9 billion in electricity procurement costs. In the three years preceding its filing, however, PG&E had up-streamed $4 billion in earnings to PG&E Corporation, an unregulated intrastate holding company exempt from PUHCA restrictions. The transferred funds were, as a result, not available for PG&E and its ratepayers, nor was the transfer subject to SEC scrutiny.[37]

In September 2001, PG&E and PG&E Corporation filed a plan of reorganization that would have unbundled PG&E's business into four separate entities, removed from state regulatory control its hydroelectric and nuclear generating facilities and natural gas transmission assets, and locked in, for 12 years, power purchase costs that would have resulted in high retail rates. The CPUC successfully opposed the plan, and PG&E remained a vertically integrated utility subject to CPUC jurisdiction.[38]

FERC Proceedings

By mid-2000, the California crisis had sharply focused official attention. In July, FERC ordered an investigation of bulk-power market conditions in California and elsewhere.[39] In August, the Oversight Board asked FERC to impose price caps to curtail market power exercised by sellers and scheduling coordinators. In October, the California Municipal Utilities Association urged FERC to set cost-based rates for jurisdictional sellers into the ISO and the PX. In November, FERC issued a remedial order (the November 1 Order).[40]

The November 1 Order found California's market structure and rules to be seriously flawed. Because sellers could "exercise market power when supply is tight," the resulting higher electric rates were deemed "unjust and unreasonable."[41] FERC concluded that the mandatory buy-sell rule had induced overreliance on spot markets and prevented incumbent utilities from using forward contracts to "protect themselves from the economic consequences of pricing volatility."[42] Despite evidence that even small suppliers could cause price spikes in spot markets, FERC declined to attribute market power abuse to individual sellers or to impose a price cap.

Instead, the November 1 Order proposed to eliminate the buy-sell rule and impose a penalty for underscheduling. In lieu of a price cap, it limited single-price auctions in spot markets operated by the PX and the ISO to sale offers at or below $150. Under that level, the highest bid would still set the market clearing price. If the market did not clear at the $150 bid level, however, a bid above $150 would not set a new market-clearing price. The supplier would instead receive its as-bid price. All other as-bid prices would then be averaged with it and charged to load in the relevant auction. The PX and the ISO would report bids over $150 to FERC each month, identifying the seller, price, and amount of electricity covered, bid sufficiency in the market, and load at the time of offer.[43] "In choosing our price mitigation approach," said FERC, "it is our intent to guide these markets to self-correct, not reintroduce command and control price regulation."[44] The November 1 Order's proposed remedy was called a *soft cap*.

The November 1 Order established October 2, 2000, as the earliest refund date permitted under Section 206 of the Federal Power Act (60 days after the date on which SDG&E had filed a complaint with FERC that wholesale rates were not just and reasonable). However, it did not require refunds, merely proposing that "sellers remain subject to potential refund liability during the period it takes to effectuate . . . longer term remedies."[45] It also refused to contemplate retroactive refunds—that is, refund liability for sales before October 2, 2000—even if rates then charged were found to be unjust and unreasonable, thus leaving five months of price spikes and soaring prices beyond FERC's refund power. Finally, the November 1 Order limited refund liability to "no lower than the seller's marginal costs or legitimate and verifiable opportunity costs."[46] The Federal Power Act, it said, was not created "to redress traumatic and inequitable circumstances . . . but to provide rate certainty in a relatively static monopoly environment."[47]

The CPUC did not find much to like in the November 1 Order. Given the finding that market prices in California were unjust and unreasonable, it characterized as unlawful the denial of a hard price cap. "There is no factual basis," it said, "upon which FERC can reasonably conclude that the California markets are sufficiently workable to produce reasonable prices in the absence of hard price caps."[48] Because the proposed soft cap did not prohibit bids above $150, it was deemed insufficient to constrain market power and unsupported factually as the price threshold necessary to stimulate new supply.[49]

The CPUC also predicted that the proposed underscheduling penalty, in an energy market with unconstrained spot prices, would increase pressure on uncapped forward and bilateral prices and render forward purchases ineffective as a means of ensuring just and reasonable rates. Finally, it argued for retroactive refund liability and use of "true" market rates to determine the amount of that liability:

> FERC may not simply accept for filing, and approve as just and reasonable, a tariff that guarantees only that sales will be made at whatever rate a market dictates. . . . The market-based rate tariffs on file here must be read as implicitly specifying . . . the "true" market rate that would result from an efficient market in which the participants are unable to exercise significant market power.[50]

FERC soon issued a further order (the December 15 Order) that implemented its November 1 Order largely unchanged, eliminating an interim $250 price cap and retaining the controversial $150 soft cap previously proposed. Consistent with its market-based philosophy, FERC refused to entertain the hard price cap urgently sought by California agencies:

> We reject proposals to return to cost based regulation. . . . Prices based upon traditional cost of service are incompatible with fostering a competitive market. . . . The one thing that California needs most is new supply and a return to traditional cost of service ratemaking will not encourage supply to enter the California market.[51]

As the CPUC viewed matters, however, the December 15 Order simply perpetuated unjust and unreasonable prices. "FERC's purported remedial program," it said,

> increased . . . opportunities for sellers to exert market power in negotiating forward contracts. First, FERC forced California to procure enormous volumes of energy in the forward markets all at once. Second, FERC eliminated the existing price cap on the spot markets. Third, FERC imposed a $100/MW penalty on load procured in the only spot market that remained.[52]

The December 15 Order did nothing to abate the crisis. In March and April filings with FERC, the California ISO claimed the California wholesale market had sustained $6.7 billion in costs above competitive levels from May 2000 through February 2001.[53] Shortly thereafter FERC issued an order (the April 26 Order) replacing the existing $150 soft cap. The April 26 Order required each gas-fired generator in California, when reserves were 7% or less (a Stage 1 emergency), to bid into real-time markets at its marginal cost, calculated on the basis of heat and emission rates for each generating unit and a proxy for gas and emission costs, plus a $2 adder for operation and maintenance costs. Gas costs were to reflect an average of the daily prices published in *Gas Daily* for all California delivery points.[54]

In dissent, Commissioner Massey (one of only three sitting FERC members at the time) remarked, "We are now eleven months into the California calamity. It has had a breathtaking and staggering effect on the western economy, and there is no end in sight."[55] He sharply criticized the April 26 Order, urging cost-based price mitigation during all hours, and noted that the "high cost of natural gas delivered into California is . . . used to justify high wholesale electricity bids into the ISO market."[56] Massey's dissent foreshadowed a key finding in FERC's Final Report, almost two years later, that "markets for natural gas and electricity in California are inextricably linked."[57] The Final Report concluded that, as spot gas prices rose to extraordinary levels, they led to parallel price increases in California's electricity markets, made worse by manipulation of gas price indexes through false data reporting and wash trading.

The April 26 Order also drew intense criticism from California agencies, which urged FERC to impose full-time price mitigation and return to cost-of-service rate making. By further order (the June 19 Order), FERC reluctantly acknowledged continuation of unjust and unreasonable rates in the California market and imposed maximum market-clearing prices for spot sales of electricity at all times.[58]

The June 19 Order continued the marginal cost price limitation established by the April 26 Order during Stage 1 emergencies and, in addition, set a nonreserve deficiency price cap equal to 85% of the highest hourly price prevailing during the last Stage 1 emergency.[59] It also prevented "megawatt laundering"—shipping electricity out-of-state and then reselling it in California to avoid price mitigation measures for sales within California. Imposition of these measures was not accompanied by ideological retrenchment. FERC maintained its opposition to individual cost-of-service rate making, which, it argued, does not provide "proper incentives for generators to become more efficient" or permit them to recover "appropriate scarcity rents."[60]

Nonetheless, the June 19 Order was immediately effective. Average spot prices at the California-Oregon border dropped by 75%, followed by further declines in later months. Long-term prices also declined. FERC-ordered price caps and must-offer requirements deprived generators of an incentive to hold power off the market to raise prices. FERC action, however grudging, thus finally addressed a market failure based on manipulation and generation withholding.[61] (See fig. 6–2.)

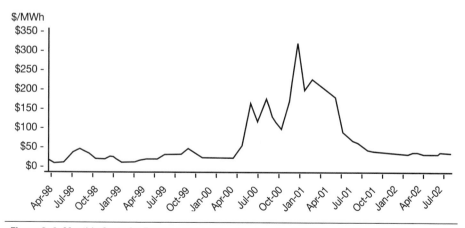

Figure 6–2. Monthly Costs for Energy and Ancillary Services for CAISO Control Area ($/MWh) April 1998–August 2002[62]

Source: CAISO-DMA (2002a), CAISO-DMA (2002b).

Notes

1 *Attorney General's Energy White Paper*. State of California (2004) (hereafter, *White Paper*), pp. 6–8; *California's Electricity Markets: Structure, Crisis, and Needed Reforms*. LECG Economics (2003) (hereafter *LECG*), p. 1; Weaver. "Can Energy Markets Be Trusted? The Effect of the Rise and Fall of Enron on Energy Markets." *Houston Business and Tax Law Journal*, 1 (4): 17 (2004) (hereafter *Weaver*), p. 30.

2 *Weaver*, p. 86.

3 *LECG*, p. 48.

4 *LECG*, p. 49. Energy is measured in megawatt-hours, delivered at a specified network location over a set period of hours and days. Capacity is an option to acquire up to a specified amount of energy, where the strike price may or may not be determined. Both energy and capacity can be acquired through firm transactions, involving an obligation by the parties to sell and deliver or purchase and receive the product, subject to stipulated damages for failure to perform. A nonfirm transaction permits immediate interruption of delivery on notification, without damages. In a swap transaction, one party provides the product in one time period, and the other returns a comparable product in a different time period. Market participants can charge market prices either if they have received market-based authority from FERC or if they are not regulated by FERC.

5 *LECG*, p. 53. During the transition period, SDG&E recovered its stranded costs pursuant to Section 368 of the California Public Utility Code and was no longer subject to the retail rate freeze. Because SCE and PG&E did not similarly recover their stranded costs, they remained subject to the freeze.

6 *San Diego Gas & Electric Company*, 93 FERC ¶ 61,121 (November 1, 2000), mimeo (hereafter *November 1 Order*), p. 8 and cases cited therein.

7 *LECG*, p. 60.

8 *LECG*, pp. 54–55.

[9] Ancillary services include regulation, spinning reserves, nonspinning reserves, and replacement reserves, purchased in separate day-ahead auction markets. Ancillary services vary according to the time required by the generating units supplying capacity in order to ramp up to the desired output level.

[10] *LECG*, p. 55.

[11] *LECG*, pp. 56–57.

[12] Stern. "California Market Redesign—Changing the Market Structure and Rules to Avert Another Energy Crisis." Presentation at the 2003 Electric Market Forecasting Conference. Skamania Lodge, Washington (September 2003), p. 3.

[13] *LECG*, pp. 57–58.

[14] *White Paper*, pp. 14–15.

[15] Bohn et al. "The Design of Tests for Horizontal Market Power in Market-Based Rate Proceedings." *The Electricity Journal* 15 (4): 43–54 (2002), p. 52.

[16] *White Paper*, pp. 15–16.

[17] Ibid., p. 29.

[18] McDiarmid. *Looking Ahead while Looking Back: Markets, Theories, Price and Bid Caps and Other Things That Go Bump in the Night.* White paper (April 4, 2001), p. 5.

[19] Joskow. Statement before the Committee on Governmental Affairs, U.S. Senate (November 12, 2002), p. 7.

[20] *Final Report on Price Manipulation in Western Markets*, FERC Docket No. PA02-2-000 (March 2003) (hereafter *Final Report*), pp. V-9.

[21] *AES Redondo Beach, L.L.C. et al.*, 84 FERC ¶ 61,046 (1998), order on rehearing, 85 FERC ¶ 61,123 (1998) (ancillary services price caps); *California ISO*, 89 FERC ¶ 61,169 (2000) (energy price caps).

[22] *LECG*, p. 60.

[23] Complaint filed at FERC on February 25, 2002, *CPUC v. Allegheny Energy Supply Company, LLC et al.* (hereafter *CPUC Complaint*) at pp. 1-2.

[24] *LECG*, p. 9.

[25] See, e.g., *Staff Report to the Federal Energy Regulatory Commission on Western Markets and the Causes of the Summer 2000 Price Abnormalities*, filed as app. D to the November 1 Order.

[26] *LECG*, p. 62. See also *CPUC Complaint*, p. 2; *San Diego Gas & Electric Co.*, 95 FERC ¶ 61,418, at 62,565 (2002).

[27] *Weaver*, p. 38.

[28] McCullough. Rebuttal testimony on behalf of Public Utility District No. 1 of Snohomish County, Washington. *Nevada Power Company and Sierra Pacific Power Company v. Enron Power Marketing, Inc. et al.*, FERC Docket Nos. EL-02-28-000, EL02-33-000, and EL02-38-000 (2004) (hereafter *McCullough*), p. 63.

[29] *Weaver*, pp. 39–40.

[30] *Application of Southern California Edison Co.*, Cal. P.U.C. Dec. No. 01-03-082 (2001).

[31] *LECG*, pp. 62–63.

[32] *CPUC Complaint* at p. 2.

[33] Ibid., p. 2.

[34] *CPUC Agenda ID #2983*. Investigation 02-04-025 (November 18, 2003). Shortly thereafter, FERC issued an order prohibiting the ISO from purchasing energy in real time on behalf of PG&E and SCE unless the purchases were supported by CDWR. *California Independent System Operator*, 94 FERC ¶ 61,132 (2001); *CPUC Complaint*, p. 3.

[35] *CPUC Complaint*, p. 3.

[36] *AEP Marketing, et al.*, 97 FERC ¶ 61,219, at 61,792 (2001).

[37] *White Paper*, pp. 53–54.

[38] *CPUC Opinion Modifying Proposed Settlement*. Decision 03-12-035 (December 18, 2003).

[39] *Order Directing Staff Investigation*, 92 FERC ¶ 61,160 (2000). The resulting report found, among other things, that prices in the ISO had spiked in May and June, reaching $750 per MWh on several occasions, and were above the level "that would have prevailed in a competitive short-term

market, if prices were determined from short-term marginal costs." *Staff Report to the Federal Energy Regulatory Commission on Western Markets and the Causes of the Summer 2000 Price Abnormalities*, p. 2.

[40] *Order Proposing Remedies for California Wholesale Electric Markets*, 93 FERC ¶ 61,121 (November 1, 2000), mimeo.

[41] Ibid., p. 5.

[42] Ibid., p. 27

[43] Ibid., pp. 51–52.

[44] Ibid., p. 55.

[45] Ibid., p. 56.

[46] Ibid., p. 57.

[47] Ibid., p. 57.

[48] Response of the Public Utilities Commission of the State of California to the November 1 Order, *San Diego Gas & Electric Company et al.*, FERC Docket No. EL00-95-000 (November 21, 2000) (hereafter *CPUC Comments*), pp. 4, 10.

[49] Ibid., p. 12.

[50] Ibid., pp. 13–14.

[51] *San Diego Gas & Elec. Co. v. Sellers of Energy and Ancillary Services into Markets Operated by CAISO and CalPX*, 93 FERC ¶ 61,294 (December 15, 2000), mimeo, p. 53.

[52] *CPUC Comments*, p. 5.

[53] *San Diego Gas & Elec. Co. v. Sellers of Energy and Ancillary Services into Markets Operated by CAISO and CalPX*, 95 FERC ¶ 61,115 (April 26, 2001), mimeo, p. 5.

[54] Ibid., p. 15.

[55] Ibid. (dissent), p. 1.

[56] Ibid. (dissent), p. 4.

[57] *Final Report*, p. ES-1.

[58] *San Diego Gas & Electric Company et al.*, 95 FERC ¶ 61,418 (2001), mimeo (hereafter *June 19 Order*).

[59] For example, if the highest hourly market clearing price during a Stage 1 emergency were $140 per MWh, spot prices in all subsequent nonreserve deficiency hours beginning when the Stage 1 emergency was lifted could be no higher than $119 per MWh (i.e., 85% of $140 per MWh). *June 19 Order*, p. 7.

[60] *June 19 Order*, p. 24.

[61] *McCullough*, pp. 4, 20–21.

[62] *LECG*, p. 10.

7 Implosion of the California Electricity Market—Part II

In May 2002, several months after Enron's bankruptcy, its counsel presented to FERC three memoranda dating from late 2000 that described trading strategies employed by Enron's traders in Western electricity markets. The memoranda provided compelling evidence of widespread market manipulation, later confirmed by Enron's chief West Coast trader in a sworn plea agreement:

> I and other individuals at Enron agreed to devise and implement a series of fraudulent schemes through these [ISO and PX] markets. We designed the schemes to obtain increased revenue for Enron from wholesale electricity customers and other market participants in the state of California. . . . As a result of these false schedules, we were able to manipulate prices in certain markets, arbitrage price differences between markets, obtain "congestion management" payments in excess of what we could have received with accurate schedules, and receive prices for electricity above price caps set by the ISO and the Federal Energy Regulatory Commission.[1]

Recall that the ISO operated much of the transmission grid in California, while managing congestion and balancing generation in the real-time market, whereas the PX ran day-ahead and hour-ahead markets to establish, in the absence of transmission constraints, a single clearing price for each hour across the entire ISO control area. When congestion was present, however, each transmission-constrained zone had a separate clearing price, based on adjustment bids submitted by buyers and sellers that reflected the perceived value of increasing or decreasing (i.e., adjusting) use of the system. The ISO's real-time market cleared after all other markets in the region. Bilateral trading hubs outside California operated between the close of the PX forward markets and the ISO real-time market.[2]

Enron's Trading Schemes

Enron's trading schemes had a direct impact on spot electricity prices in California. In addition, they often depended on deliberate use of false information and were not a legitimate form of arbitrage.[3]

Load shift

To create the appearance of congestion and increase the value of its transmission rights, Enron deliberately overscheduled load in the southern zone of the California market and underscheduled load by a corresponding amount in the market's northern zone. Enron also acquired firm transmission rights (FTRs), auctioned by the ISO, that accorded it priority in scheduling transmission on a specified path, allowed it to avoid congestion payments on that path, and entitled it to share in congestion revenues.

In the ISO's first annual auction of FTRs, for $3.6 million, Enron purchased 1,000 (62%) of the 1,621 MW in rights to north-to-south transmission on Path 26, one of two main transmission interfaces linking Northern and Southern California. Enron's FTRs entitled it to collect revenues on Path 26 attributable to north-to-south congestion, typical during periods of peak demand in summer months. To earn congestion fees, Enron shifted load, creating north-to-south congestion. The technique allowed Enron to net $33 million during July and August 2000 alone and represented a disproportionate return on the purchase price of its FTRs. Enron's false schedules also harmed the market and impaired the ISO's ability to manage congestion.[4]

Ricochet, or megawatt laundering

After purchasing electricity from the PX in the day-ahead market, Enron exported it to an out-of-state accommodation counterparty, which *parked* it for a fee. Enron later resold the electricity to the ISO above the applicable price cap as out-of-market power. On days when insufficient supply had been bid into the market, Enron knew the ISO was vulnerable to a price squeeze and would pay virtually any price to avoid blackouts and system outages. In FERC's view, "This behavior (raising prices at the last minute where buyers are ... incapable of saying no) was not legitimate arbitrage, but was an exercise of market power."[5] (See fig. 7–1.)

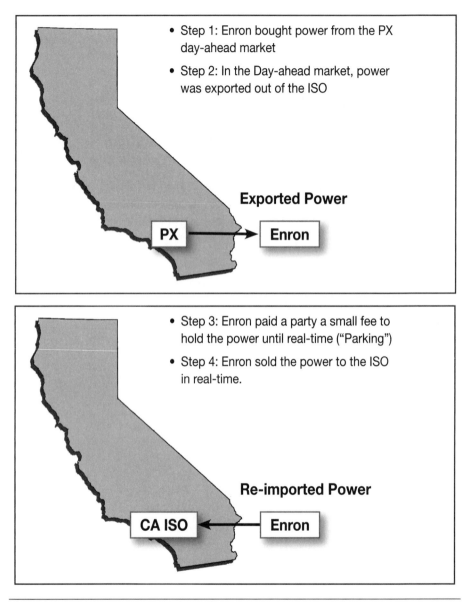

- Step 1: Enron bought power from the PX day-ahead market
- Step 2: In the Day-ahead market, power was exported out of the ISO

Exported Power

PX → Enron

- Step 3: Enron paid a party a small fee to hold the power until real-time ("Parking")
- Step 4: Enron sold the power to the ISO in real-time.

Re-imported Power

CA ISO ← Enron

Figure 7–1. Ricochet, aka "MW Laundering"[6]

Source: Southern California Edison (2003)

Fat boy, or Inc-ing load

Under California market rules, all schedules submitted to the ISO were balanced—that is, scheduled load and generation had to be equal. As a scheduling coordinator, Enron artificially increased load to match scheduled generation. It then dispatched the generation, including that in excess of actual load, causing the ISO to pay the higher clearing price in the real-time market. Enron's *fat boy* trading strategy took advantage of California utilities' chronic underscheduling of load, which meant that the real-time market had to serve more load than it was designed to supply. Fat boy enabled Enron to preschedule on a day-ahead basis an imbalance in the real-time market and thereby capture its higher clearing price. By submitting false information, Enron gamed existing market rules and exacerbated the ISO's reliability problems.[7] (See fig. 7–2.)

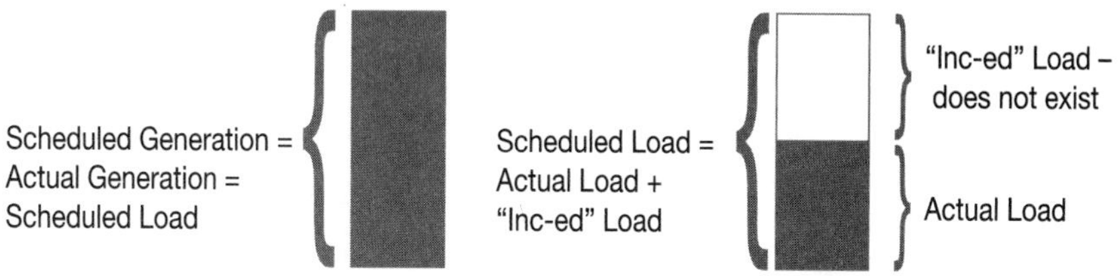

Scheduled Generation =
Actual Generation =
Scheduled Load

Scheduled Load =
Actual Load +
"Inc-ed" Load

"Inc-ed" Load –
does not exist

Actual Load

- Enron scheduled "real" generation time against some "real" load and some fictitious "Inc-ed" load

- In real-time, the "Inc-ed" load is paid the real-time imbalance uninstructed price **Note** that the generation performs exactly to schedule

- Why do this? To withhold power from the day-ahead market and sell the power in real-time

Figure 7–2. Enron Strategy: "Fat Boy"[8]

Source: Source: Southern California Edison (2003)

Nonfirm exports, Death Star, and wheel out

With these trading strategies, Enron generated payments for relieving congestion by scheduling counterflow transmission in fictitious transactions. In *wheel out*, the most egregious scheme, Enron scheduled transmission flow over a constrained or out-of-service intertie, thereafter receiving a congestion payment without actually having dispatched any electric power at all. In May 1999, for example, to earn a congestion payment from the ISO, Enron scheduled 2,900 MW across a 15 MW intertie between Southern

California and Nevada.

Subsequently, in a scheme called the *Forney perpetual loop* or Death Star, Enron articulated the wheel-out strategy to include counterparties outside the ISO's control area, including Portland General (its affiliate), El Paso Electric, and Avista. A typical transaction was as follows:

- Enron scheduled nonfirm electric power from Palo Verde, Arizona, through California, and across the Oregon border;

- Avista bought the power from Enron and sold it to Portland General at the Oregon border;

- Portland General transmitted the power across its system.

- Enron then returned the power to the Oregon border;

- Los Angeles Department of Water and Power, a municipal utility that owned transmission facilities interconnecting with the ISO's system but outside its control, scheduled the power from the Oregon border to Palo Verde;

- Finally, the power was scheduled to return to California.

Despite the appearance of sequential transactions, no power actually flowed, since the schedule began and ended at the same location. A structural flaw in the ISO's software prevented it from identifying the sham transactions, which nonetheless gave rise to very real congestion-relief payments. The trading strategy would not have worked if a single comprehensive congestion management system had been implemented in the Western states.[9] (See fig. 7–3.)

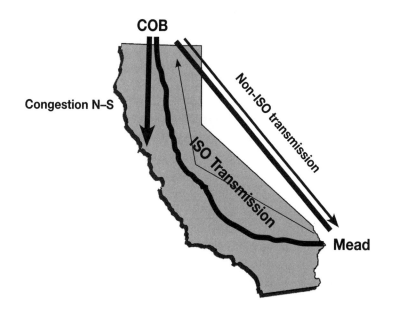

- **Step 1:** Enron predicted congestion on COB N to S
- **Step 2:** Enron bought power at Mead, sold power at COB and scheduled a counterflow using ISO transmission
- **Step 3:** Simultaneously, Enron purchased non-ISO transmission at embedded cost rates (e.g. DWP)
- **Step 4:** Enron bought power at COB and sold power at Mead; transaction was scheduled over the non-ISO transmission.
- "The net effect of these transactions is that Enron gets paid for moving energy to relieve congesion without actually moving any energy or relieving any congestion."

—Enron memo

Figure 7–3. Enron Strategy: "Death Star" [10]   *Source: Southern California Edison*

Get Shorty

This strategy involved the *paper trading* of ancillary services—that is, generation capacity held in reserve to meet market contingencies such as loss of critical generation or transmission facilities. Enron undertook to sell required ancillary services in the PX's day-ahead market while purporting to cover its commitment through standby purchase of the same services in the ISO's real-time market. Although

ISO rules require identification of the specific generating units used to provide ancillary services, Enron committed to sell those services without in fact acquiring them on a standby basis. In the process, Enron deliberately submitted false information to the ISO.[11]

Selling nonfirm power as firm power

Enron deliberately sold nonfirm power to the PX as firm power, a strategy that compromised system reliability, particularly when nonfirm power was imported from another control area and the receiving control area, supposing it to be firm, did not procure reserves.[12]

The Investigation Widens

Because the Enron memoranda implicated many other companies, FERC immediately issued data requests to more than 130 sellers of wholesale electricity and ancillary services in Western states during 2000–2001, including requests for admissions, and in June 2002 issued an order directing four companies—Avista, El Paso Electric, Portland General, and Williams Energy Marketing and Trading—to show cause why their market-based rate authority should not be revoked.[13]

FERC staff obtained voluminous electronic data, written records, and data responses from all segments of the industry, together with ISO and PX bidding data, expert testimony, and analyses, that formed the basis for its *Final Report on Price Manipulation in Western Markets*, issued in March 2003. Meanwhile, in a parallel investigation of equal scope, the California Attorney General's office issued dozens of subpoenas, reviewed millions of pages of documents, deposed hundreds of witnesses, and sifted through data from multiple sources. Its investigation revealed widespread illegal, criminal, and manipulative behavior by energy market participants, including gaming, false reporting, withholding, and supply disruption.[14] To seek redress at FERC, the California attorney general and other California parties filed massive documentary evidence of market manipulation and requests for refunds.[15]

Between May 2000 and June 2001, according to the California filing, the total cost of electricity needed to serve California exceeded $44 billion (compared to $25 billion for all of 1998, 1999, and 2002 combined)—an extraordinary increase that "imposed great hardship on the State's citizens and businesses, crippled the State's two largest utilities, and took the State's budget from a multi-billion dollar surplus to a multi-billion dollar deficit . . . [and] caused a life-threatening power crisis that sent the nation's most populous state into rolling blackouts."[16] The cause of the crisis was market "abuse by sellers, who . . . drove prices far above competitive levels through a pervasive pattern of market manipulation."[17]

The California filing identified specific patterns of manipulative conduct that paralleled those revealed in the Enron memoranda. The following sections describe those patterns in detail.

Withholding

AES/Williams, Duke, Dynegy, Mirant, and Reliant—purchasers of the California utilities' fossil fuel generating plants—engaged in systematic and deliberate withholding of generation from the market, artificially reducing supply and driving prices far above competitive levels. As a group, they withdrew large volumes of power from the day-ahead market and forced buyers to purchase what they required in the real-time market at exorbitant prices. To exercise market power, they falsely reported available units as out of service, failed to bid available capacity during system emergencies, submitted bids far above competitive levels, and placed available units on reserve shutdown. In doing so, they used hockey stick bids, bid spikes, and bids based on the perceived need for power rather than costs to manipulate the market. Withholding violated PX and ISO tariffs, which proscribed it as gaming or anomalous market behavior.[18]

Submitting false load schedules

To drive up prices, Sempra, Powerex, Mirant, Dynegy, Reliant, and others adopted Enron's fat boy strategy and intentionally submitted false load information to the ISO, whose tariff required that scheduled generation be balanced against scheduled load, with remaining generation, if any, bid into the day-ahead and real-time markets. By scheduling generation against bogus load, sellers gamed prevailing market rules. They knew that, when actual generation was found to equal the amount scheduled while actual load fell short, the ISO would treat the difference as an *uninstructed deviation*, allowing sellers to earn the real-time market price through de facto sales at or near price caps. By intentionally submitting schedules that specified greater demand than forecasted, sellers violated ISO tariff prohibitions, "decreasing supply in the organized auction markets while at the same time profiting from the high prices yielded by those markets."[19]

Megawatt laundering

Enron, Powerex, Sempra, Mirant, Williams, Reliant, and numerous others scheduled exports of day-ahead power to locations outside the ISO system, often in multiparty transactions. They then parked the power and reimported it for sale at higher prices in the real-time market. Parking entailed purchase and sale transactions on prearranged terms, with the parking party earning an up-front fee for each transaction (e.g., the $1 million fee paid by Powerex to PNM). Between May 2000 and June 2001, merchant traders shifted more than two million megawatt-hours between California's day-ahead and real-time markets in violation of PX and ISO tariffs. Intermarket arbitrage allowed sellers to extract rents from "imbalance markets during price spikes."[20] By reducing supply in the day-ahead market, sellers received artificially high prices for the displaced supply in the real-time market. Such gaming had a broad impact on prices between May 2000 and June 2001. Using this technique, for example, Sempra marked up the power it sold in California markets by over 70%.[21]

Congestion games

Adopting Enron's trading strategy "to create a false perception of scarcity," Mirant, Coral, Duke, Powerex, Sempra, and others submitted circular export-import schedules that reflected apparent, but fictitious, power counterflows. The strategy enabled them to earn payments from the ISO for relieving congestion without actually doing so. Intentional submission of such schedules, relied on by the ISO to relieve day-ahead or hour-ahead congestion, violated tariff requirements, increased prices for energy in congested zones, and impaired system reliability.[22]

Ancillary services scams

Ancillary services require generating capacity that can deliver output to the grid in response to uncertain events, such as major plant outages, when the ISO issues a dispatch order. The supplier of ancillary services, which is compensated for doing so, must comply with such an order and hold capacity in reserve.[23] While committing capacity from reserve units, Mirant, Reliant, and Dynegy sold electricity from the same units as uninstructed deviations, thereby receiving double payments and depriving the ISO of promised reserves when it needed backup power. Double-selling violated the ISO tariff and a FERC order specifically prohibiting such activity.[24] A related, Get Shorty strategy used by Enron, Sempra, Coral, Powerex, Dynegy, and others involved the sale of ancillary services that did not exist or the seller did not intend to deliver, as evidenced by sales in the day-ahead market and offsetting buybacks in the hour-ahead market. Such scams forced the ISO to buy ancillary services in the day-ahead market or risk a real-time shortfall and erosion of systemwide reliability.[25]

Uninstructed generation games

Mirant, Reliant, and Dynegy also intentionally ignored the ISO's operating orders and dispatch instructions to bid up real-time prices, selling *uninstructed generation* even when the ISO had rejected an inflated bid or chosen another generator. Such generation games violated the ISO tariff and accounted for up to one-quarter of the sellers' total generation during portions of 2000 and 2001.[26]

Sharing nonpublic outage information—and collusion

Industrial Information Resources, Inc. (IIR), a company located in Houston, Texas, e-mailed a daily generation outage notification service to power industry subscribers at a cost of $70,000 per year. IIR's information was plant and unit specific, disclosing the expected start date for an outage, the expected return to service date, the cause of the outage, and a description of the unit affected. Subscribers could also request immediate information on an outage affecting a competitor's plants.

Duke, Dynegy, and Williams, among others, used the IIR service to exchange nonpublic information regarding planned and ongoing unit outages. As pivotal suppliers, each was able to observe a competitor's outage and respond to it in near real time by bidding a higher price or withdrawing additional capacity from the market. As the California filing explained, this "enhanced the sellers' ability to exercise market power and facilitated the coordination of conduct among competitors thereby leading to . . . market manipulation . . . in violation of the ISO Tariff and possibly the antitrust laws."[27]

Exchange of nonpublic information was but one example of collective behavior. "Alliances and trading of information . . . [transformed] a marketplace of several independent competitors into a set of entities . . . with aligned interests in maximizing profits."[28] Two-party agreements enabled Enron, Sempra, Powerex, and others to share competitive information with counterparties, split profits on sales of surplus power, and engage in wash trading. Industry organizations pooled member company price information and facilitated joint opposition to regulatory initiatives, such as proposed price caps, at a time when certain member companies were withholding power to raise prices. This action was described in the California filing as a "conspiracy to fix and maintain prices at levels which permitted exercise of market power."[29] In the summer of 2000, sellers in the California power markets, as a group, also withdrew large volumes of power from the day-ahead market, thus compelling buyers, as a last resort, to purchase power from the same sellers at exorbitant prices in the real-time market. In effect, sellers shifted supply between markets to extract unjust and unreasonable prices.[30]

Root cause

While the California electric power market can properly be called badly designed and dysfunctional, the root cause of the 2000–2001 crisis lay elsewhere: the market oversight and enforcement mechanisms then in place, both in California and at the federal level, were simply incapable of deterring widespread market manipulation. FERC staff numbers declined each year between 1993 and 2001 (see fig. 7–4).

Number of full-time employees

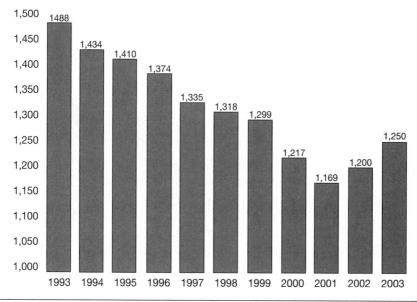

Figure 7–4. FERC Staff Years, 1993–2003[31]

Source: GAO-02-656, (June 2002), p.13

Further, there is no record of any FERC enforcement action, before or during the California energy crisis, against any generator operating in the California market. FERC oversight was "episodic, fractured, and largely ineffectual."[32] In December 1998, for example, in response to allegations that generators had *double-sold* ancillary services capacity in violation of the ISO tariff, thereby receiving millions of dollars for services never rendered, FERC simply implemented tariff changes but took no action to compel the violators to disgorge illegal profits.[33] Not surprisingly, by mid-2000, sellers were emboldened "to try the many schemes that, at least until June 2001, effectively increased . . . profits . . . by many billions of dollars above what they would otherwise have been, or above what would have existed in workably competitive markets with strong and effective oversight."[34]

Refunds for Overcharges

Given the mounting evidence of market manipulation, FERC had little choice but to acknowledge that energy prices in the seriously flawed California markets were unjust and unreasonable. To address the problem on a go-forward basis, FERC imposed price caps. Immediately thereafter, in late June 2001, prices in California spot and forward markets fell back to preexisting competitive levels. FERC also imposed, rather belatedly, structural reforms intended to avoid price spikes, such as eliminating the requirement that incumbent utilities buy and sell power through the PX.[35]

Still without remedy, however, were consumers and incumbent utilities that had borne huge overcharges inflicted by sellers in the California market. On July 25, 2001, FERC finally ordered an evidentiary hearing triggered by the refund complaint SDG&E had filed under Section 206 of the Federal Power Act almost a year earlier. The purpose of the hearing was to determine refunds payable by sellers in California spot markets between October 2, 2000, and

June 20, 2001.[36] FERC contended that, under Section 206, refunds were limited to sales beginning 60 days after the filing of SDG&E's complaint, a start date precluding billions in refunds for prior periods. "Section 206," FERC stated, "does not permit retroactive refund relief for rates covering periods prior to the filing of a complaint or the initiation of Commission investigation, even if the Commission determines that such past rates were unjust and unreasonable."[37]

Sections 205 and 206 of the Federal Power Act embody the filed-rate doctrine and its corollary, the rule against retroactive rate making, which, taken together, confirm that a utility may charge only those rates on file with and approved by FERC and, conversely, that FERC may not alter a utility's filed rates retrospectively. As further extended by judicial interpretation, unless official agency procedures change the filed rate prospectively, it is the only legal rate. A reviewing court will decline to impose damages or refund obligations on a utility that sells electricity to aggrieved consumers at the filed rate.[38] The filed-rate doctrine therefore represents a formidable legal barrier to plaintiffs, whether in administrative proceedings at FERC or litigation before a court.

To its critics, the filed-rate doctrine is an anachronism. A market-based regulatory regime, it is argued, "fundamentally changes the relationship of the regulatory agency to the commodity." Since FERC no longer brings its unique expertise to bear on rate setting, the market, not the agency, sets the rate. In such a system, it is argued, courts no longer need to defer to agency expertise.[39]

In its July 25 Order, FERC vigorously defended the filed rate doctrine and the rule against retroactive rate making, noting that Section 205(c) of the Federal Power Act, which requires utilities to file schedules showing all rates and charges subject to FERC jurisdiction, "does not distinguish between cost-based and market-based rates."[40] FERC concluded that its rule requiring utilities and power marketers to file quarterly reports summarizing market-based transactions satisfied Section 205(c)'s requirements for market-based rates.[41] As will be seen, however, FERC's reliance on after-the-fact quarterly reports did not pass muster upon later judicial review.

FERC's July 25 Order also drew sharp criticism from the California Electricity Oversight Board (CEOB) for other reasons, in particular its denial of refunds for bilateral spot market purchases made by the California Department of Water Resources (CDWR) (totaling more than $5 billion during the first five months of 2001 alone). CDWR, "by voluntarily entering into bilateral transactions outside the ISO and PX," FERC reasoned, "made a conscious decision to forego the protection . . . provided for purchases through the ISO and PX."[42] CEOB estimated that FERC's decision cost "California consumers two billion dollars [in] excess unjust and unreasonable charges."[43]

In fact, CEOB argued, as the buyer of last resort, CDWR had little choice but to purchase in the spot market, since FERC's own orders had eliminated the PX day-ahead market and imposed underscheduling penalties on transactions in the ISO real-time market. As a result, sellers refused to sell through the ISO, preferring to deal directly with the CDWR in a must-buy posture. By excluding CDWR from its scope, the July 25 Order "unreasonably ignore[d] a massive quantity of spot transactions at extremely high prices tainted by market power."[44]

FERC's regulatory response to the California crisis was thus ill considered and problematic. It abdicated its enforcement responsibilities, failed to monitor the market-based system it had sanctioned, delayed far too long before imposing firm price caps, and unjustifiably limited refunds. Eventually, FERC was compelled to change course as the massive economic damage caused by pervasive manipulation of the California market became impossible to rationalize or ignore.

California goes to court

To recover overcharges, the State of California embarked on an aggressive litigation strategy. In addition to filing for refunds at FERC,[45] California commenced multiple state court actions to recover civil penalties against power generators and marketers, alleging failure to file rates with FERC, as required under the Federal Power Act, and sale of wholesale power at unjust and unreasonable rates.[46] California also filed a separate complaint at FERC, alleging that sellers of power into the PX and ISO had failed to file transaction-specific information with FERC as required under Section 205(c). FERC agreed that "the quarterly reports submitted . . . by a number of respondents do not comply with the requirements . . . [since they] filed aggregated data in their transaction reports for the fourth quarter of 2000 and all four quarters of 2001." Relying on its initial determination that the sellers lacked market power—a finding deemed equivalent to a filed rate—FERC nonetheless dismissed their failure to report transactions as "essentially a compliance issue," curable by refiling, and rejected California's request for refunds.[47]

California appealed FERC's order to the Ninth Circuit Court of Appeals in *California v. FERC*,[48] contending that FERC's approval of market-based rates violated the Federal Power Act and that, even if such rates were valid, the sellers had failed to comply with applicable reporting requirements. California sought recovery of $2.8 billion in overcharges. Although the Court upheld FERC's approval of market-based rates, it found that, to be valid, a market-based tariff must ensure enforceable postapproval reporting. Without the transaction-specific information provided in quarterly reports, the Court stated, FERC had no way of knowing whether the rates in question were market-based and thus just and reasonable, nor could FERC or any affected party challenge the rates. In effect, the Court said, the market-based tariffs at issue "virtually deregulate an industry and remove it from statutorily required oversight."[49] The Court remanded the case to FERC, noting that its "power to order retroactive refunds when a company's non-compliance . . . eviscerates the tariff is inherent in [its] authority to approve a market-based tariff in the first instance."[50]

Remedial action and settlements at FERC

While California was seeking recovery in court, FERC authorized more than $1 billion in refunds,[51] clarified the methodology to be used for calculating refunds, and instructed the ISO and PX to recalculate bills for all sales during the refund period.[52] When the Enron evidence surfaced, FERC commenced its investigation into manipulation of short-term prices in Western energy markets, leading to issuance of its *Final Report* in March 2003. Shortly thereafter, FERC ordered a further investigation of anomalous bidding behavior and practices by individual market participants. FERC staff reviewed all bids in the ISO and PX markets above $250 per MWh during the 18-month period ending in June 2001, to determine whether sellers had manipulated prices in violation of ISO and PX tariffs by withholding power. FERC required that named sellers justify why they should not be deemed to have participated in prohibited gaming practices, including those conducted collusively through partnerships and alliances.[53] FERC's action led, eventually, to settlements between California litigants[54] and Enron (nominally, $1.5 billion), Williams ($137 million), Dynegy ($267 million), Duke ($200 million), and Mirant ($320 million).

In November 2003, as a sequel to its investigation, FERC required that sellers under market-based rate tariffs comply with specific behavioral rules prohibiting collusion, manipulation, and submission of false or misleading information. The rules imposed disgorgement of profits as a penalty for violations. FERC defined market manipulation to include wash trades, submission of false information to transmission providers, creating artificial congestion, and collusive agreements between or among sellers to manipulate electricity prices, conditions, or supply—market strategies for which Enron had supplied the explicit blueprint.[55] Beyond adoption of behavioral rules, FERC was urged to use its conditioning power to ensure structurally competitive markets (e.g., by mandating divestiture of pivotal generation) before granting market-based rate authorization, as it had often done in the merger context.[56] The Energy Policy Act of 2005 grants FERC further enforcement and remedial powers.

FERC Revisits Market-Based Rates

Given the egregious manipulation of California's wholesale power markets by a handful of predatory sellers, FERC was also moved to revisit its hub-and-spoke methodology for determining the existence of market power.[57] In November 2001, FERC adopted a new generation market power test, the Supply Margin Assessment (SMA), in deciding whether to grant market-based rate authority.[58]

To determine the relevant geographic market for the purpose of assessing market power, the SMA took into account transmission constraints that could preclude competitive supply. It also inquired, as a threshold measure of market power, whether an applicant was *pivotal* in the market—that is, whether its capacity exceeded the market's surplus of capacity above peak demand, called the *supply margin*.[59] If an applicant's capacity was necessary to meet the market's annual peak day load in a control area, the SMA treated the applicant as a must-run supplier with power to withhold supply and raise prices.

If an applicant failed the SMA, FERC would deny market-based rate authority and require mitigation measures. To prevent physical withholding, an applicant would have to offer uncommitted capacity (i.e., generation in excess of projected peak load) for spot market sales in the relevant market. To prevent economic withholding, an applicant would have to price uncommitted capacity using a split-the-savings formula (the traditional cost-based rate making technique for spot market energy sales),[60] post cost and price data on the Web, and, if the applicant were a transmission provider, facilitate necessary interconnections on the grid.

The SMA came under immediate attack from utilities, which claimed it unfairly counted capacity committed to native load as if the capacity were available to the market. When analyzing wholesale markets, they argued, it does not matter that a utility's generation is required to serve total load if it is already dedicated to supply that load. The objecting utilities had seized on a fatal flaw. Not more than a month after promulgating the SMA, therefore, FERC deferred its implementation, pending further review and the results of a technical conference. Two years passed before FERC scheduled the conference. Meanwhile, it declined to use the SMA to support a finding of market power.[61] Given the critical importance of identifying and remedying market power, FERC's delay was inexplicable.

In April 2004—almost three years after the California market crisis—FERC replaced the SMA with two indicative screens, so called because FERC believed that no single market power test was definitive.[62] The first indicative screen, like the SMA, uses a pivotal supplier analysis based on a control area's annual peak load, but it subtracts generation dedicated to native load in determining an applicant's uncommitted capacity. If that capacity is less than the difference between wholesale load and total uncommitted capacity, the applicant does not have market power. The second indicative screen is a market share analysis, seasonally applied, that determines whether an applicant has a dominant market position (typically, 20% or more) enabling it to exercise market power alone or together with others.[63] Both screens are applied to the applicant's core control area and, separately, to each directly interconnected area. The applicant must then supply a simultaneous import capability study showing how much imported power can properly be included in the analysis— a more restrictive test than the SMA's assumption that power can be imported up to the level of total transmission capacity.

An applicant that fails one or both of the indicative screens has the option of performing a delivered price test using market prices, input costs, and transmission availability to define relevant markets and suppliers and demonstrate that it has not exercised market power. The delivered price test incorporates capacity deliverable at a price less than or equal to 105% of the market price in the destination market and references economic capacity (the entire capacity of suppliers that can compete in the market, using the 105% threshold if simultaneous import capability is available) and available economic capacity (capacity that excludes the supplier's native load and other firm commitments).[64]

Although they are an improvement on the SMA, indicative screens do not ensure that wholesale power costs are just and reasonable— that is, they do not link the outcomes of bidding and pricing in the energy, ancillary services, and capacity markets to permit a simultaneous, integrated assessment whether market power exists in all such submarkets. Similarly, the delivered price test determines market concentration thresholds separately for each electric product market. To address real-world market power concerns, screening methodology must also go beyond structural tests and account for collusive bidding (as employed in California).[65]

Observations

More than 100 applicants have made filings at FERC under the indicative screens, several of which have triggered rate reviews. In most cases, further granularity of appropriate product and geographic markets is required, an observation that is also true of an applicant's annual, seasonal, or aggregate load, since each hour represents a product market with a unique supply curve. FERC now recognizes that market power assessments must take into account transmission tests, affiliate abuse, and barriers to entry and will incorporate these factors in a four-pronged test.[66] Defining market power—the predicate for a market-based regulatory regime—has thus proven to be a difficult, iterative process, not a global fix. In retrospect, it seems obvious that rigorous empirical analysis of market power should have preceded, not followed, FERC's extensive reliance on market-based rates.

Notes

---

[1] Exhibit No. CA-229, p. 3, Plea Agreement No. CR-02-0313 (N.D. Cal. 2002).

[2] *Initial Report on Company-Specific Separate Proceedings and Generic Reevaluations; Published Natural Gas Price Data; and Enron Trading Strategies; Fact-Finding Investigation of Potential Manipulation of Electric and Natural Gas Prices*, FERC Docket No. PA02-2-000 (August 2002) (hereafter *Initial Report*), pp. 88–89.

[3] McCullough. Rebuttal testimony on behalf of Public Utility District No. 1 of Snohomish County, Washington. *Nevada Power Company and Sierra Pacific Power Company v. Enron Power Marketing, Inc. et al.*, FERC Docket Nos. EL-02-28-000, EL02-33-000, and EL02-38-000 (2004), pp. 4, 63.

[4] *Initial Report*, pp. 94–95.

[5] Ibid., pp. 102–4.

[6] Stern. "California Market Redesign—Changing the Market Structure and Rules to Avert Another Energy Crisis." Presentation at the 2003 Electric Market Forecasting Conference. Skamania Lodge, Washington (September 2003) (hereafter *Stern*).

[7] *Initial Report*, pp. 105–6.

[8] *Stern*.

[9] *Initial Report*, pp. 108–9.

[10] *Stern*.

[11] *Initial Report*, pp. 109–10.

[12] Ibid., pp. 110–11.

[13] Ibid., pp. 14–15. See also *Fact-Finding Investigation of Potential Manipulation of Electric and Natural Gas Prices, Order to Show Cause Why Market-Based Rate Authority Should Not Be Revoked*, 99 FERC ¶ 61,272 (2002).

[14] *Attorney General's Energy White Paper*. State of California (2004) (hereafter, *White Paper*), p. 47.

[15] California Parties' Supplemental Evidence of Market Manipulation by Sellers, Proposed Findings of Fact, and Request for Refunds and Other Relief, *San Diego Gas & Electric Company et al.*, FERC Docket No. EL00-95-000 (March 3, 2003), mimeo (hereafter *California Filing*).

[16] Ibid., p. 2.

[17] Ibid., p. 2.

[18] Ibid., pp. 20–46.

[19] Ibid., pp. 47–48

[20] Ibid., pp. 53–56. In *Utah Municipal Power Systems v. Pacificorp*, 83 FERC ¶ 61,337 (1998), FERC viewed simultaneous purchase and sale transactions as a transmission service governed by open-access transmission tariff provisions.

[21] *California Filing*, pp. 54, 58.

[22] Ibid., pp. 58–61.

[23] See, e.g., *People of the State of California et al. v. Dynegy, Inc. et al.*, No. 02-16619, (9th Cir. July 6, 2004), p. 8,837.

[24] *California Filing*, pp. 62–63. *California Independent System Operator Corp.*, 86 FERC ¶ 61,122 (1999), rehearing denied, 101 FERC ¶ 61,021 (2002).

[25] *California Filing*, pp. 63–66.

[26] Ibid., pp. 66–69.

[27] Ibid., pp. 69–75.

[28] Ibid., pp. 76–77 (citing staff witness Deters in *El Paso Electric*, FERC Docket No. EL02-113-000).

[29] Ibid., pp. 84–85.

[30] Ibid., p. 104.

[31] *Energy Markets: Concerted Actions Needed by FERC to Confront Challenges That Impede Effective Oversight.* United States General Accounting Office, GAO-02-656 (June 2002), p. 13.

[32] *California Filing*, p. 111.

[33] *White Paper*, p. 33.

[34] *California Filing*, p. 113.

[35] See *In Re California Power Exch. Corp.*, 245 F.3d 1110, 1114–16 (9th Cir. 2001).

[36] *San Diego Gas & Elec. Co. v. Sellers of Energy & Ancillary Services*, 96 FERC ¶ 61,120 (2001) (hereafter *SDG&E*).

[37] *SDG&E* (slip opinion), p. 13.

[38] See, e.g., *Arkansas Louisiana Gas Co. v. Hall*, 453 U.S. 571, 577–78 (1981).

[39] *White Paper*, p. 40.

[40] *SDG&E* (slip opinion), p. 15.

[41] Ibid., p. 15; *Power Co. of America, L.P. v. FERC*, 245 F.3d 839, 846 (D.C. Cir. 2001).

[42] *SDG&E* (slip opinion), p. 29.

[43] *Request of the California Electricity Oversight Board for Expedited Rehearing of the July 25 Order Establishing Evidentiary Hearing Procedures*, FERC docket EL00-95-004 et seq. (July 30, 2001), mimeo (hereafter *CEOB Rehearing Request*), pp. 2, 13.

[44] *CEOB Rehearing Request*, p. 3. The CEOB also objected that, in relying on artificially high daily spot market natural gas prices, FERC had in effect inflated the gas component of generators' marginal costs in its calculation of the refund proxy price. Similarly, to calculate market-clearing power prices for refund purposes, FERC relied on the heat rate of the last generating unit actually dispatched, despite uncontroverted evidence that generators engaged in economic and physical withholding and foreclosed dispatch of lower cost, or more efficient, resources in order to set a higher market price. Ibid., pp. 21, 25.

[45] *Attorney General's Motion for Refunds of the California Parties*, *SDG&E*, FERC Docket Nos. EL00-95-031 et al. (July 12, 2001).

[46] These cases were removed to federal court and were ultimately dismissed as preempted by the Federal Power Act and barred by the filed-rate doctrine, based in part on FERC's exclusive jurisdiction over wholesale transactions.

[47] *State of Cal. v. British Columbia Power Exch. Corp.*, 99 FERC ¶ 61,247 (May 31, 2002).

[48] No. 02-73093 (slip opinion) (September 9, 2004).

[49] Ibid., p. 15.

[50] Ibid., p. 18.

[51] *SDG&E*, 101 FERC ¶ 63,026 (2002).

[52] *SDG&E*, 110 FERC ¶ 61,336 (2005); 109 FERC ¶ 61,218 (2004); 107 FERC ¶ 61,165 (2004); 105 FERC ¶ 61,066 (2003); 102 FERC ¶ 61,317 (2003). Petitions for review of refund proceeding orders have generally been consolidated in the Ninth Circuit Court of Appeals, with the lead docket captioned *Public Utilities Commission v. FERC*, No. 01-71051. When recalculations are finalized, FERC will order final refunds and close the refund proceeding.

[53] *Investigation of Anomalous Bidding Behavior and Practices in Western Markets*, 103 FERC ¶ 61,347 (2003).

[54] Pacific Gas & Electric Company, Southern California Edison Company, San Diego Gas & Electric Company, the State of California, ex rel. Bill Lockyer, Attorney General, the California Department of Water Resources, the California Electricity Oversight Board, and the California Public Utilities Commission.

[55] *Order Amending Market-Based Rate Tariffs and Authorizations*, 105 FERC ¶ 61,218 (2003).

[56] See, e.g., *American Elec. Power Co., Central and South West Corp.*, 90 FERC ¶ 61,242 (2000), order on rehearing, 91 FERC ¶ 61,129 (2000).

[57] In a hub-and-spoke analysis, an applicant computes its market share of both installed and uncommitted generation capacity in its control-area market and separately for each market to which it is directly interconnected (i.e., first-tier markets). While FERC did not employ a bright-line test, it used a 20% market share in each relevant market as a benchmark of the existence of market power. By 2001, FERC concluded that hub-and-spoke analysis, which worked reasonably well when market participants were vertically integrated monopolies trading on the margin, had been rendered obsolete by structural changes in the market and no longer protected customers against generation market power.

[58] *AEP Power Marketing, Inc. et al.*, 97 FERC ¶ 61,219 (November 20, 2001).

[59] The supply margin included the amount of generation capable of being imported into the control area from each first-tier market—limited, however, by the total transfer capability of the transmission system. All sales in ISO or RTO markets with approved market power mitigation measures were exempt from the SMA.

[60] Under the split-the-savings formula, a seller's incremental cost (the out-of-pocket cost of producing an additional megawatt) is compared with a buyer's decremental cost (the cost of not producing the last megawatt). The average of the incremental and decremental costs is the split-the-savings rate.

[61] Morris. "The Good, the Bad, the Ugly." *Public Utilities Fortnightly,* July 2005, p. 38. The technical conference was held on January 13–14, 2004, and focused on two fundamental proposals for change: that FERC treat any generation market power analysis as an indicative screen, rather than a definitive test, and that native-load obligations be taken into account.

[62] *Order on Rehearing and Modifying Interim Generation Market Power Analysis and Mitigation Policy,* 107 FERC ¶ 61,018 (2004).

[63] Both screens allow utilities with native-load obligations to exclude capacity dedicated to native load and therefore unavailable to the market. To account for the alternation of much utility-owned capacity between serving native load and serving the market, FERC calculates a reasonable proxy for native load: in the case of the pivotal supplier analysis, an applicant's installed capacity minus its average daily peak native load for the control area's month of highest demand; in the case of the market screen, an applicant's installed capacity minus its native-load obligation on the minimum peak demand day of the season.

[64] "Putting U.S. 'Market Power' Tests into Perspective." *ICF Perspectives 2005* (hereafter *ICF*), p. 2.

[65] *Request for Rehearing of the New Mexico Office of Attorney General et al.,* Conference on Supply Margin Assessment, FERC Docket No. PL02-8-000 (April 14, 2004), mimeo, pp. 13–14.

[66] *ICF,* p. 3.

8 Market Design

Background

Electricity restructuring in the U.S. has long been forecast and shaped by economists. Over 20 years ago, two professors at the Massachusetts Institute of Technology proposed the transfer of ownership and operation of all high-voltage transmission lines to a "regional power pooling and transmission entity" with no interest in generation.[1] Under this scenario, linkages among distribution, transmission, and generation occur across markets, rather than through internal organization. Market forces call forth appropriate quantities and types of generating capacity. Actual physical delivery of power, however, always takes place through a real-time pooling-transmission entity that dispatches generation, makes financial settlements, and provides for transmission and resale of power. More recently, market theoreticians have proposed use of spot prices in connection with direct dispatch of generation, contract networks for electric power transmission, wholesale pool spot markets, and capacity reservation open-access transmission tariffs.[2]

Control of complex interactions in a deregulated market suggested the need for a system operator to

- balance production and consumption through a voluntary bid-based real-time market;

- use least-cost redispatch of generation within transmission system limits;

- coordinate spinning reserves and reactive support for reliability purposes;

- apply locational marginal prices (LMPs) to determine the marginal cost of serving load at each system node.[3]

Within this construct, LMP reflects the price of energy at the location where it is delivered or received. Absent constraints, LMP is the same throughout the system and yields a single clearing price. When the grid is constrained, however, generation must be dispatched out of economic merit order. LMP then varies by location relative to the constraint. Congestion dictates the difference in LMP between sink and source; in other words, the cost of delivering power across a constrained path is equal to the difference in price at the path's beginning and end. (See fig. 8–1.)

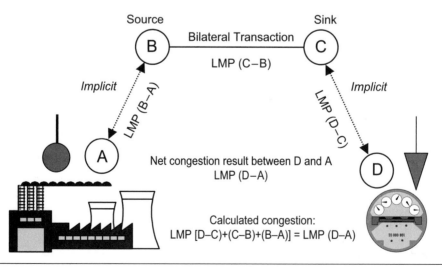

Figure 8–1. Anatomy of a Financial Bilateral Transaction[4]   *Source: PJM (2003)*

Influenced by these theoretical considerations, FERC embarked on an ambitious program to shape the structure of a deregulated electric power industry. In Order 888, issued in 1996, FERC required all public utilities owning, controlling, or operating interstate transmission facilities to provide transmission, generation, and power marketing services separately under a nondiscriminatory open-access tariff.[5] In doing so, FERC asserted jurisdiction over the rates, terms, and conditions of interstate transmission of electricity, including electricity destined for sale at retail.[6] FERC also suggested (but did not require) that vertically integrated utilities transfer control of their high voltage wires to ISOs (i.e., entities independent of utility ownership that would manage the grid and ensure equal access to essential transmission facilities).

As public utilities subject to FERC jurisdiction, ISOs were intended to decouple vertically integrated utilities' joint control of transmission and generation assets. Order 888 treats ISOs as the linchpin of market-based deregulation and prescribes general principles of organization and operation requiring that ISOs

- be independent of any market participant or class of participants (e.g., transmission owners or end users), as reflected in a representative or nonstakeholder governing board;

- provide open-access, self-scheduled transmission at non-pancaked rates under a single, unbundled, gridwide nondiscriminatory tariff;

- have primary responsibility for short-term reliability of grid operations and control the operation of transmission facilities within its service area;

- dispatch generation to regulate and balance power flows and relieve transmission constraints;

- operate an energy auction and a settlements system;

- make transmission information publicly available on a real-time basis, including information about available capacity and system constraints.

These broad principles have largely determined the functions, structure, and governance of ISOs organized following Order 888, mostly through brokered negotiations among industry stakeholders. As FERC itself recognized, however, Order 888 was simply a first step. It alone could not create competitive power markets, given the pervasive inflexibility of demand, low-price elasticity, and long lead time needed to expand supply. Competitive electricity markets require adequate supply, demand side options, and a commercial nexus between the two. To maintain balance, a system must have plentiful reserves close at hand, sufficient transmission capacity, and load that can be quickly shed. Often these conditions are not realized. Consumers cannot cut back or find substitutes for power, leaving sellers with a strong economic incentive to withhold supplies. The consequences, as the California market implosion showed, are price volatility and supply-side abuse of market power.[7]

FERC's initiative in Order 888 played out against parallel state retail competition programs, which strongly encouraged or even required utilities to separate regulated transmission and distribution functions from wholesale generation and marketing activities. Utilities in California, Massachusetts, New York, Maine, and Rhode Island divested practically all of their generating assets through an auction process, while those in Pennsylvania, Maryland, and New Jersey transferred generating assets to separate unregulated wholesale power affiliates within a holding company structure.

Each program typically unbundled retail generation from transmission and distribution services and allowed retail customers to choose among competing retail suppliers. Whether or not the affected utilities transferred or divested generating assets, they still had to sell power, at regulated prices, to retail customers who had not chosen a competitive retail supplier. The programs also mandated stranded-cost recovery and reduction of regulated retail rates during a transition period.

By 2000, retail competition programs had spread to a dozen states, and others had announced plans to implement similar programs.

State regulators anticipated that competition would reduce retail prices, passing on the benefit of cheaper wholesale power. After 2000, however, retail restructuring reversed course in the wake of the California electricity crisis, Enron's bankruptcy, the financial collapse of merchant generators and traders, widespread phantom trading, and fraudulent price reporting. Nine states with reform plans delayed, cancelled, or scaled back competition programs. The average real retail price of electricity in the U.S. for residential and industrial customers increased for the first time in 15 years.[8]

Before this reversal, unregulated merchant and nonutility generators had become an increasingly important source of supply for distribution companies and vertically integrated utilities that were required to meet incremental generation needs through wholesale market purchases. Between 1997 and 2002, merchant power comprised 80% of new generating capacity—tangible evidence, it was thought, of the impact of market-based regulatory policy. Thereafter, the merchant power and trading market went into sharp decline, and many planned facilities were cancelled or indefinitely postponed.[9]

Following Order 888, the three Northeastern power pools, as well as California, Texas, and several Midwestern states, commenced restructuring on a regional basis. In each instance, an ISO was formed to

- schedule and dispatch generation and demand on transmission networks with multiple owners;
- allocate scarce transmission capacity;
- operate voluntary real-time and day-ahead markets for energy and ancillary services;
- coordinate planning for new transmission facilities;
- monitor market performance;
- implement mitigation measures and market reforms.

Each regional market shared certain common characteristics but differed from the others in critical structural details.

PJM, which was built on the base of a tight power pool in operation since 1927, emerged as the most successful first mover among regional ISOs following Order 888. PJM operates the high-voltage transmission system in the mid-Atlantic region and runs a real-time wholesale power market that determines a market-clearing energy price for each generating unit within its control area. Using LMP, PJM settles imbalances, prices congestion for both spot and contract transactions, and procures and prices ancillary services. Because LMP enables PJM to monetize the cost of all congestion within the system, a participant need not trade actively in decentralized forward markets to harmonize its contract and real-time positions. The adjustment is instead accomplished automatically in the real-time market, which balances supply and demand.

PJM also operates day-ahead, capacity, and ancillary service markets, together with an auction-based FTR market. In the day-ahead market, PJM calculates clearing prices for each hour of the next operating day, based on generation offers, demand bids, and bilateral transaction schedules. In the real-time market, by contrast, PJM determines hourly clearing prices through actual bid-based, least-cost, security-constrained unit commitment dispatch. The day-ahead market enables participants to purchase and sell energy at binding nodal prices and schedule bilateral transactions with binding congestion charges, which can be hedged through the medium of FTRs. Separate accounting settlements are performed for each market. (See fig. 8–2.)

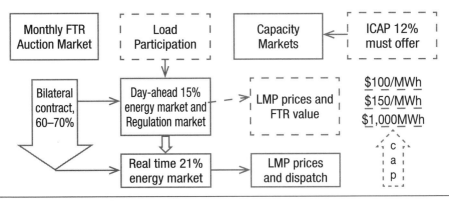

Figure 8–2. PJM Model[10]

Source: Texas PUC White Paper (2002), p. 19

Order 2000

In the wake of Order 888, FERC acknowledged that continuing impediments to competition existed. It recognized insufficient structural separation between generation and transmission, pancaked transmission rates within service areas, congestion management inadequacies, loopflow problems, and residual market power, among other factors. Within less than a decade, industry restructuring had imposed new stresses on the transmission grid, including utilities' divestiture of more than 50,000 MW of generating capacity, sharply increased power trading, and state-sponsored retail competition. Even as traffic on the grid increased, FERC did little to enhance the transmission system's load-serving and transfer capability.

To address these concerns, FERC proposed RTOs (entities similar to ISOs that would control and operate high-voltage transmission facilities within broad geographic regions, separate the merchant and transmission functions of vertically integrated utilities, and relieve transmission constraints through redispatch of generation). In Order 2000, FERC codified the organizational and operational requirements for RTOs.[11] "Our objective," it stated, "is for all transmission-owning entities in the Nation . . . to place their transmission facilities under the control of an RTO in a timely manner. . . . We expect jurisdictional utilities to form RTOs."[12] As a mechanism for separating ownership and control of transmission, RTOs were expected to reduce the incidence of discrimination and market power abuse. Although nominally voluntary, Order 2000 required that each transmission owner electing not to join an RTO justify its decision.

To receive approval as an RTO, FERC required that an applicant have four minimum characteristics:

1. *Independence.* An RTO must be independent of market participants.[13] To satisfy this requirement, neither the RTO, its employees, or any nonstakeholder directors may

have a financial interest in any market participant; the RTO's decision-making process must not be controlled by any market participant, either individually or as a class; and the RTO must have exclusive and independent authority under the Federal Power Act to propose rates, terms, and conditions of transmission service.

2. *Scope and regional configuration.* An RTO must serve a "region of sufficient scope and configuration to permit [it] to maintain reliability, effectively perform its required functions, and support efficient and non-discriminatory power markets."[14] FERC declined to prescribe RTO boundaries, leaving the matter to transmission owners and market participants.

3. *Operational authority.* An RTO must have operational authority over and coordinate security for all transmission facilities under its control to maintain system reliability and competitive parity among market participants.[15]

4. *Short-term reliability.* An RTO must have "exclusive authority for maintaining the short-term reliability of the grid that it operates."[16] To satisfy this requirement, an RTO must have "exclusive authority for receiving, confirming and implementing all interchange schedules"; the right to redispatch generation; and authority to approve or disapprove scheduled transmission outages.

Order 2000 also specified eight minimum functions of an RTO:

1. Tariff administration and design

2. Congestion management

3. Parallel path flow coordination

4. Last-resort provision of ancillary services

5. Sole determination of total and available transmission capacity posted on an open-access same-time information system (OASIS)

6. Market monitoring

7. Planning and arranging transmission expansion, additions, and upgrades

8. Interregional coordination to address seams issues

The Ramp-Up to Standard Market Design

An early applicant for approval as an RTO, PJM achieved provisional RTO status in July 2001 and became the template for FERC's later promulgation of standard market design principles.[17] More nearly so than any other candidate for RTO status, PJM embodied in practice the generic characteristics and functions identified by FERC in Order 2000. Unlike California's failed experiment, PJM worked and, in FERC's view, provided the essential blueprint for market reform nationwide.

In its Order 2000 compliance filing, PJM emphasized its independent nonstakeholder board, exclusive and independent control over tariff terms and conditions, wide scope and configuration, control of transmission facilities and short-term reliability, unbundled rates, congestion management through LMP and FTRs, and coordinated regional planning. "While PJM does not have physical control over the transmission grid," it noted, "it effectively operates the grid by way of a central control center that provides explicit operating instructions to local control centers operated by PJM members . . . [and] has 'the right to order redispatch of any generator connected to the transmission facilities it operates.'"[18] PJM also reminded FERC of its critical finding, in an earlier order confirming PJM as an ISO, that LMP "will reflect the opportunity cost of using congested transmission paths, encourage efficient use of the transmission system, and facilitate the development of competitive electric markets."[19]

With PJM as a model and under the direction of a new chairman, FERC issued a working paper in March 2002 proposing a prescriptive standard design for wholesale electric power markets. The FTC, in response, cautioned that price signals provided by LMP and *ex post* market monitoring would not be "sufficient to prevent harm to customers from the exercise of generation market power." The FTC expressed a preference for "structural remedies . . . that [preserve] incentives to invest in efficient new generation and transmission capacity," such as medium- to long-term forward contracting.[20] The FTC also advised FERC to look beyond the unilateral exercise of market power to coordinated interaction as a potential source of competitive harm.[21]

The FTC's cautionary advice was later confirmed by PJM's market-monitoring unit (MMU), which found significant market power issues in PJM's energy, capacity, and regulation markets. With respect to capacity markets, the MMU concluded that high levels of ownership concentration implied a "likelihood of the exercise of market power."[22]

Standard Market Design

Undeterred, FERC issued a proposed rule (the Standard Market Design [SMD] Rule) seeking to establish a single, standard market design for all power markets nationwide.[23] The SMD Rule, a one-size-fits-all formulation, addressed all aspects of the wholesale electricity industry, including the structure of wholesale markets, transmission ownership and operations, transmission pricing, generation and transmission planning and expansion, market power monitoring and mitigation, and governance.

Drawing heavily on PJM's experience, the SMD Rule contemplated an independent transmission provider (ITP) that would assume the functions of the ISO/RTO delineated in prior FERC orders. While managing the transmission system in a given region, the ITP would also run all wholesale power markets (day-ahead markets to coordinate generator startup and real-time spot markets to address energy imbalances), monitor market power, and assume broad responsibilities for regional transmission planning and resource adequacy. Participation in the ITP would no longer be voluntary. All FERC-jurisdictional investor-owned utilities would therefore relinquish control of their transmission assets to an ITP, a nonprofit entity with an independent board selected by a stakeholder committee of generators, transmission owners, end users, and others.

Under an open-access transmission tariff, the ITP would provide network access service, combining the principal features of network integration service (flexibility in designating load) and point-to-point transmission service (reassignability of transmission rights) as authorized by Order 888.[24] Load-serving entities (LSEs) would pay a license-plate (zonal) or postage-stamp (regional) access charge to recover embedded transmission costs, based proportionally on their respective shares of the system's total peak load.[25] The ITP would recover transmission expansion costs through rolled-in pricing on a regional basis or through participant funding for cases in which a particular entity benefits from the upgrade. It would also operate day-ahead and real-time spot energy markets, modeled on PJM's successful design; monitor those markets for "exercises of market power, flaws in . . . tariff rules or operations that contribute to economic inefficiency"; and manage congestion, using LMP and congestion revenue rights (CRRs), the analogue within the SMD Rule to PJM's FTRs.[26] The Department of Energy (DOE) forecast that SMD would confer a net benefit on all consumers of approximately $1 billion per year.[27]

To ensure resource adequacy, the ITP would forecast demand, maintain a reserve margin of at least 12%, and allocate a percentage of the reserve margin, within its service area, to each LSE, which could then procure the required capacity through self-generation or purchase from other generators. The ITP would enforce the LSE's obligation through the tariff and application of curtailment penalties.[28] The

SMD Rule relied on administrative provisions because spot market prices alone appeared insufficient to call forth new resources in time to avert a shortage. The SMD Rule made no provision for capacity markets or for transmission investment incentives.

Although far-reaching, the SMD Rule did little to refine the concept of market power—which it defined simply as the ability to raise prices above a competitive level—in part because FERC could not readily identify what constitutes a competitive price. The SMD Rule focused instead on circumstances (e.g., anomalous bidding patterns) that would lead MMUs to mitigate or forestall the exercise of market power. ISOs in California, PJM, and New England urged FERC to develop a comprehensive market power policy statement, while the New York ISO preferred to define market power in the context of specific market-monitoring proposals.[29]

Industry Reaction and FERC Response

Given its scope and top-down prescriptive nature, the SMD Rule called forth widespread criticism and more than 1,000 formal comments from state utility regulatory agencies, consumer groups, and public utilities. More than 20 states asked FERC to abandon the SMD Rule, arguing that it exceeded FERC's authority over wholesale power rates, demand forecasting, resource planning, demand-side management, and marketing. Opposition was particularly widespread in the southern and northwestern states, which feared loss of cheap power to out-of-state buyers. Consumer groups argued that the SMD Rule guaranteed neither lower prices nor reliable service and feared it would allow merchant generators to manipulate spot markets. Critics took their complaints to Congress, where the Senate Energy Committee warned FERC not to proceed with any SMD proposal before the end of 2006—and then only after issuing a new notice of proposed rule making.

In April 2003, FERC issued a white paper acknowledging the need for changes in its SMD Rule. The white paper indicated that FERC

- would not assert jurisdiction over the transmission rate component of bundled retail service;

- would not seek to change state authority over resource adequacy and regional transmission planning requirements;

- would allow regional state committees to determine how firm transmission rights should be allocated to current customers;

- would tailor implementation to each region;

- would require that each RTO tariff contain a clear transmission-cost-recovery policy;

- would abandon the requirement that public entities create or join an ITP (although requiring them to join an RTO or ISO).[30]

Major industry players nonetheless continued to oppose the SMD Rule's prescriptive one-size-fits-all approach, preferring a voluntary transition to regional competitive markets. In July 2005, FERC withdrew the SMD Rule, recognizing that it had been "overtaken by events."[31]

The SMD Rule's demise, largely driven by political opposition, was also welcomed by its economic critics, who contended it "devotes almost no attention to the issue of competitive structure" and "is entirely focused on market design and market monitoring."[32] In initial comments, the Consumer Federation of America argued that the SMD Rule "leaves markets vulnerable to the abuse of market power through two fundamental oversights": a reserve level set "far too low" (12%) and failure to deal with "vertical integration between the gas market and the electricity market," as evidenced by manipulation of natural gas prices by players in Western gas and electric markets.[33]

Such manipulation strikes at the heart of the SMD Rule, since a market clearing price in a single price auction is likely to be driven by the cost of natural gas, leaving structural separation between the natural gas and electricity markets as the only feasible way to control abuse.[34]

Other critics focused on mandated use of LMPs and FTRs, championed by the SMD Rule, which they saw as insufficient to ensure an adequate transmission infrastructure. "All the LMP/FTR system does is show which source/sink pairings create transmission congestion," wrote the American Public Power Association. Moreover, "RTOs themselves do not have the ability to construct transmission facilities," whose transmission owner members may have reasons of their own to oppose construction of new wires needed to alleviate congestion, including "pricing structures that impact the cost of serving their own loads, and, in some instances, protecting their own generation from wholesale competition."[35]

While FERC's ambitious initiative failed, PJM, on whose design the SMD Rule was largely based, has continued to thrive:

- Serving 51 million customers and with over 130,000 MW of peak load, PJM operates the largest centrally dispatched control area in North America, including all or parts of Delaware, Illinois, Indiana, Kentucky, Maryland, Michigan, New Jersey, North Carolina, Ohio, Pennsylvania, Tennessee, Virginia, West Virginia, and the District of Columbia.

- With 160,000 MW of generating capacity, more than 1,000 generating sources, and 56,000 miles of transmission lines, PJM runs the world's largest competitive wholesale electricity market (including day-ahead and real-time components) and has completed $28 billion of energy and energy-service trades since 1997.

- PJM coordinates the continuous buying, selling, and delivery of wholesale electricity, balances the requirements of suppliers, wholesale customers, and other market participants, and monitors market activities. PJM uses LMP to reflect the value of energy at the specific location and time it is delivered. In the real-time market, PJM calculates nodal LMPs at five-minute intervals on the basis of actual grid operating conditions. In the day-ahead market, it calculates hourly LMPs for the next operating day on the basis of generation offers, demand bids, and bilateral transactions. Market participants in PJM use FTRs—entitling the holder to a stream of revenue based on day-ahead hourly scheduled energy price differences across the transmission path—as a hedge against price risk when delivering energy.

- To ensure continued system reliability, PJM also manages a sophisticated regional planning process for generation and transmission expansion.

In 2003, the Center for Advancement of Energy Markets (CAEM), a nonprofit think tank, reported $28.5 billion in expected future consumer savings from PJM's restructured markets:

> The benefits from restructuring in the PJM region result from improving market efficiency. . . . The incentives inherent in the auction market encourage cost reduction relative to the incentives inherent in traditional utility regulation.[36]

Observations

PJM's success can be attributed to superior technology, good management, independent governance, and viable market structure—all empirically tested and refined over time with constant feedback from regulators and market participants. In contrast, the SMD Rule, although based on PJM's experience, ignored political realities and historic regional differences, placed undue weight on conceptual design, and did not adequately account for endemic structural concerns, including residual market power, covert discrimination, and continued monopoly leverage.[37]

Notes

[1] Joskow and Schmalensee. *Markets for Power: An Analysis of Electric Utility Deregulation.* MIT Press (1983), pp. 104–5.

[2] See Hogan. *Successful Market Design ("SMD") and Electricity Markets.* International Energy Agency Workshop on Transmission Network Reliability in Competitive Electricity Markets. Paris (March 29–30, 2004), pp. 3-4.

[3] Hogan. *FERC Policy on Regional Transmission Organizations: Comments in Response to the Notice of Proposed Rulemaking,* FERC Docket No. RM99-2-000 (August 16, 1999).

[4] Laughlin. *LMP Overview (PJM).* Internal PJM instructional document (January 8, 2003), p. 29.

[5] *Federal Energy Regulatory Commission Final Rule Promoting Wholesale Competition Through Open-Access Non-Discriminatory Transmission Services by Public Utilities,* Order No. 888, 61 *Federal Register* 21,450 (May 10, 1996) (codified at 18 *Code of Federal Regulations,* pts. 35, 385) (hereafter *Order 888*).

[6] FERC's assertion of jurisdiction, which did not apply to bundled retail sales of electricity, was upheld in *New York et al. v. FERC,* 535 U.S. 1 (2002).

[7] *Initial Comments of the Consumer Federation of America and Consumers Union, Remedying Undue Discrimination through Open Access Transmission Service and Standard Electricity Market Design,* FERC Docket No. RM01-12-000 (November 14, 2002), mimeo (hereafter *Consumer Federation Comments*), pp. 5–9.

[8] *Erecting Sandcastles from Numbers: The CAEM Study of Restructuring Electricity Markets.* National Rural Electric Cooperation Association white paper (December 3, 2003) (hereafter *NRECA White Paper*), p. 6.

[9] Ibid., p. 4.

[10] *A Primer on Wholesale Market Design: Market Oversight Division White Paper.* Public Utility Commission of Texas (2002), p. 19. For general background, see Lambert. *Creating Competitive Power Markets: The PJM Model.* PennWell Publishing (2001).

[11] *Federal Energy Regulatory Commission Final Rule on Regional Transmission Organizations,* Order No. 2000, 65 *Federal Register* 810 (January 6, 2000) (codified at 18 *Code of Federal Regulations* § 35.34) (hereafter *Order 2000*).

[12] *Order 2000.*

[13] 18 *Code of Federal Regulations* § 35.34(j)(1) (2002).

[14] 18 *Code of Federal Regulations* § 35.34(j)(2).

[15] 18 *Code of Federal Regulations* § 35.34(j)(3).

[16] 18 *Code of Federal Regulations* § 35.34(j)(4).

[17] *PJM Interconnection, L.L.C.,* 96 FERC ¶ 61,061 (July 12, 2001). PJM received official approval as an RTO in December 2002.

[18] PJM Interconnection, L.L.C. *Order No. 2000 Compliance Filing* (October 11, 2000), mimeo, pp. 31–33.

[19] Ibid., p. 41.

[20] *Comment of the Staff of the Bureau of Economics and the Office of the General Counsel of the Federal Trade Commission,* FERC Docket No. RM01-12-000 (July 23, 2002), pp. 3, 7.

[21] Ibid., p. 5.

[22] PJM Market Monitoring Unit. *2004 State of the Market Report* (March 8, 2005), pp. 20–21, 33.

[23] Federal Energy Regulatory Commission Proposed Rule, *Remedying Undue Discrimination Through Open Access Transmission Service and Standard Electricity Market Design,* 67 *Federal Register* 55,452 (August 29, 2002) (hereafter *SMD Rule*).

[24] Ibid., at 55,471–75.

[25] Ibid., at 55,476–77. The costs of transmission system expansions would be recovered through rolled-in pricing (general benefit) or participant funding (particular generator).

[26] Ibid., at 55,487, 55, 530.

[27] U.S. Department of Energy. *Report to Congress: Impacts of the Federal Energy Regulatory Commission's Proposal for Standard Market Design* (April 30, 2003), p. 20.

[28] *SMD Rule*, at 55,514.

[29] *Energy Markets: Additional Actions Would Help Ensure That FERC's Oversight and Enforcement Capability Is Comprehensive and Systematic.* United States Government Accounting Office, GAO-03-845 (August 2003), pp. 12–13.

[30] *Wholesale Power Market Platform White Paper,* FERC Docket No. RM01-12-000 (April 28, 2003).

[31] *Order Terminating Proceeding,* FERC Docket No. RM01-12-000 (July 19, 2005).

[32] *Consumer Federation Comments,* p. 43.

[33] Ibid.

[34] Ibid., pp. 43–44.

[35] American Public Power Association. *Restructuring at the Crossroads: FERC Electric Policy Reconsidered* (December 2004), pp. 10–11.

[36] Center for Advancement of Energy Markets. *Estimating the Benefits of Restructuring Electricity Markets: An Application to the PJM Region* (September 2003) (hereafter *CAEM Report*), p. 8. This report was challenged by the National Rural Electric Cooperation Association: "The Study's quantitative analysis merely finds that prices in the high-cost PJM region fell by more than did the prices of some of its low-cost neighbors during a recent 5-year period, and that they will fall in the future when certain stranded costs are fully amortized. The Study's quantitative results fail to demonstrate any relationship between the price changes and the economic effects of restructuring." *NRECA White Paper,* pp. iii–iv.

[37] See, e.g., *Preventing Undue Discrimination and Preference in Transmission Services,* FERC Notice of Inquiry dated September 16, 2005, Docket No. RM05-25-000, 70 *Federal Register* 55,796 (September 23, 2005).

9 Changing the Ground Rules

Energy Policy Act

The Energy Policy Act of 2005, the first comprehensive national energy legislation in 13 years, will have a profound impact on electric and natural gas markets. Among other changes, the Energy Policy Act has

- repealed PUHCA, a 70-year-old law regulating public utility holding companies;

- increased criminal and civil penalties for manipulative trading practices in power and natural gas markets;

- revised FERC's merger review authority;

- granted FERC backstop transmission-siting authority;

- established an electric reliability organization to set and enforce mandatory reliability standards;

- authorized incentive-based transmission rates;

- addressed knotty industry issues such as electricity market transparency, economic dispatch, and native-load service obligations.

PUHCA Repeal

PUHCA was enacted following the collapse, in the early years of the Depression, of hugely leveraged unregulated utility holding companies that resulted in over 50 bankruptcies and enormous investor losses. To address recurrent abuses—pyramiding, misallocation of costs, excessive debt, and abusive affiliate transactions—PUHCA placed utility holding companies under SEC control, prohibited them from owning nonutility businesses or operating noncontiguous systems, and required SEC approval before they could issue securities, acquire assets, or engage in transactions with affiliates. In the absence of an exemption, PUHCA applied to any company that owned, controlled, or held with power to vote 10% or more of the outstanding voting securities of a public utility and prohibited any person, without prior SEC approval, from acquiring 5% or more of the voting securities of a public utility if it already held more than 5% of another public utility (the so-called two-bite rule).

PUHCA therefore constituted a powerful restraint on utility de-integration, mergers and acquisitions, and diversification into nonutility businesses. Although only a handful of electric and three gas utility holding companies were directly subject to PUHCA's restrictions, more than 150 holding companies otherwise exempt from PUHCA as intrastate operators, were vigilant in avoiding any action that would subject them to SEC regulation.[1] In addition, to avoid holding company regulation, investors in the public utility sector had to employ dauntingly complex ownership structures, such as those Berkshire Hathaway used when it recently acquired an 81% equity interest in MidAmerican Energy Holding Company, only 9.9% of which was voting stock, and arranged for individuals, including a member of its board, to hold the balance of the voting interest.[2]

As a result of PUHCA repeal, utility subsidiaries need not be geographically integrated with or functionally related to the public utility business of the holding company, SEC approval of a utility's acquisition of nonutility businesses is no longer required, and there is no regulatory requirement for simplified corporate and capital structures. Similarly, preexisting SEC financing standards and restrictions on interlocking directorates no longer apply.[3] Also eliminated are requirements for SEC approval of and cost limitations on contracts for construction or sales of goods or services within a holding company system.

According to Fitch, a leading bond rating service,

> Repeal paves the way for mergers of utilities that do not operate as a single, integrated system . . ., acquisitions of utilities by companies from outside the industry . . ., [and formation of] more gas/electric multi-utilities.[4]

Fitch associates heightened merger and acquisition activity with "rating degradation . . ., higher merger premia . . ., more debt-financed merger transactions," and an "attendant increase in event risk for utilities."[5]

Long sought by the utility industry, PUHCA repeal is expected to invite a new wave of utility diversification and consolidation. Although FERC has assumed certain oversight functions from the SEC, the reach of its authority is uncertain.[6] Apart from its merger review authority (discussed in the following sections), the locus of FERC's regulatory power over utility holding companies, as modified by the Energy Policy Act, involves review of books and records—a right described by consumer advocates as "virtually meaningless" when applied to "conglomerates the size of GE, ExxonMobil, JPMorgan Chase, and Berkshire Hathaway in the off chance that FERC could discover whether these vast conglomerates have affiliates whose activities have in any way affected their affiliated utility's rates."[7]

When a utility holding company acquires or establishes a nonutility affiliate, the affiliate may shift risk to the public utility by charging the utility above-market transfer prices for goods and services, misallocating common administrative, capital, or operating costs, and using the utility's assets or revenue streams as collateral for upstream or affiliate loans or guarantees. Such cross-subsidies often leave a paper trail of interest to regulators.

Sections 1264 and 1275 of the Energy Policy Act therefore give FERC access to the books and records of public utilities and affiliated entities to review cost allocations for an affiliate's provision of nonpower goods or services, effectively reversing a federal court decision that conferred exclusive oversight responsibility for such matters on the SEC.[8] FERC regards its new powers as supplemental to existing authority under the Federal Power Act and the Natural Gas Act "to protect customers against improper cross-subsidization or encumbrances of public utility assets" by obtaining the books and records of regulated companies. To this end, FERC has adopted the accounting, cost-allocation, and record-keeping rules previously applied by the SEC.[9] FERC has also been urged to use its access authority "as necessary to . . . its consumer-protection responsibilities," including review of corporate relationships and transactions within holding company structures.[10]

Notwithstanding the Energy Policy Act's grant of authority, holding companies that own power projects operated as QFs, exempt wholesale generators (EWGs), or foreign utility companies have no obligation to make their books and records available to FERC unless those entities are also classified as public utilities.[11] In that event, they will remain subject to FERC's books and records and rate-making authority under the Federal Power Act.[12]

Although PUHCA repeal leaves state regulators with the power to monitor jurisdictional utility financial records, the Energy Policy Act makes state access contingent on prior identification of specific records in a proceeding before the state public utility commission. Such access is essential if regulators are to detect and prevent abusive affiliate transactions and cross-subsidies. While nearly all state commissions have generic authority over such matters, substantive ring-fencing restrictions designed to protect utility affiliates from financial abuse are not common.

Oregon and Wisconsin are among a handful of jurisdictions that have in place rules intended to prevent inequitable reallocation of risk and, if necessary, compel divestiture as a remedy. Such rules typically

- prohibit a utility from lending money to or guaranteeing the obligations of a holding company or its nonutility affiliates;

- limit nonutility investments to a specified percentage of public utility assets;

- require commission approval of utility security issuances;

- impose minimum equity requirements;

- require state commission approval of mergers, consolidations, or takeovers by anyone owning more than 10% of the utility's outstanding securities;[13]

State commissions may also condition merger approval on:

- compliance with reporting and information access requirements;

- restrictions on intracorporate transactions resulting in direct charges or cost allocations;

- preclusion of the local utility's assumption of premium, transaction, or merger transition costs;

- restrictions on a holding company's access to a local utility's power, natural gas assets, and customer information.[14]

Given postrepeal concerns about a regulatory vacuum, certain states (California, Maryland, Kansas, and New Jersey) are also contemplating the need for further regulation modeled on PUHCA. The California Public Utilities Commission, for one, has announced that it "will re-examine the relationships of major energy utilities with their parent holding companies and affiliates" and "consider whether new rules or regulations are needed."[15]

Merger Review Authority

Although most utility mergers have over time proven unsuccessful, utility managements continue to see them as growth opportunities that confer financial rewards through acquisition of new capacity and synergy-related savings.[16] The Energy Policy Act of 1992 and FERC orders promoting market-based regulation encouraged mergers and acquisitions during the 1990s. The prevailing corporate mantra was "growth through diversification." Electric utilities combined with other utilities, gas pipelines, natural gas companies, and independent power producers. They also bought or built merchant generating assets, which were later sold or moved to unregulated affiliates pursuant to state restructuring laws.

- Between 1997 and 2000, electric utilities completed over 40 mergers.

- In 2000 alone, assets of utility mergers totaled $260 billion.

- Between 1999 and 2002, utilities transferred the 160,000 MW of generating capacity from regulated ownership, 90% of which was sold or divested to unregulated affiliates of investor-owned utilities.[17]

The California energy crisis and exposure of Enron's market-rigging activities had a profound impact on the energy trading sector, causing an asset sell-off as companies sought to raise cash and avoid bankruptcy. Between 2002 and mid-2004, merger activity came to a virtual halt but has since sharply rebounded (e.g., MidAmerican Energy Holdings/Pacificorp [$10 billion in annual revenues], Duke Energy/Cinergy [$25 billion in annual revenues], Exelon Corp./ PSEG [$25 billion in annual revenues], and PNM Resources/ TNP Enterprises). Given PUHCA repeal, further consolidation of the utility industry can be seen as a threat to competitive markets. Approval of the Exelon/PSEG merger, for example, would create the nation's largest electric utility—controlling over half the generating capacity in PJM-East, the regional electricity market, and owning

40% of firm natural gas supply capacity in the Philadelphia–northern New Jersey region, where gas-fired generation often sets the price of electricity.[18]

Using its merger review authority in this and similar cases, FERC has been called on "to forestall increased concentration of generation ownership, greater opportunities for the exercise of market power and affiliate abuse, potentially uneconomic mergers, and deteriorating financial health of core public utility companies."[19] To analyze a merger's impact on competition, FERC relies, in principle, on the DOJ/FTC Horizontal Merger Guidelines. Although they address five primary areas—concentration, competitive effects, entry, efficiencies, and potential exit of assets—FERC has applied the guidelines mechanically, measuring market concentration by formula and ignoring other criteria, as in the proposed Exelon-PSEG merger, where it found that "by restoring [the market concentration index] to the pre-merger levels, Applicants will restore competition to the pre-merger level and meet their burden to show that the merger, as mitigated, will not harm competition in wholesale energy markets."[20] In so finding, FERC accorded no weight to the possibility that a seller with market share below a formula threshold can still raise prices above competitive levels by strategic bidding and withholding output.

Under prior policy, FERC measured utility consolidation against the public interest standard in Section 203 of the Federal Power Act and considered a proposed transaction's effect on competition, rates, and regulation.[21] Section 1289 of the Energy Policy Act amends Section 203(a) by

- prohibiting a utility, without FERC authorization and for values over $10 million, from (i) selling, leasing, or otherwise disposing of all or any part of its FERC jurisdictional facilities; (ii) merging or consolidating those facilities with those of another person; (iii) purchasing, acquiring, or taking any security of any other public utility; or (iv) purchasing, leasing, or otherwise acquiring an existing wholesale generation facility subject to FERC's rate making authority;

- prohibiting a holding company within a system that includes a transmitting or electric utility, without first obtaining FERC's authorization and for values over $10 million, from purchasing, acquiring, or taking any security of or merging or consolidating with a transmitting or electric utility or holding company system that includes same;
- requiring that FERC notify the governor and state commission of each state where physical property affected by the proposed merger is located;
- requiring that FERC issue rules implementing its amended merger authority.

Under Section 1289 of the Energy Policy Act, FERC must approve a proposed disposition, consolidation, acquisition, or change of control if the proposed transaction is consistent with the public interest and will not result in cross-subsidization or encumbrance of utility assets to benefit a nonutility associate company unless FERC finds such cross-subsidization or encumbrance in the public interest.

As FERC has noted, however, Section 1289 provides no guidance as to how it should determine whether a proposed transaction will result in cross-subsidization or encumbrance contrary to the public interest. Historically, FERC has sought to guard against such concerns when reviewing applications for cost-based or market-based rate authority under Section 205 of the Federal Power Act or dispositions of jurisdictional facilities under Section 203.[22] In that context, FERC's primary concern has been to monitor a possible transfer of benefits from a traditional public utility's captive customers to shareholders of its holding company by reviewing prudently incurred costs, imposing conditions on market-based rate authorizations, and auditing utilities' books and records.[23]

Nonetheless, individual rate proceedings are at best a *post hoc* means of addressing structural problems, ill suited to an era of intensified merger activity:

> The regulatory goal should be to prevent the problem, rather than allow it to fester and then upon emergence trace after-the-fact all of its effects, assign blame and impose penalties.[24]

FERC's authority to *condition* mergers is therefore the preferred means of protecting the public interest—a rubric that includes just and reasonable rates, adherence to antitrust principles, and unimpaired reliability of the nation's electric infrastructure. In reviewing the antitrust implications of proposed horizontal mergers, however, FERC must now go beyond conventional market concentration analysis to assess *cross-country* transactions, which unite geographically remote electric utility partners but lack markets common to both applicants.[25]

For mergers raising cross-subsidization or affiliate abuse concerns, FERC has in the past sought to insulate wholesale utility customers from risks associated with affiliates' nonutility businesses. Such protection requires that a public utility and its non-utility affiliates be kept legally separate and distinct, without commingling assets and liabilities, reallocating nonutility affiliates' operating losses or financing costs, or facilitating utility loans to its nonutility affiliates. To do so, FERC can impose substantive preconditions, such as the Westar Energy restrictions imposed on future issuances of utility debt securities under Section 204 of the Federal Power Act,[26] and require that public utility holding companies, whether formerly registered or exempted under PUHCA, file cost-allocation and interaffiliate agreements affecting jurisdictional rates.[27] Whether FERC will have the requisite political will remains an open question.

Electricity Market Transparency, Manipulation, and Enforcement

As California's example shows, wholesale power markets can be opaque, fraudulently rigged in favor of pivotal suppliers, and operated on false information. In response to massive manipulation of Western power markets, FERC issued an order in 2003 requiring that sellers under market-based tariffs comply with specific behavioral rules.[28] Although a plausible response to market dysfunction, the order was just a first step toward the eventual statutory overhaul accomplished by the Energy Policy Act.

Market transparency

Competitive markets presuppose timely availability of price information for multiple and interrelated products, including energy (both day ahead and real time), natural gas, reserves (spinning and quick start), regulation, transmission, and capacity. RTOs publish day-ahead and spot market energy prices but provide no information on bilateral forward contracts, as to which market participants typically rely on brokers who post bid and ask prices for standardized blocks of power for various time periods. Neither RTOs nor private indexing companies capture information on long-term contracts. FERC's "Electric Quarterly Reports" reflect voluminous transaction information collected from industry players but do not format the information for easy use or accessibility.[29]

Section 1281 of the Energy Policy Act directs FERC "to facilitate price transparency" in wholesale power markets. Section 316 contains the equivalent directive for natural gas markets. To comply, FERC will use newly acquired power to obtain price information from market participants, publishers, and trade processing services and issue rules requiring its public dissemination. FERC has also reached an information-sharing agreement with the CFTC, whose exclusive jurisdiction under the Commodity Exchange Act continues.[30] In support of FERC's price-transparency mandate, Section 1282 amends the Federal Power Act to prohibit fraudulent reporting of false information relating to wholesale electric prices or transmission availability to a federal agency.

Manipulation

To fill a void in the regulation of market-based trading activity, Sections 315 and 1283 of the Energy Policy Act amend the Natural Gas Act and Federal Power Act to prohibit use or employment of any "manipulative or deceptive device or contrivance" in connection with the purchase or sale of natural gas, electric energy, or related transportation or transmission services subject to FERC's jurisdiction, antimanipulation provisions that closely track Section 10(b) of the Securities Exchange Act of 1934 and serve as the basis for FERC's own regulations.[31] Noting the "vast body of Section 10(b) case law," FERC observes that the Energy Policy Act's incorporation of an equivalent provision "provides substantial certainty" and renders its antifraud rules consistent with those enforced by the SEC and CFTC.[32] FERC's new rules also apply to "any entity," not simply jurisdictional market-based rate sellers, natural gas pipelines, or holders of blanket certificates.[33]

Edison Electric Institute (EEI), which represents investor-owned utilities, reflects industry reservations about FERC's unqualified adoption of Section 10(b) jurisprudence.

> The electric industry and its regulation have as an underpinning commercial contracts for the provision of goods and services, in contrast to the securities industry where regulation focuses on the provision of complete and accurate information and dissemination of knowledge. In transactions in wholesale electricity markets, it is difficult to envision what information would have to accompany a bid to either buy or sell, other than the nature of the product, the price and quantity offered and the timeframe in which the product is available. . . . In bilateral contractual negotiations in wholesale energy markets, each party is pursuing private interests. Neither

> fully shares with the other the full nature and extent of those interests and the information they possess. . . . In an obvious example, one party may have price curves or other knowledge that indicates future shortages and price increases, while the other may believe that supply and prices will remain stable. *It is not the responsibility of either party to disabuse the other of his or her beliefs by sharing confidential and proprietary information. . . . Once the basics of a transaction in terms of price, firmness, duration, etc. are communicated accurately, a party should have no other affirmative disclosure obligation to its counterparty.*[34]

EEI's caveat emptor comments signal strong industry resistance to FERC's application of Section 10(b) to energy transactions and the likelihood that its antifraud rules will be tested in court.[35]

As collateral support for its new antifraud authority, FERC continues to rely on existing market behavior rules, which establish guidelines for jurisdictional market-based rate sellers in wholesale power markets and wholesale sellers of natural gas under blanket certificates. Unlike generic antifraud rules based on Section 10(b), FERC's behavioral rules address industry-specific circumstances, prohibiting "actions or transactions that are without a legitimate business purpose and that are intended to or foreseeably could manipulate market prices, market conditions, or market rules for electric energy or electricity products."[36] The behavioral rules also expressly prohibit wash trades, transactions predicated on false information, creation and relief of artificial congestion, and collusion.[37]

The behavioral rules reflect FERC's underlying concern that the transmission system serving bulk power markets is flawed. In a Notice of Inquiry issued in September 2005, FERC observed that "it is in the economic self-interest of transmission monopolists, particularly those with high-cost generation assets, to deny transmission or to offer transmission on a basis that is inferior to that which they provide themselves."[38] The nexus between generation and transmission in vertically integrated utilities has "proven problematic for transmission access by new generators and new load-serving entities" since utilities have both the "discretion and incentive to interpret and apply [tariff] provisions . . . in a manner that can result in unduly discriminatory behavior."[39] During peak load periods in particular, FERC found, such discrimination reduces available transfer capability and increases denials, interruptions, and curtailments of service. To address these problems, FERC has looked beyond behavioral rules and is considering changes in the pricing and nature of tariffed transmission services, additional penalties for tariff violations, and mandatory joint transmission planning.[40]

Enforcement

To enforce the statutes it administers (namely, Federal Power Act, Natural Gas Act, and NGPA), FERC can order disgorgement of unjust profits; condition, suspend, or revoke previously authorized rates; or refer matters to the DOJ for criminal prosecution.[41] FERC's authority to assess civil penalties for statutory violations, which was greatly enhanced by the Energy Policy Act, now covers violations of Part II of the Federal Power Act (as well as any rule or order thereunder) and violations of the Natural Gas Act (and all rules and orders thereunder). FERC has been empowered to assess civil penalties up to $1 million per violation for each day that it continues.[42]

To implement its enhanced civil penalty authority, FERC will not, following SEC and CFTC practice, prescribe specific penalties, develop formulas for different violations, or refrain from ordering other sanctions, such as disgorgement of unjust profits or revocation of market-based rates. In assessing the gravity of a violation, FERC will determine the harm caused and whether it was willful, a repeat offense, or the result of manipulation or fraud. Possible mitigating factors include internal compliance, self-reporting, and cooperation.[43]

Enhancement of FERC's enforcement powers, while long overdue, will not itself deter manipulation so long as electricity and gas markets are not competitive. Market structure shapes commercial behavior. It often determines who can exercise market power and under what circumstances. Given high-demand conditions and transmission constraints, as we have seen, a supplier can exert market power in specific locations while controlling only marginal capacity. To be effective, top-down legal reform must therefore be accompanied by parallel improvements in market structure and system capacity.

Economic Dispatch, Native Load, and Locational Installed Capacity

Although FERC's standard market design initiative failed, the Energy Policy Act embeds similar structural features. It

- establishes an Electric Energy Market Competition Task Force to study the "critical elements for effective wholesale and retail competition";[44]

- extends open access beyond investor-owned utilities to include municipally and cooperatively owned utilities;[45]

- directs FERC to convene regional state-FERC joint boards to make recommendations concerning "security constrained economic dispatch" (PJM's principal operating characteristic);[46]

- amends the Federal Power Act to entitle load-serving entities (i.e., distribution utilities or other electric utilities with a service obligation) to use firm transmission rights in serving native load (i.e., retail customers the utility is required to serve by law or contract);

- requires FERC to issue an order or rule promoting long-term transmission rights as a means of facilitating transmission planning and expansion.[47]

The Energy Policy Act also addresses a pending market structure controversy posed by ISO New England's proposed use of locational installed capacity (LICAP) methodology to operate its capacity market.[48] Historically, under cost-based regulation, vertically integrated utilities provided energy and capacity to loads they served, recovering their costs and a return on investment in approved rates. This system allowed utilities to pass the related costs of capital investment in new generation capacity to customers through increased rates but eventually led to excess capacity and cost overruns. Following deregulation, ISOs and RTOs developed markets for discrete energy products, including capacity markets that allow retail load-serving utilities to buy—and generators to sell—capacity credits to create financial incentives for development of new generation resources and to maintain adequate reserve margins.[49]

By placing a tradable commodity value—a capacity credit—on the availability of new generation capacity, a market mechanism can be used to call forth the capital investment necessary to serve forecasted system peak load plus a required reserve margin (ICAP). For this purpose, a regional capacity market coordinator presides over periodic auctions of capacity credits, implements applicable market rules, and sets the ICAP requirement for a service area, as adjusted for generation reliability. The resulting requirement is then allocated proportionally among incumbent load-serving entities, each of which can meet its allocated service obligation by bidding for capacity credits at auction, acquiring capacity pursuant to negotiated bilateral contracts with sellers, installing new capacity, or some combination of the foregoing.

In capacity market auctions, buyers and sellers submit price and quantity bids for the capacity they are willing to buy or sell. The capacity market coordinator then determines the capacity credit price where relevant supply and demand curves intersect.[50] Demand curves, however, are administratively determined, not market-based, and are designed to produce capacity payments for both new and existing resources equivalent to the cost of new resource entry (using gas-fired generation as a proxy).

In regions with retail access where RTOs or ISOs use locational marginal pricing, load-serving entities have often proved unwilling or unable to enter into long-term contracts for new generation resources without assurance of adequate future loads to support such obligations. Operators of existing generation units in transmission-constrained areas have also threatened to shut down unless they receive revenues at or above a certain threshold. Demand curves have been adjusted to accommodate such concerns, provoking criticism that capacity payments grant windfall profits to existing generators and unnecessarily increase costs to ratepayers.[51]

ISO New England's capacity market, like its counterparts in New York and PJM, uses an administratively set demand curve that includes an estimated price for new entry (estimated benchmark capacity cost), the long-term average amount of capacity desired, the maximum quantity of capacity resources that will receive compensation, an upper limit on prices, and the quantity of capacity resources to be paid the maximum price. (See fig. 9–1.) In a 2004 filing at FERC, ISO New England also proposed to establish five separate capacity zones, each with its own demand curve and locational requirement, to account for transmission congestion in calculations of needed capacity levels—an initiative intended to attract generating capacity to underserved locations.

ISO New England's proposed LICAP system drew heavy opposition from stakeholders, who viewed it as providing a subsidy to generators while subjecting consumers to billions in incremental capital costs. Most of the economic benefit transferred from ratepayers, critics said, would go to owners of existing generating plants with fully recovered costs, rather than to developers of new capacity.[53] FERC nonetheless found ISO New England's demand-curve approach to be just and reasonable (while leaving its technical parameters open to further litigation).[54] In response to this unresolved controversy, Section 1236 of the Energy Policy Act directs FERC to carefully consider objections that ISO New England's LICAP system will not provide adequate assurance of improved reserve capacity or reliability commensurate with the subsidized costs it imposes on ratepayers.

Transmission Siting and Incentives

To finance and build the nation's high-voltage transmission grid, the electricity industry relies on vertically integrated utilities whose investment in transmission has declined consistently for more than three decades. Although the volume of transmission transactions has increased sharply in recent years, transmission capacity today lags significantly behind new generation.[55] Several factors explain this critical infrastructure deficit, among them lengthy and uncertain transmission-siting proceedings at state and local levels, regulated returns on transmission investment that many utilities deem inadequate, and utilities' disinclination to build new transmission facilities that would expose their generation capacity to greater competition.[56] Whatever the underlying cause, transmission inadequacy often translates into system congestion, underserved load pockets, subsidized must-run generation facilities, price spikes, and higher consumer costs.

Transmission siting

Siting transmission lines has historically been a state responsibility, governed by state law. Typically, a utility must demonstrate to a siting authority, usually the state public utility commission, that the proposed transmission facility is needed and will serve the public interest. The process is usually contested and involves numerous stakeholders. The siting authority has to consider cost, rates, environmental impact, property rights, and possible nontransmission alternatives. It often acts without according full weight to out-of-state benefits and in one state (Mississippi) is prohibited by law from doing so. With the advent of regional bulk-power markets, the state-based regime for permitting new transmission projects is seen as an impediment to rational transmission planning.[57]

To address the transmission siting problem, Section 1221 of the Energy Policy Act creates a new provision of the Federal Power Act, Section 216, under which

- the DOE must within one year conduct a study of transmission congestion, in consultation with affected states, and may designate a congested area as a "national interest electric transmission corridor" (except within the Texas borders);

- the DOE, acting as lead agency, must coordinate and set deadlines for all federal permits, authorizations, and approvals required in order to site a transmission facility, prepare a single environmental review document under federal law, enter into a memorandum of understanding with the heads of all relevant federal agencies, Indian tribes, multistate entities, and state agencies to coordinate transmission review and permitting, and issue implementing regulations;

- FERC may exercise backstop siting authority, by issuing permits for construction or modification of transmission facilities in a national interest electric transmission corridor, if it finds that (i) a state regulator does not have siting authority; (ii) the permit applicant, although a transmitting utility under federal law, does not qualify for a permit under state law because it does not serve end-use customers; (iii) the state has withheld approval for more than one year after the later of the filing of an application or the designation of a national-interest electric transmission corridor or has conditioned approval so that the proposed project will not significantly reduce congestion or is not economically feasible; and (iv) the proposed project will significantly reduce interstate transmission congestion and benefit consumers, while maximizing existing transmission capacity;

- permit holders are empowered to obtain necessary rights-of-way through eminent domain proceedings in federal district courts;

- three or more contiguous states are permitted to enter into an interstate compact establishing regional agencies for the purpose of siting future transmission facilities, in which event FERC is precluded from using its backstop authority unless the members disagree or take more than one year to reach approval.

To implement its new statutory powers, FERC will have to develop a transmission permitting process from scratch. Before issuing any transmission siting permit, it will also be required to conduct a National Environmental Policy Act review. Because such reviews can extend for the length of the permitting process, the Energy Policy Act wisely gives the DOE sole responsibility for preparing the single environmental review document to be used as the basis for federal decisions.[58] Not surprisingly, state regulators view the prospect of federal preemption implicit in FERC's backstop authority as a severe limitation on state sovereignty and see regional siting commissions as more likely to take into account local benefits, burdens, and costs.[59]

Incentive-based transmission rates

Section 1241 of the Energy Policy Act creates a new provision of the Federal Power Act, Section 219, requiring that FERC provide incentives for construction of transmission infrastructure by authorizing higher transmission rates. In this way, the Energy Policy Act seeks to increase investment in new transmission capacity, thereby mitigating congestion and reducing the cost of delivered power.[60]

It is unclear whether incentive-based transmission rates will have this result. Higher wholesale transmission rates, realized only when a line is placed in service, will not by themselves provide the cash flow required in order to construct new transmission facilities, reduce siting problems, or serve as an incentive to utility sellers presently receiving higher electricity prices because of the very congestion new transmission is intended to relieve. Once incurred, moreover, increased wholesale transmission charges will simply be passed on, without state regulatory review, to load-serving entities that will in turn include the charges as a cost component in their retail rates for both bundled and unbundled services. The primary purchasers of FERC-approved wholesale transmission services, municipal and cooperative transmission-dependent utilities, will absorb the increased cost directly.[61]

Critics have called incentive-based transmission rates a "blunt-edged tool" and have urged FERC to consider other, more focused incentives, including formula rates that track current costs and rates that permit current recovery (rather than capitalization) of prudently incurred precertification expenses and interest on construction funds (construction work in progress).[62] To this end, the Energy Policy Act permits allocation of transmission upgrade costs to the primary beneficiary thereof without burdening native-load customers (Section 1241) and private investment in federal transmission systems (Western Area Power Administration and Southwestern Power Administration) (Section 1222).

Long-term transmission rights

Under Section 1233 of the Energy Policy Act, FERC must issue a final rule requiring long-term transmission rights (LTTRs) in organized electricity markets that will provide the equivalent of firm transmission at a known price for a period of years. By pairing LTTRs with base-load generating units, load-serving entities would be able to offer an all-in delivered price for power for a specific term and would agree to pay a share of the RTO's fixed transmission costs, including network upgrades.[63]

Reliability

Section 1211 of the Energy Policy Act creates a new provision of the Federal Power Act, Section 215, granting FERC jurisdiction over a newly established electricity reliability organization (ERO) with authority to propose and enforce mandatory reliability standards, subject to FERC's review and approval, for all users, owners, and operators of the bulk-power system in North America. The ERO or FERC on its own motion may impose penalties for violations, although neither has authority to order construction of additional generation or transmission capacity or to set or enforce safety and adequacy standards. Working with subordinate regional councils (similar to the nine existing NERC regional councils), the ERO will develop and submit reliability standards to FERC for approval, after which they will become binding on all parties, including municipal and cooperative utilities otherwise exempt from federal regulation. FERC has issued proposed rules governing certification of the ERO and establishment of reliability standards.[64]

Under the prior regime, the NERC set voluntary operating and planning guidelines that were often honored in the breach, leading to cascading blackouts on the West Coast in 1996 and a major blackout in 2003 that affected 50 million people in the Midwest, the Northeast, and part of Canada. Following the 2003 blackout, FERC created a new division focused on reliability issues but still acted primarily as an economic regulator of wholesale power markets and the interstate grid. The Energy Policy Act finally fulfills recommendations by successive postblackout task forces that FERC be empowered to enforce mandatory reliability standards.[65] It is also expected to drive further consolidation of control areas and organized markets, redraw regional boundaries, and reduce states' authority to set and enforce standards, preserved only when not inconsistent with those imposed by the ERO.

PURPA

PURPA granted special rights to QFs, essentially cogenerators and producers using primarily renewable resources, including a put that obligated investor-owned utilities to sell backup power to QFs and buy their output at a price based on the purchasing utility's long-run avoided cost. PURPA became a portal of entry for independent power producers seeking to compete in wholesale markets by using the superior credit of utility purchasers as leverage. When bulk-power markets emerged, the policy justification for the put eroded.

Section 1253 of the Energy Policy Act prospectively repeals the put for all new QFs and new contracts except where FERC finds that a QF lacks nondiscriminatory access to competitive wholesale power markets from which it can buy backup power and into which it can sell its output. The Energy Policy Act also amends PURPA to eliminate prior restrictions on utility ownership, allowing traditional utilities to own up to 100% of a QF's equity, and apply more rigorous standards to QFs' output.[66] The new standards seek to eliminate so-called PURPA machines, cogeneration facilities intended to sell power to a utility rather than serve the thermal or electrical needs of a host. To protect utilities still required to purchase power from grandfathered QFs, the Energy Policy Act directs FERC to issue regulations ensuring that utilities recover all prudently incurred costs.

Other Provisions

Other provisions of the Energy Policy Act (Sections 1251, 1252, and 1254) amend PURPA to add new standards, to be considered by the states, addressing conservation, efficiency, and demand-side management. The smart-metering standard addresses power market demand inelasticity and would require that utilities offer customers a time-based rate schedule to reflect variations in the costs of generating and purchasing electricity at wholesale, including time-of-use pricing, real-time pricing, critical peak pricing, and credits for peak-load reduction agreements.

Notes

[1] Fox-Penner. *Electric Utility Restructuring* (1998), pp. 98–99.

[2] Fine and Wang. *Private Equity and the Repeal of PUHCA, Electric Light & Power* (November/December 2005), p. 30.

[3] However, FERC policy requires advance approvals of proposals by directors to hold interlocking positions. See *Commission Authorization to Hold Interlocking Positions,* Order No. 664, 70 *Federal Register* 55, 517 (September 23, 2005), 112 FERC ¶ 61,298 (2005).

[4] *Fitch Comment: 2005 Energy Policy Act to Have Slightly Positive Credit Implications.* Fitch press release. (August 1, 2005).

[5] Ibid. Fitch notes that mergers usually produce higher returns for the selling company, rather than the purchasing company, and that "often the buyer winds up overleveraged and exposed to the risk of failure to achieve expected merger benefits, which are counted on to repay acquisition debt." See *Back to Basics: A Durable Strategy or a Flash in the Pan?* Fitch Ratings, *Global Power Quarterly,* June 2004, p. 3. Some companies (e.g., Wisconsin Energy Corp.; TXU Corp.; Progress Energy, Inc.; PEPCO Holdings, Inc.; FirstEnergy Corp.; and DTE Energy Co.) are still carrying acquisition debt that has proved difficult to repay.

[6] See, e.g., Orrick. *Energy Regulatory Update* (August 2005) (hereafter *Orrick*), p. 1.

[7] Public Citizen. *Section-by-Section Analysis of Key Provisions Affecting Consumers in the Energy Policy Act of 2005 Discussion Draft Released February 8, 2005,* http://www.citizen.org/print_article.cfm?ID=12962 (February 14, 2005).

[8] *Ohio Power Company,* 954 F.2d 779 (D.C. Cir.), cert. denied, 498 U.S. 73 (1990).

[9] *Notice of Proposed Rulemaking, Repeal of the Public Utility Holding Company Act of 1935 and Enactment of the Public Utility Holding Company Act of 2005,* FERC Docket No. RM05-32-000 (September 16, 2005), mimeo (hereafter *PUHCA NOPR*), pp. 3–4. In allocating the cost of nonpower goods and services among affiliated entities in registered holding company systems, the SEC and state commissions have used an at-cost standard. By contrast, FERC's long-standing policy is that registered

holding company special-purpose subsidiaries must provide nonpower goods and services at the lower of cost or market, a standard also applied as a condition for approval of mergers that result in creation of a new registered holding company. Ibid., p. 10.

[10] *Comments of American Public Power Association and the National Rural Electric Cooperative Association,* FERC Docket No. RM05-32-000 (October 14, 2005), mimeo (hereafter *APPA PUHCA Repeal Comments*), pp. 17–18.

[11] *Orrick,* p. 1.

[12] *PUHCA NOPR,* p. 7.

[13] See *Wisconsin Statutes* § 196.795 (2005); *Code of Virginia,* Title 56, Chaps. 3, 4; and Oregon Public Utility Commission Order No. 97-196 (cited in *NRRI Briefing Paper,* pp. 6–7).

[14] See, e.g., *In the Matter of the Application of Enron Corp. for an Order Authorizing the Exercise of Influence over Portland General Electric Company,* Public Utility Commission of Oregon, Order No. 97-196, UM-814 (June 4, 1997).

[15] California Public Utility Commission. *PUC to Re-Examine Utilities/Holding Company Operations.* Press release, http://www.cpuc.ca.gov/wordpdf/NEWS_RELEASE/50629.pdf (October 27, 2005).

[16] American Public Power Association. *The Post-Merger Experience* (October 2005), pp. 1–2. The major reasons are overestimation of benefits and underestimation of the difficulties in integrating merged firms. See Hartman. "The Efficiency Effects of Utility Mergers: Lessons from Statistical Cost Analysis." *Energy Law Journal,* 17: 425 (1996), pp. 437–39.

[17] American Public Power Association. *The Electric Utility Industry after PUHCA Repeal: What Happens Next?* (October 2005), pp. 3–4.

[18] On February 4, 2005, Exelon Corporation requested formal permission from the New Jersey Board of Public Utilities to acquire Public Service Enterprise Group. See *Consolidation of Power: How Exelon's Bid to Acquire PSEG Could Raise Rates, Reduce Reliability, and Risk Public Safety.* NJPIRG Reports, http://www.njpirg.org/NJ.asp?id2=20564&id4=NJ HP (November 2005).

[19] *Comments of American Public Power Association and the National Rural Electric Cooperative Association,* FERC Docket No. RM05-34-000 (October 2005), mimeo (hereafter *APPA Comments*), p. 3.

[20] *Exelon Corp., Public Service Enterprise Corp.,* 112 FERC ¶ 61,011 (2005), p. 132.

[21] See *Merger Policy Statement* (Order No. 592, issued in 1996); *NRRI Briefing Paper,* pp. 7–8.

[22] *PUHCA NOPR,* p. 23. FERC also has in place cash management rules to monitor proprietary capital ratios and money lending or other financial arrangements that can harm regulated companies. Ibid., n. 39.

[23] Ibid., pp. 26–27.

[24] *APPA Comments,* p. 26.

[25] See, e.g., MidAmerican-PacifiCorp merger application, FERC Docket No. EC05-110-000, and Duke Energy-Cinergy merger application, FERC Docket No. EC05-103-000; see also *APPA Comments,* pp. 36–37.

[26] *Westar Energy,* 102 FERC ¶ 61,186 (2003); *APPA Comments,* pp. 22, 30. The Westar Energy restrictions are as follows: (i) public utilities seeking authorization to issue debt backed by a utility asset must use the proceeds of the debt for utility purposes only; (ii) if any utility assets that secure debt issuances are spun off, the debt must follow the asset and also be spun off; (iii) if any of the proceeds from unsecured debt are used for nonutility purposes, the debt must follow the nonutility asset, and if a nonutility asset is spun off, then a proportionate share of the debt must follow the spun-off nonutility asset; and (iv) if utility assets financed by unsecured debt are spun off to another entity, then a proportionate share of the debt must also be spun off.

[27] *APPA PUHCA Repeal Comments,* pp. 6–7.

[28] *Order Amending Market-Based Tariffs and Authorizations,* 105 FERC ¶ 61,218 (2003).

[29] *Comments of American Public Power Association,* FERC Docket No. AD05-17-000. Electric Energy Market Competition Task Force (November 18, 2005), mimeo (hereafter *APPA Market Competition Comments*), pp. 18–19.

[30] On October 12, 2005, FERC and the CFTC concluded a memorandum of understanding that allows FERC to obtain futures, options, and other trading data from the CFTC, subject to a confidentiality requirement limiting public disclosure to certain court and FERC administrative proceedings.

[31] Notice of Proposed Rulemaking, *Prohibition of Market Manipulation*, FERC Docket No. RM06-3-00 (October 20, 2005), mimeo (hereafter *FERC Manipulation NOPR*), p. 2. Pursuant to newly created Section 4A of the Natural Gas Act and Section 222 of the Federal Power Act, FERC has proposed regulations to make it unlawful for any entity, directly or indirectly, in connection with the purchase or sale of electric energy or transmission services or natural gas or transportation services subject to FERC's jurisdiction (i) to use or employ any device, scheme, or artifice to defraud; (ii) to make any untrue statement of a material fact necessary in order to make the statements made, in light of the circumstances under which they were made, not misleading; or (iii) to engage in any act, practice, or course of business that operates or would operate as fraud or deceit on any person. Ibid., p. 5.

[32] *FERC Manipulation NOPR*, p. 8. Section 4(b) of the Commodity Exchange Act makes it unlawful for any person to "cheat or defraud or attempt to cheat or defraud" or to make false statement or reports, or to deceive or attempt to deceive another in transactions under the CFTC's jurisdiction. The elements of a claim under Section 4(b)(A) are the same as those under Rule 10b-5. See, e.g., *Drexel Burnham Lambert, Inc. v. Commodity Futures Trading Comm'n*, 850 F.2d 742, 748 (D.C. Cir. 1988).

[33] *FERC Manipulation NOPR*, p. 5.

[34] *Initial Comments of the Edison Electric Institute*, FERC Docket No. RM06-3-000 (November 17, 2005), mimeo, pp. 14–15 (italics added for emphasis). The Edison Electric Institute urged that Section 47.1(a)(3) of FERC's proposed antifraud rules (making it unlawful for an entity to "engage in any act, practice, or course of business that operates or would operate as a fraud") be eliminated or revised to include elements of knowledge and intent; that FERC explicitly disavow (as does the Energy Policy Act) creation of new private rights of action; and that the rules not be used to federalize claims otherwise beyond FERC's purview. Ibid., pp. 22–25.

[35] *Notice of Inquiry Preventing Undue Discrimination and Preference in Transmission Services*, Docket No. RM05-25-000, 70 *Federal Register* 184 (September 23, 2005), p. 55,797 (hereafter *Transmission NOI*).

[36] *Investigations of Terms and Conditions of Public Utility Market-Based Rate Authorizations*, 105 FERC ¶ 61,218, app. A (2003). Sections 284.288(a) and 284.403(a) of FERC's regulations, promulgated in Order 644, contain substantially similar language. The market behavior rules are currently being appealed. See, e.g., *Cinergy Mktg. and Trading L. P. v. FERC*, Docket No. 04-1167 (D.C. Cir. 2005).

[37] *FERC Manipulation NOPR*, p. 4.

[38] *Transmission NOI*, p. 55,797.

[39] Ibid., p. 55797.

[40] Ibid., pp. 55,797–805.

[41] *Policy Statement on Enforcement*, 113 FERC ¶ 61,068 (October 20, 2005), mimeo (hereafter *Policy Statement*), pp. 2–3. The Energy Policy Act expands the scope of criminal sanctions under the Federal Power Act, the Natural Gas Act, and the NGPA by increasing maximum fines and imprisonment time. Section 1284 amends Section 316 of the Federal Power Act by increasing criminal penalties for "willful and knowing" violation thereof from $5,000 to $1 million and maximum imprisonment time from two to five years. Section 1284 also increases criminal penalties for violation of regulations under the Federal Power Act from $500 to $25,000 per day. Similar increases apply for criminal violations of the Natural Gas Act and the NGPA.

[42] Section 314(b)(1), inserting Section 22(a) into the Natural Gas Act; Section 314(b)(2), amending Section 504(b)(6)(A) of the NGPA; and Section 1284(e)(2), amending Section 316 of the Federal Power Act.

[43] *Policy Statement*, pp. 6–12.

[44] Section 1815. See *Notice Requesting Comments on Wholesale and Retail Electricity Competition*, FERC Docket No. AD05-17-000 (October 13, 2005), p. 1.

[45] Section 1231.

[46] Section 1298. FERC has adopted, as the definition of security constrained economic dispatch, that provided in Section 1234(b) of the Energy Policy Act, i.e., "the operation of generation facilities to produce energy at the lowest cost to reliably serve consumers, recognizing any operational limits of generation and transmission facilities." Section 1234 also requires that the DOE, in consultation with the states,

conduct a study on current economic dispatch procedures and identify possible revisions therein to include nonutility generators and the potential customer benefits of doing so.

[47] Section 1233 creates Section 217 of the Federal Power Act for this purpose that grandfathers any existing or future methodology for allocating or auctioning transmission rights employed by an RTO authorized by FERC as of January 1, 2005.

[48] Section 1236.

[49] See *Capacity for the Future: Kinky Curves and Other Reliability Options,* Synapse Energy Economics, Inc. (December 20, 2004) (hereafter *Synapse Capacity*), p. 2.

[50] *Wholesale Electric Capacity Markets.* The National Regulatory Research Institute (August 2005), pp. 2–10.

[51] *Synapse Capacity,* pp. 1–3; *APPA Comments,* p. 31.

[52] *Synapse Capacity,* p. 48.

[53] See *An RPM Case Study: Higher Costs for Consumers, Windfall Profits for Exelon.* Synapse Energy Economics, Inc. (October 18, 2005), p. 3. This argument has been advanced with respect to PJM's reliability pricing model (RPM), under which Commonwealth Edison (ComEd) is seeking approval before the Illinois Citizens Utility Board of a 20% wholesale rate increase that could result in annual payments to Exelon, ComEd's owner, of as much as $1.2 billion: "The design of the RPM system is to award all capacity, existing or new, profitable or marginal, the same payment for capacity on a per-MW basis. The vast majority of this money would be made to owners of existing base load units such as Exelon's. These payments, because they bear no relation to any investment in new capacity, would amount to an excessive, ratepayer-funded artifact of an inefficient and poorly targeted approach to capacity pricing." Ibid., p. 11.

[54] *Synapse Capacity,* pp. 12–16.

[55] *NRRI Briefing Paper,* p. 11; Republican Policy Committee, U.S. Senate. *Fixing the Power Grid* (September 30, 2003); U.S. Department of Energy. *National Transmission Grid Study* (May 2002) (hereafter *DOE Grid Study*).

[56] *APPA Market Competition Comments,* pp. 43–45.

[57] Meyer and Sedano. *Transmission Siting and Permitting* (May 2002), exhibit to *DOE Grid Study* (hereafter *Meyer and Sedano*), pp. 2–14.

[58] For an example of federally caused permitting delay, see the Alturas 345 kV intertie project, cited in *Meyer and Sedano* (pp. 38–39), which involved a transmission line of 163 miles between Reno, Nevada, and Alturas, California. The line was needed to support fast-growing demand around Reno and to enable the applicant, Sierra Pacific, to gain access to low-cost hydroelectric power from the Pacific Northwest. Because a portion of the line as proposed would have traversed federal lands, the Bureau of Land Management (BLM) became the lead agency for the purpose of preparing an environmental impact statement (EIS). Although BLM approved the project and issued an EIS, the manager of the Humboldt-Toiyabe National Forest, through which 8 miles of the line would have passed, issued a no-action decision, causing months of delay and leading Sierra Pacific to reroute the line onto private land and incur additional costs of over $20 million.

[59] *NRRI Briefing Paper*, p. 13.

[60] *NRRI Briefing Paper*, pp. 32–33.

[61] *APPA Market Competition Comments*, p. 43; *NRRI Briefing Paper*, p. 33.

[62] *APPA Market Competition Comments*, pp. 43–47.

[63] Ibid., p. 36.

[64] *Rules Concerning Certification of the Electricity Reliability Organization; and Procedures for the Establishment, Approval, and Enforcement of Electric Reliability Standards*, FERC Docket No. RM05-30-000 (September 1, 2005), 112 FERC ¶ 61,239.

[65] Ibid., pp. 4–5.

[66] See *Revised Regulations Governing Small Power Production and Cogeneration Facilities*, FERC Docket No. RM05-36-000 (October 11, 2005), mimeo.

10 Conclusion

Enron, the California electricity market meltdown, and the multistate power blackout of 2003 are all recent memories. Given the pain endured by many consumers and market participants, it is hardly surprising that a consensus has not emerged among politicians, regulators, or industry analysts in favor of competitive power markets. There is instead a spectrum of sharply focused but divergent opinions, passionately argued but largely irreconcilable, that tend to follow predictable scripts, ranging from embrace of competitive markets to continued cost-based regulation.

The Energy Policy Act, a grand national bargain reflecting this divergence, embraces both market-based and regulatory initiatives (e.g., uniform grid rules, expanded transmission to facilitate markets, PUHCA repeal, and enhanced legal recourse for small players). Although it does not mandate deregulation, the Energy Policy Act clearly reflects congressional sentiment in favor of competitive wholesale markets, even if these coexist with regulated markets and public power.[1] Whether the Energy Policy Act will achieve its framers' pro-competitive objectives remains an open question. One of the most contentious issues currently facing federal regulators, as the Electric Energy Market Competition Task Force has noted, is whether the different forms of competition in wholesale markets have resulted in an efficient allocation of resources. Markets are not themselves a fix. Much will depend on the elimination of intractable system limitations requiring an infrastructural solution—notably transmission enhancement—and regulators' ability to recognize and control the exercise of residual market power.

The Competitive Power Market Brief

Recent events have not discouraged the advocates of market-based competition. Based on a study of the Eastern Interconnection from 1999 to 2003, Global Energy Advisors, an industry analyst, claims that wholesale competition has already saved customers more than $15 billion in energy operating costs while concurrently improving power plant operating efficiency.[2] In support of the claimed savings, the study compares actual results with a simulation that assumes traditional, vertically integrated utilities continued to operate in an environment unaffected by regulatory changes, revised tariff protocols, and market rules facilitating wholesale competition. To implement the comparison, the study divides the Eastern Interconnection into two parts, a regulated sector, in which utilities have an obligation to serve native-load retail customers, and a competitive sector, in which at-risk merchant generators realize income only from energy and capacity sales to utilities in the regulated sector. In the "without wholesale competition" case, the study makes the following assumptions: no competitive or merchant plants have been built; FERC did not issue Orders 888 and 2000; RTOs were not formed; and marginal-cost contracts did not replace market-based wholesale energy.

During the five-year study period, the competitive sector comprised generation capacity of almost 89,000 MW, including combined and simple cycle units, from which the competitive sector sold energy and capacity worth $13.7 billion to the regulated sector. The study assumes that, without competitive power suppliers, regulated utilities would have built rate-base generating plants and incurred related operating costs of $28.9 billion—$15.1 billion more, in aggregate, than the $13.7 billion paid to merchant generators during the relevant period.

The study attributes a significant fraction of the resulting savings to the mix of new power plants that it assumes regulated utilities would have built, 20% of which are deemed to be combined cycle.[4] The study does not address amortization of generation plant capital costs, although it assumes regulated utilities would have invested $31 billion, compared with the $38 billion actually spent by competitive power suppliers during the relevant period; further, it does not address "the cost-savings or benefits associated with retail competition" or regions other than the Eastern Connection.[5] The projected wholesale operational cost saving is therefore heavily dependent on the validity of underlying assumptions. Methodology aside, however, the study illustrates a basic fact: load-serving entities' access to more efficient competitive generation sources probably reduced the average wholesale cost of energy during the relevant period.[6] In the Eastern Interconnection, one can infer, PJM has successfully implemented FERC's regional open-access initiatives.

Even so, the implications of the study with respect to energy policy are open ended. It does not prescribe a granular market blueprint and therefore leaves the field open to contesting visions of the industry's future (even though a leading proponent of competitive markets cites the study to show that the California energy crisis "was not a failure of markets" but instead "a failure of market design"[7]).

Market Design

Despite withdrawal of FERC's proposed SMD Rule, market design remains a predicate for competition. Professor William Hogan, a leading theoretician, asserts that electricity markets must be designed, that good design begins with the real-time market and works backward, and that the market itself cannot solve the problem of market design, a task that falls instead to regulators. In a properly designed system, regional operators maintain an instantaneous balance between generation and load, adjust flexible generating plants and loads through economic dispatch, and set power flows that work even if transmission is constrained. Economic dispatch presupposes efficient market equilibrium and a market-clearing price of general applicability determined by conditions of supply and demand. In a real-time market, spot prices are based on the marginal costs of power at each location, with locational differences also determining transmission spot prices. Volatile transmission prices are hedged by defining FTRs to collect the congestion rents inherent in efficient, short-run spot prices.

Successful market design therefore implies a consistent framework, as established in New England, New York, and the mid-Atlantic region, and presupposes standardized energy commodities, accurate metering, explicit market rules, commercially viable settlement procedures, and, not least, sufficient investment in transmission and generation capacity.[8] Professor Hogan recognizes, nonetheless, that greater reliance on markets confronts a minefield of difficult, real-world issues, among them "entry, exit, governance, contracts, demand participation, fuel supply, environmental impacts, technology innovation, market power, competition policy, merger rules, cost allocation, customer choice, customer equity, settlements, transparency, liquidity, risk allocation, [and] investment"[9]—factors that have caused other observers to express reservations about electricity restructuring. To address such factors, SMD must include a fully integrated market monitoring process, implemented by independent entities and based on consistent measures of market performance.[10]

SMD sought to replicate, nationwide, the market design employed by Northeastern ISOs, derived in part from previous power pool experience. Under SMD, in the context of an ISO-administered wholesale market, producers submit energy bids and related schedules. Knowing the location, heat rate, ramp rate, and capacity of all producers bidding in the market, the ISO optimizes unit commitments and schedules to meet predicted hourly loads, subject to reliability and transmission constraints and revised as necessary in real time to accommodate forecast errors and contingencies. Each producer then receives payment based on hourly energy prices at its location (reflecting net payments for energy and charges for transmission). Producers have strong incentives to minimize costs and enter into forward bilateral contracts.[11]

Market design requires centralized control of the transmission grid, which an independent operator must continuously synchronize and adjust in response to frequency, voltage, and line loadings. To call forth adequate transmission capacity in the long run, centralized planning must establish reliable forecasts of grid topology while according utilities (and others) economic incentives to make required additions. Adequate transmission is essential to grid reliability and competitive generation but, as experience has shown, cannot be provided by market forces without some form of regulatory intervention.[12] Similarly, neither fast-response generation reserves nor total available capacity flow reliably from competitive wholesale markets alone; workable electricity markets require, among other preconditions, adequate infrastructure, demand response, and limitation of retail price volatility.[13]

Rethinking Electricity Restructuring

Electric utility restructuring can be viewed, historically, as a political response to the problem of high rates in the Northeast and California, where large industrial customers sought to gain access to and import distant low-cost power from competitive generators. The market forces unleashed in response were expected to displace cost-based regulation, as FERC recognized a new category of competitive generators, opened the transmission grid, and altered the monopoly status of vertically integrated incumbent utilities. While realizing certain intermediate objectives, however, electricity restructuring

- underestimated the difficulties involved in managing and optimizing investment in the alternating current transmission grid with its public commons characteristics;

- did not benefit the retail market, whose customers opted for regulated universal service;

- established market institutions that invited manipulation and abuse, as in California.[14]

These results (and other consequences chronicled previously) have led certain observers to reconsider the virtues of the regulated monopoly system, among them universal service, economies of scale, and low cost of capital. Vertically integrated utilities with exclusive franchises rested on a linear supply chain—from fuel to generation to distribution to service delivery—under a regulatory regime that fostered investment in irreversible, long-lived capital assets, centralized dispatch of generation and transmission, and implicit cross-subsidies in lieu of explicit financial subventions. Single-utility ownership of generation and transmission, it is argued, reduced wholesale price volatility just as cost-based retail price regulation avoided abrupt rate changes. From a regulatory perspective, vertically integrated utilities are also thought to have been more accountable for deficiencies and, from an economic perspective, better able to obtain capital at lower cost than their suppliers.[15]

In view of these factors, the Cato Institute, ordinarily a free-market advocate, has advanced the revisionist conclusion that "vertical integration may be the most efficient organizational structure for the electricity industry," since "mandatory open access requires much additional regulation to govern the interaction of independent generators with the AC grid 'commons.'"[16] Other analysts have proposed an evolutionary third-way approach to restructuring, in which utilities subject to performance-based regulation continue to provide basic services at regulated rates that recover allowed costs over time, depending on whether such costs are less or more than average wholesale spot prices.[17]

Real-World Response

In the aftermath of a disastrous market reversal, the California Independent System Operator has advanced a Market Redesign and Technology Upgrade (MRTU), revised by FERC in a multiyear iterative process that commenced in 2003. Described as a "major and important reform needed to address the difficulties inherent in the original market design,"[18] the MRTU contemplates an electricity market with bid-based, security-constrained economic dispatch having locational prices, license-plate access charges, bilateral schedules, financial transmission rights, consistent day-ahead and real-time markets, a multi-settlement system, and unit commitment with simultaneous optimization of energy and ancillary services. In these respects, the MRTU largely replicates features proposed by FERC's SMD Rule.

Important as it may be, however, viable market design alone will not resolve the underlying problems in California's energy sector, which is characterized by "spiraling energy prices, potential supply shortages, and an inadequate and ageing delivery infrastructure."[19] The California Energy Commission (CEC) notes that "systematic under-investment in transmission infrastructure is reducing system reliability and increasing operational costs" and that the state "lacks a well-integrated transmission planning and permitting process that considers both generation and transmission needs, evaluates non-wires alternatives, plans for transmission corridors well in advance of need, and allows access to essential renewable resource areas."[20] Underinvestment has created a 7,000 MW generation shortfall, exacerbated by the lack of long-term power contracts. To address the problem of inadequate generation capacity, California has therefore extended regulatory jurisdiction over independent load-serving entities and required publicly owned utilities to file periodic capacity reports.[21] In the CEC's view, reduction of gas prices in the California market will also require infrastructure upgrades, including advanced metering technology, increased gas pipeline and storage capacity, and liquefied natural gas import terminals.[22]

A Holistic View

Energy deregulation has evolved, over decades, while seeking to reform network electricity and natural gas industries along pro-competitive lines. In an interconnected economy, deregulation has reconceived energy as a tradable product, rather than a service, and has led to linked physical and derivative wholesale energy markets alongside a regulated retail sector. In the process, contracting has displaced vertical integration as an organizing principle, and new integrative institutional arrangements have become necessary to manage bid-based markets and transmission.

Until events compelled an overdue reassessment, federal energy policy substituted market-based mechanisms for regulatory controls without sufficient understanding of the complex markets being deregulated or the decisive continuing impact of market power. Regulators found it difficult to distinguish high prices caused by the exercise of market power from those caused by genuine scarcity. As controls were phased out, opportunistic energy companies, undeterred by prevailing legal sanctions or behavioral rules, moved to capture the large profit potential in energy trading. Massive fraud and market manipulation soon followed, exposing many errors in regulatory policy.

When FERC launched SMD, it was no mere coincidence that PJM provided the preferred model. PJM represents the triumph of tested solutions over *a priori* theory, a process one economist calls the "experimental test-bedding of policy."[23] Experimental economics constructs a hypothetical environment with a given benchmark and then determines how well policy works in real-world testing—that is, how well real humans, using heuristics and rules of thumb, operate in a complex network, as measured by such metrics as efficiency and price volatility. To determine how a particular mechanism will perform, for example, whether a uniform-price or pay-as-bid auction rule performs better in a wholesale market, both rules can be tested through simulation before field implementation. Empirical proof is essential in a decentralized-yet-coordinated network industry subject to congestion, market power, and infrastructural constraints.[24]

In energy deregulation, pragmatism trumps ideology. Competition cannot be summoned by decree, except through top-down legal orders to manage externalities—regulation in a different guise. Markets may work, but industry structure determines outcomes. The energy business is not a competitive universe— particularly when (as is too often the case) companies retain pricing power, have significant concurrent stakes in natural gas and electricity, and can freely increase market share through merger and consolidation. To be effective, competition presupposes unambiguous rules, adequate infrastructure, and vigilant regulatory oversight.

Notes

1. Fox-Penner. *Remarks before the ExNet and Bruder, Gentile & Marcoux, L.L.P. Special Briefing of the Energy Policy Act of 2005.* White paper (September 28, 2005), pp. 3–4.

2. Global Energy Advisors. *Putting Competitive Power Markets to the Test* (July 2005), p. RS-3.

3. Ibid., p. RS-6.

4. Ibid., pp. RS-6, 1-16. If only simple cycle combustion turbine plants are assumed to have been built, the indicated cost saving falls to $9.4 billion.

5. Ibid., p. A-5. Deregulation may result in higher retail prices for power. In Texas, e.g., power generation and sales are unregulated enterprises, with few price controls. Texas utilities are permitted to raise retail rates whenever gas prices rise above specified thresholds, without regard to underlying costs. TXU Corp. (TXU), which derives much of its power from low-cost coal, lignite, and nuclear plants, has thus been able to charge more for power as gas prices have escalated. In 2005, TXU earned $1.71 billion, or $2.50 per share, compared with $386 million, or $0.64 per share. At the same time, TXU's retail power sales fell nearly 17% in 2005 "as customers fled TXU for other suppliers or simply cut their usage." *The Wall Street Journal,* February 3, 2006, p. A2.

6. McDiarmid. *Taking Stock: The Successes and Limitations of Open Access.* White paper presented to National Rural Electric Cooperative Association (January 11, 2005), p.6.

7. COMPETE. *California in Perspective: Don't Blame Competition.* White paper (undated), pp. 1, 6, n. 16.

8. Hogan. *Market Design and Electricity Restructuring.* White paper presented to Association of Power Exchanges (November 1, 2005), p. 13.

9. Ibid., p. 10.

10. Wolak. *Lessons from International Experience with Electronic Market Monitoring.* University of California Energy Institute, CSEM WP 134 (June 2004), p. 8.

[11] Chao, Oren, and Wilson. *Restructured Electricity Markets: Reevaluation of Vertical Integration and Unbundling.* White paper (July 1, 2005) (hereafter *Chao et al. Markets*), p. 45.

[12] As Professor Joskow has observed, "Transmission investment decisions do not immediately strike me as being ideally suited to relying entirely on the invisible hand. Transmission investments are lumpy, characterized by economies of scale and can have physical impacts throughout the network. The combination of imperfectly defined property rights, economies of scale and long-lived sunk costs for transmission investments, and imperfect competition in the supply of generating services can lead to either underinvestment or overinvestment at particular points on the network if we rely entirely on market forces." Quoted in Van Doren and Taylor. "Rethinking Electricity Restructuring." *Policy Analysis*, November 30, 2004 (hereafter *V&T*), p. 7

[13] *Chao et al. Markets*, pp. 55, 61.

[14] *V&T*, p. 11.

[15] *Chao et al. Markets*, pp. 1-13.

[16] *V&T*, p. 9.

[17] Chao, Oren, and Wilson. *Alternative Pathway to Electricity Market Reform: A Risk-Management Approach.* EPRI technical paper (September 2005).

[18] Harvey, Pope, and Hogan. *Comments on the California ISO MRTU LMP Market Design* (February 23, 2005).

[19] California Energy Commission. *2005 Integrated Energy Policy Report* (November 2005) (hereafter *CEC Report*), p. 1.

[20] Ibid., pp. 2, 12.

[21] AB 380 (Nunez), Chapter 367, Statutes of 2005, cited in *CEC Report*, p. 3.

[22] *CEC Report*, pp. 7–12.

[23] Kiesling. "Using Economic Experiments to Test Electricity Policy" *The Electricity Journal*, 18 (November 2005), p. 43.

[24] Ibid., pp. 44, 48.

Index

A

accounting firms. *See also* Arthur
  Andersen (Andersen)
  acquiescence by auditors, 70
  auditors in, 29
  consulting services by, 70
  role of auditors, 67–68

accounting practices. *See also*
  Financial Accounting Standards
  Board (FASB)
  Arthur Andersen (Andersen) on,
    31, 76, 82
  creative, 38
  fair-value accounting, 83–84
  generally accepted accounting
  principles (GAAP), 71
  generally accepted accounting
  standards (GAAS), 71
  gross vs. net basis accounting,
    76, 80
  hedge accounting, 84
  high-risk, 31
  historical cost accounting, 83
  mark-to-market accounting, 71,
    80–86
  net vs. gross basis accounting, 76
  regulatory accounting, 25
  round-trip trading accounting, 76

AEP Energy Services, Inc., 138

AES, 156

AES/Williams, 177

affiliate abuse, 121–124, 216–217

affiliated power marketers, 97

after-the-fact quarterly reports,
  183–184

agency model, 85

Alaska Gas Pipeline Port Authority,
  128

American depository receipts
  (ADRs), 45

American Electric Power (AEP), 138

American Public Power Association,
  9

Amsterdam exchange, 45

ancillary services
  capacity viewed as, 152
  double selling of, 182
  paper trading of, 175–176
  scam of, by Dynegy, 179
  scam of, by Mirant, 179
  scam of, by Reliant Energy
    (Reliant), 179

anomalous market behavior, 135,
  154, 177, 186, 206

antifraud rules, 223–225

a priori theory, 250

Aquila Merchant Services, Inc., 140

Arthur Andersen (Andersen)
  as auditor for CMS Energy Corp.
    (CMS), 75
  as consultant and auditor for
    Enron, 70
  deference to Enron, 86
  Enron auditors, 29
  on Enron's mark-to-market
    accounting, 82
  on high-risk accounting practices,
    31
  resigns as auditor for CMS
    Energy Corp. (CMS), 77
  on round-trip trading accounting,
    76

O

P

S

T